Blend In or Fade Out

BLEND IN OR FADE OUT

A MEMOIR

COLNESE M. HENDON

strive
PUBLISHING

Blend In or Fade Out: A Memoir
Published by Strive Publishing, Robbinsdale, Minnesota

  Strive Publishing
  3801 27th Avenue North
  Robbinsdale, MN 55422
  www.strivepublishing.com

The stories in this book reflect the author's recollection of events. Some names and identifying characteristics have been changed to protect the privacy of those depicted. Dialogue has been recreated from the author's memory.

Bible passages are quoted under the Copyright Act Fair Use Clause.

Developmental Editor: Phoebe McGowan
Copyeditor: Yasmin Angoe McClinton
Cover Art: Barbara Thomas
Author photo: Tiffany Townsend
Book Cover Design: Jermaine Taris
Page Design: Beth Wright

ISBN: 978-1-948529-17-4

Library of Congress Control Number: 2021923916

To my parents, Coleridge and Bernese Hendon, and my brother Ira:
Without a doubt, there would be no me without you.

Contents

◆ ◆ ◆

CONTENTS

Who Am I?

I am the daughter of strangers
Of estranged races who left traces
Of themselves in me
I am the sun-kissed bastard child of children
Who gave in to fever, the heat of rebellion
Thirst for the unknown
For what could not be
But what was and ultimately became me
I am the baby who was left behind
The dust kicked off retreating feet
Fleeing my helplessness
My cries unheeded
My need for belonging and acceptance unquenched

CHAPTER 1

The Adopted Family

One night when I was three years old, my mom read a special bedtime story to my six-year-old brother Ira and me. We were in our twin beds, and our mother was sitting on a chair between us.

"Tonight, I'm going to read you a story about an adopted family," she said while opening the book.

"Like our family, right?" asked Ira.

"That's right, Ira, just like our family."

"What's an adopted family?" I wondered aloud.

"It's a family like ours," Ira explained. "Adopted families are chosen. We were chosen to be in this family—right, Mom?"

"That's right. Some children were born into their families, and others were adopted like you. We wanted children very badly, so we went out and found the two of you, and now you're our very own little boy and girl."

"But who was I born to?" I asked. "Why didn't they want to keep me?"

"Sometimes a mother doesn't have a husband to help her take care of her children, or she might be too young to take care of them properly. Things can be very hard for a mother without a husband who goes to work, so he can earn money to provide for the family. And because she loves her baby so much, she wants what's best for the baby's future, so she decides to give him or her up for adoption.

"And that's what happened to you and Ira. It's not that your birth mother didn't want to keep you. She loved you so much that she decided to put you up for adoption. And tonight, I'm going to read you a story called *The Adopted Family*."

Tears welled up in my eyes. "Does she miss me?"

"I'm sure she misses you," was my mom's attempt to comfort and reassure me.

"When can I meet her?"

"When a baby is placed for adoption, the birth records are sealed. That means we have no way of finding out who she is or where she is. Now you are our little girl, and we are so happy about that. We wouldn't trade you for the world!"

Then my mom opened the book and began reading about the happy, adopted family. Afterwards we talked a little bit more about what it means to be adopted and how Ira and I had been chosen, not born, into our family. After getting down on our knees and saying our bedtime prayers, our mom kissed us good night and turned off the lights. As I drifted off to sleep, I wondered about my real mother and why she hadn't wanted to keep me. I felt sad inside and abandoned, not at all like the happy adopted child in the book.

◈ ◈ ◈

I learned my first lesson about listening in kindergarten. My kindergarten teacher, Mrs. Berg, called us from our activities to sit around her in a semicircle. As we sat around her on the wooden floor of the classroom, she spoke to us about a very important safety issue, crossing the street.

"What are you supposed to do when you want to cross the street?" Mrs. Berg asked.

"Look both ways," the other kindergartners and I answered in unison.

"Very good, children," she replied. "But you must also listen. When you get to the street corner, before crossing the street, you must stop, look, and listen. Now, repeat after me. Stop, look, and listen."

"Stop, look, and listen," we chimed together.

After we learned our safety lesson, next was story time. Mrs. Berg read a story to our class about a duck that was looking for its mother.

"Are you my mother?" the little duckling asked each animal it encountered.

I felt a twinge inside. I could identify with the duckling and its search for its mother. Just that past weekend, I had been in Sears Roebuck with my dad, who was picking up a catalog item from the second floor. As he stood at the counter waiting while the clerk went back into another area to retrieve his parcel, I leaned against the back of his legs and stared at a lady with brunette hair and red lipstick, who was sitting at a nearby desk. As the lady looked up from the paper she was writing on and smiled at me, just like the duck, I wondered, *Are you my mother*?

After the story my mother read to Ira and me about the adopted family, we had never again spoken about the subject, but I had not forgotten. It wasn't lost on me that I had another mother somewhere out there in the big, wide world. The pretty lady with her hair flipped up on the ends, who looked a little like Mary Tyler Moore—Dick Van Dyke's wife on the television show—could possibly be her.

I pressed even closer against the back of my dad's legs and smiled bashfully at the lady, who could be my mother. Soon the store clerk came back with my dad's catalog item. He paid for it, and we headed down the escalator to the first floor to buy a box of popcorn. Every time we shopped at Sears, my dad bought us popcorn. Judging from all the people gathered around the popcorn stand, it seemed to me that everyone else shopping at Sears bought popcorn, too. The promise of hot, fresh popcorn was one of the reasons I loved shopping with my dad at Sears.

As the teacher finished up the story about the duck's search for its mother, a lump formed in the back of my throat. I wondered where was the mother I came from and why had she given me away? From my family's periodic trips to drop off clothes for the needy into a big yellow Goodwill container at Red Owl grocery store, I knew people usually gave away only things they did not want. Things that had little or no value. Things like me.

CHAPTER 2

Colorism

◈ ◈ ◈

When I turned five, freckles began to pepper my face. At first, I thought the spots on my face came from the grape Tootsie Roll Pop I was licking as I looked into the mirror attached to my parents' dresser, but when I rubbed my cheeks, the marks stayed put. "Sun kisses" was the term my Aunt Edith used to describe them. However, I would have preferred not to be kissed by the sun in that way. Nobody else I knew had been kissed by the sun quite like me. Most of my friends were almond, cocoa, or sepia-toned, and I wanted to be brown like them.

"How can my skin get darker?" I asked my mom one day as she was ironing. "I want brown skin."

"You need to have more pigment in your skin," she explained.

"What's pigment? How do I get more pigment?" I wanted to know.

"It generally follows the darker parent," replied my mom absently as she sprinkled water from a green water bottle onto my dad's white shirt and began to iron out the wrinkles.

My mother's skin was nearly as light as mine. She also had freckles just like I did, only not as many. What I understood from our conversation was that for me to get darker skin, I had to follow my darker parent around, which happened to be my dad. So that is what I did. I began to follow my dad around the house. I trailed him into the basement, outside to the garage, around the yard as he worked, and finally back inside again. I also tagged along with him when he drove the car to the Red Owl grocery store or to Mr. Anderson's Mobil Station or Mr. Schofield's Delicatessen. I'm pretty sure my dad had no idea why I was suddenly stuck to him like glue, but he took it all in stride.

Checking the mirror one day to see what, if any, progress was being made, I noticed that my face continued to be a light shade of tan, not the pretty shade of brown I was endeavoring to have. Most of the children who lived on my block, who went to my Sunday school, and who lived in my neighborhood were various shades of brown, and I wanted to be like them.

"Am I white or colored?" I asked my mom one day as I splashed around and played in the bathtub. I waited for her answer as I poured water from a little white cup into a red and blue toy boat.

"You're colored," she responded.

But when I looked in the mirror to inspect the color of my skin, my face definitely did not look brown. Although I wanted to be brown, not everyone thought being brown was so cool. Like Nettie, who sat next to me in Miss Bonin's first-grade class. One day Nettie got mad at me because I did not want to share my crayons with her anymore. I had decided to stop sharing with her because sometimes she gave them back to me either broken in half or with the tips broken off. When I told Nettie she couldn't use my big fat green crayon, she got heated and said, "Don't nobody want to be your friend anyway, with your ole' black daddy!"

I could tell by the way she said it—the look on her face and the tone of her voice—that she meant it as an insult.

"You're black, too," I responded and waited nervously for whatever was coming next.

I thought Nettie might want to fight me for saying she was black, too, but she just looked at me with a surprised look on her face and let the comment slide. I was relieved because Nettie came from a large family with several brothers and sisters. She even had a few bad nephews that regularly stood on the hill in front of their house and threw rocks at passersby. In my neighborhood, if you got into a fight with one member of a large family, you might have to fight more than one. Because I was one of only two children in my family, I did not have much backup, so I chose my battles carefully. But when Nettie called my dad black, she crossed a line that had to be addressed.

Calling a person black or referring to their skin tone in a negative way in the 1960s amounted to fighting words. The children on the playground at Warrington Elementary School regularly taunted each other about skin color and hair texture. The lighter-skinned kids teased the darker-skinned kids by saying, "Jet black jungle baby, but ten shades darker" or "You're so black, you're blue!"

We jumped rope singing, "I went downtown to see Miss Hootie, gave her two cents to see her bootie, her bootie was so black that I couldn't see the crack, so I asked Miss Hootie for my two cents back."

Another rhyme I heard chanted by my schoolmates out on the playground went like this:

> *You're the ugliest child I ever did see.*
> *You look like a monkey every time you smile.*
> *The clothes that you wear are out of style.*
> *You're knock-kneed, bowlegged, pigeon-toed, too.*
> *The curse of the devil must have fallen on you,*
> *And, boy, your hair is nappy.*
> *Who's your pappy?*

These were only a few of the insults around skin tone and hair texture traded daily by colored children at my school. When the topic of hair texture came up, I tried to fade into the background. Most of the girls I knew got their hair pressed with a hot comb in order to straighten it. My hair was thick and wavy, but I didn't get it straightened. My mom put a sweet-smelling lotion on my hair and brushed it until its waves rippled nicely. Then she braided it and put barrettes on the ends to keep the braids from coming undone.

Sometimes kids would say, "You got good hair," meaning my hair was wavy rather than kinky or nappy. I didn't like to hear anyone make a comment about my hair being "good" because the words had the power to spark jealousy and envy. Because I was sensitive, I couldn't stand anyone being mad at me, especially about something I could not change, like my hair texture. All I wanted to do was fit in with all the black, brown, and tan girls around me, so I begged my mom to press my hair. I wanted nothing more than to be able to join in the conversation on Monday morning when my school buddies showed off their straightened hair and talked about getting their hair pressed and curled over the weekend.

"You don't need your hair pressed," my mom reminded me. "Don't let the other children belittle you."

Wearing a natural hairdo didn't become socially acceptable until later in the 1960s and early '70s, when Black people began to wear Afros as a method of showing Black pride. It was around the time when James Brown promoted Black pride with his song, "Say it Loud: I'm Black and I'm Proud."

James Brown's song and the advent of Black pride was a monumental and controversial moment in African American history since Black people had been taught to hate themselves both overtly and covertly centuries earlier with the onset of slavery in 1619. Self-hatred continued to be reinforced in multiple ways and even trickled down into our childhood games on the playground.

Looking different and being different made me uncomfortable because it reminded me that I was adopted. *Who is my real family?* I wondered. *Do I look like them?* I had no way of knowing. One day after school, not knowing who I was and where I came from had become too unbearable. I climbed up on the kitchen stool, sat down, and lifted the receiver from the old black telephone. Clutched in my hand was a piece of paper containing the number of Hennepin County Adoption Records that I had copied from the big white telephone book stored in the hallway closet. The telephone made a clicking noise as I dialed the number.

"Records."

"Hi. I'm adopted, and I want to know my mother's name."

"I'm sorry, but adoption records are sealed."

"What does that mean?"

"That means no one can give you any information about your birth certificate or adoption records."

"Never?"

"You'd have to get a court order."

Depressed and downhearted, I hung up. "Why won't they just tell me?" I asked aloud, but no one answered.

CHAPTER 3

On the Block

When I was growing up, our family lived on 39th and Portland Avenue South. It was a block in South Minneapolis that was full of children. After school was out and all summer long, Ira and I were free to go outside to play with our friends on the block, as long as we changed into our play clothes first. The only rule was that we were not supposed to cross the street, so we played mostly in the alley and in the backyards of our friends in the neighborhood.

In the alley, there was always so much to do. If you drove down Portland, you'd think it was a very peaceful and quiet community, but if you ventured into the alley, you'd see that it was alive with the activity of children hard at play. Children on our block ruled.

The bigger kids rode our bikes around the block, and the tiny kids rode their tricycles in front of their houses. Girls on the block used chalk to draw squares on the pavement to play hopscotch. Whenever anyone brought their ball outside, we played two-square or four-square, a game that involved passing the ball back and forth across a crack in the pavement or lines drawn with chalk, or we played kickball in the alley using telephone poles and assorted makeshift items as the bases. Meanwhile, the boys played baseball, football, and basketball. They also performed handstands, turned backflips, and dug up worms to chase us girls with. Sometimes kids from other blocks came over to our block to play.

We were threatened on a constant basis by our parents, "If you keep running in and out the door, you can just stay inside," which in our way of thinking was a fate almost worse than death. Being forced to stay inside when we could hear the shouts and squeals of all our friends outside playing was torturous, so we avoided it at all costs. If we grew hungry, we knew our neighbor across the alley, Miss Mahoney, had a garden with a rhubarb patch in her backyard, which we regularly raided.

Then we would elect one of the younger kids to sneak into their house to get a plastic baggie full of sugar, which we would use to dip the rhubarb in to make a tasty snack. The green coil of my dad's water hose was attached to the side of the house. Whenever we got thirsty, we'd turn on the faucet for a nice long drink. There were also apple trees in the neighbor's yard that yielded sour green apples that we picked or ate from the ground after rinsing them off using the garden hose.

My dad built a tree house for my brother Ira, and hammered wooden blocks on the tree trunk to be used as stairs. Underneath the tree house, where the tree trunk split into three sections, there was a nice space wide enough for me to sit in. I liked perching there in my cozy space under my brother's treehouse where I could see more of the world than when I was on the ground. My brother objected to me being allowed in his tree house, but he couldn't say anything about me sitting underneath it, so that was the section of our tree I claimed as my very own.

From my vantage point in the tree, I was pretty sure I could see anything in the world worth looking at. For example, I could see the neighborhood dogs, Rex and Laddie, chained in their respective backyards. Rex was a little reddish-brown Chihuahua that lived next door, and Laddie was a big, beautiful brown, tan, and white collie. They barked all the time, until one day someone poisoned them, and then they barked no more. I remember the morning the dogs were discovered dead because the block was so quiet without their barking and yapping. Before the dogs were poisoned, seeing Rex and Laddie and listening to them bark brought back memories of our puppy, Frisky.

◀◀ ◀◀ ◀

My dad's best friend, O. Donald Smith, was a Pullman porter who worked on the railroad. Late one night, there was a knock on our front door. It was Don carrying Frisky in his arms. I was in bed asleep when Don came over. My mother got Ira and me out of bed to come into the living room but didn't tell us what to expect. When I saw Frisky for the first time, I fell head over heels in love with the puppy.

Frisky was a mutt, part black lab and part who-knew-what-else. She was black with a white neck, white paws, and the cutest little brown face I had ever seen. I listened as Don told my dad how he had brought the puppy all the way from Chicago on the train. Before long, my mother ushered Ira and me back to bed. She then put Frisky into a cardboard box with an alarm clock wrapped in a towel, so the puppy would think she was still with her mother.

It didn't work. Frisky kept everyone up all night long, yapping and crying the most pitiful cries. We kept Frisky for a while but eventually had to get rid of her because our dad was allergic to dogs. He didn't know it at first but soon found out after he grew a great big carbuncle on the back of his neck and had to have surgery at Fairview Hospital to remove it. I cried because my heart was broken when we had to give Frisky to the dog pound. For many years afterwards, whenever I thought of Frisky, I would cry. Even if I was crying about something else, I'd cry an extra round of tears about losing my beloved puppy dog, Frisky.

◆ ◈ ◈

I came out of my mournful daydream about Frisky and did a scan of all the places I could see. From my cozy seat in the tree high above our backyard, I could look down on my swing set. I could also look two houses over into my friend Tina's backyard to see whether or not she and her little sister Stacy had come outside to play. But best of all, I could survey the asphalt driveway where my brother and all the neighborhood boys played basketball. They dribbled, passed, and dunked the ball into the basketball hoop attached to our garage. If the timing was right, I could even see Trash Can Annie, one of the adults who was a constant presence in our alley.

Trash Can Annie was a lady around fifty-five or sixty years old, who spent her time digging in the trash. She smelled like stale urine and dressed like a man. She usually had on a man's hat or had a bandana scarf tied around her head and a winter coat, even on the hottest days of summer. She never bothered anybody as she made her rounds up and down the alley going from one trash can to the next, seeking hidden treasures. The kids on my block did not mind her coming into our world to dig in the trash. We understood that scavenging for trash was her thing. Rain, shine, sleet, or snow, Trash Can Annie was as dependable as the mailman.

Some of my playmates and I used to sort the good junk from the bad and sit the good things on top so Trash Can Annie could find them easier. Like most children, we could be cruel, so when we'd see her poking around in garbage cans or simply walking through the alley, we couldn't suppress the urge to sing, "Trash Can Annie, Trash Can Annie!!" We would bend over and pat our butts in her direction as we taunted her. There were urban legends that if you called her Trash Can Annie to her face, she'd chase you. If she caught you, she'd stab you with the knife she carried in her bandana, but I never saw her do or say a mean thing to anybody. I'm not sure, but I think her name was Mrs. Richardson or Miss Lee. Both names were acceptable to Trash Can Annie whenever we greeted her.

There were many other tales and legends about Trash Can Annie. The main story was that Trash Can Annie was rich. She was said to have once had a convertible car and a trunk full of money, but that the firemen took her money when her house burned down. People also said when her husband died, she went crazy and started wearing his clothes. Apparently, she seldom, if ever, took them off to wash; hence, the ever-present smell of pee. I never knew what to believe about her, so I believed what I saw. She was a mixed-up old lady who dug in the trash. If you were nice to her, she'd be nice to you. If we didn't see her around for a while, we became concerned about where she was and how she was doing.

One day we were in exceptionally high spirits and filled with goodwill, so we hunted around the alley until we found what we considered to be some really good junk: a piece of an end table and some curtain rods. We set them outside the garage and went on about our business, raking leaves and jumping in them. When it was time to go in, I noticed that the junk intended for Trash Can Annie was still there. I thought maybe she had become bored with trash hunting in our alley and had gone to wander down other alleys. I expected Trash Can Annie to return to our alley in the next few days, but she did not.

After several days of her missing in action, we learned from Mr. Workcuff, our neighborhood policeman, that Trash Can Annie had been carted off to jail. I was shocked. For the life of me, I couldn't figure out why anybody would want to lock up such a sweet, smelly old lady, who had become part of our world and, therefore, played an important role in our lives.

About two or three months later, we were outside playing, all bundled up and ready to make a snowman when someone (I can't remember who) yelled, "Look!" Of course, we all looked, and to our joy and relief, it was good old Trash Can Annie, who had finally been released from jail. To our surprise, she had on a fresh new bandana and a different old man's coat. As Trash Can Annie made her way up the alley, we all smiled radiantly at her and welcomed her.

"Hi, Mrs. Richardson."

Trash Can Annie looked over at us, smiled a toothless grin, and said, "Hi honey, hi sweetheart," giving each of us her proper attention. She then attended to her own affairs with the trash cans. But as soon as Trash Can Annie stepped foot into the next alley and out of close range, we let it out and joyfully shouted at her retreating form, "Trash Can Annie, Trash Can Annie!" It was our way of letting her know she was truly back home.

As I grew older, I spent less time playing in the alley, so I didn't see Trash Can Annie as often. I finally stopped seeing her altogether. Somebody called the police about her absence, and they checked up on her. That is how we learned Trash Can Annie had died and had been dead for a long, long time.

CHAPTER 4

Warrington Elementary School

Bonomo bonomo bonomo biscuit
Bonomo bonomo bonomo biscuit
Ooh she she wah wah, a biscuit
I got a lover, a biscuit
He's so fine, a biscuit
Like a bottle of wine, a biscuit . . .

Our hands went slap, slap, clap as we played the familiar hand game, Bonomo Biscuit, on the playground of Warrington Elementary School in South Minneapolis. One palm up, one palm down, slap, two hands together, slap, and then a clap. Slap, slap, clap; slap, slap, clap. With closed fists, we pointed over our shoulders with our outstretched thumbs each time we chanted "a biscuit."

After the game of Bonomo Biscuit, my friend Yvonne offered me a bite of her peanut M&M. She held the green candy close to my mouth so I could take a bite. Mischievously, I leaned forward and closed my teeth around Yvonne's fingers. I bit hard, causing the entire piece of candy to fall into my mouth. Yvonne's mouth fell open in surprise; I laughed and skipped away.

At Warrington, there were children of all shapes, sizes, and skin colors. There were colored children, mixed children, and even a few white children and American Indian children, who back in the 1960s were not yet known as Native Americans.

My friends Adrienne, Arlene, and Yvonne, the Barrett girls, were Jamaican. They wore silver bangles on their arms, and they ran very fast. They listened to calypso music on the record player and knew how to dance to it, too. Their mummy and daddy spoke very fast with a clipped Jamaican accent. On most weekday mornings, the Barrett girls stopped by my house to pick me up for school, but they seldom walked—they ran. I trotted along behind them, but rarely could I keep up. My short chubby legs were no match for theirs. One time we were running to school, and I tripped on a sidewalk block that stuck up a couple of inches above the rest of the pavement. I fell, ripped a hole in my tights, and skinned my knee. I wound up going back home so my mom could clean it up and put a Band-Aid on it.

There were often fights on the playground, and it was always a source of much excitement and adrenaline.

"A fight, a fight!"

The war cry would go from child to child, and the excitement would build. The grapevine had spoken, and we felt obliged to run towards where the fight was taking place to watch. The toughest boys at Warrington wore their shirttails pulled out. They liked them to hang down over their pants rather than to be tucked in. My brother wasn't allowed to wear his shirttail pulled out. If parents only knew how their rules could set their kids up for teasing and ridicule, I wonder if they would reconsider some of them.

Our third-grade class was outside for recess. A group of kids ran past yelling, "A fight, a fight. Terry Brooks is in a fight." I ran along with the pack around to the other side of the school building to watch the fight. Terry's fists flew, and gravel rose on the schoolyard as the two boys scuffled. Two recess monitors quickly broke it up, but the playground had already reached a decision: Terry had won again. Of all the third-grade boys, Terry and Randy were by far the toughest. No one wanted to tangle with them.

Randy had been my boyfriend in second grade. He was dark-skinned like my dad, rarely smiled, and I adored him. One time he slapped our second-grade teacher Mrs. McCoy's eyeglasses off her face, but I'm not sure what provoked him. I just remember Randy being almost as tall as she was. Even in second grade, I was attracted to bad boys, and Randy was by far the baddest of them all. During story time, I would sit at the foot of Randy's chair and tie his tennis shoes. For some reason, the tough boys at Warrington Elementary School almost never tied their shoelaces, and most of them came from the largest families in the neighborhood.

"Don't be messing with my brother!" an outraged child would announce.

"I just know you're not talking about my cousin," someone else might holler out while leaning forward with their hands on their hips, their foot tapping, and their jaws jutted out.

Their body language stated very clearly that they double dared anybody to mess with their family. If the offending party continued down the slippery path they were on, the situation would end with them getting their butt kicked after school or during recess with all the kids on the playground there to witness it.

I wished I had a bunch of brothers, sisters, and cousins to stick up for me, but as it stood, I had only my brother Ira, who regularly got chased home from school because he was afraid to fight. Plus, he was light-skinned and overweight, so he got bullied over that as well.

Our mother bought him husky-sized pants from Sears Roebuck and then rolled them up and ironed a cuff in them. When he fell and got a hole in them, she would repair his pants by ironing a patch on the knee. Most of the tough kids didn't have patches on the knees of their pants, as I recall, just holes.

"Fatty, fatty two by four, can't get through the kitchen door," were the words the bad kids used to taunt him. My brother was regularly picked on by the big boys in our neighborhood. They would threaten to beat him up after school, and I often had to stick up for him. Because I was three years younger and three grades lower, I wasn't much help. They would laugh at my attempts to stick up for him.

"Look at Ira's little sister," they'd say, shaking their heads and chuckling with a hint of admiration at my nerve to stand up to them since they were the baddest of the bad boys.

Ira didn't know how to fight, so he would often run home from school with the big boys right on his heels. Our mom grew up in Barnesville, Ohio, out in the country. She went to a small country school, so she didn't know how to advise Ira on how to survive in the city. Our dad grew up in Chicago, but he was quiet and unassuming. From what I understand, his sister Marguerite, who was a year older than him, protected him from any potential bullies he encountered.

"It's not nice to fight," was all she offered up to us as advice on the subject, so Ira continued to get chased home, picked on, and taunted, "Fat boy!"

Ira and I were often sent to the corner store on the next block to buy milk, bread, or eggs. I remember the screen door of the store opening and slamming shut all day long as the neighborhood children scampered in and out, making their purchases of Popsicles, sunflower seeds, pickles, and penny candy. Nickels, pennies, and occasionally dimes were clutched in sweaty palms or dug from the toes of holey tennis shoes. Our coins were exchanged for sweet relief on the long, hot summer days.

One day the storekeeper fished a dill pickle from the large jar on the counter and handed it to Ira, the chubby-cheeked boy in front of him. I busied myself with opening a piece of bubble gum I bought for a penny. I pulled the comic that came with it away from the square of pink bubble gum and popped half of it into my mouth. The gum had a line down the center of it, so you could break off a piece to chew and save the other half for later. My wavy dark brown, almost black hair was plaited into three braids and adorned with blue and white barrettes.

Just then, the door slammed shut as three noisy boys in their early teens came into the store. One of the boys, sporting a chipped front tooth, grabbed Ira's baseball cap and tossed it to his friend, who in turn tossed it to the other boy. Ira jumped from one to the other trying to retrieve it. I joined my brother's battle, yelling loudly, "Give him his cap back."

"We should kick his fat butt," said the boy with the chipped tooth as he pushed Ira into the counter. The store clerk pulled the jar of pickles protectively towards him and out of harm's way, but he did and said nothing to stop the bigger boys' harassment of my brother. Ira regained his balance and bolted out of the store. One of the boys attempted to grab him, but he broke free.

"Leave him alone!" I screamed while forcing my body between the boys and the door. I scrambled to get outside and then thrust my hip against the screen door in an attempt to prevent the big boys from exiting. One of them shoved against the unyielding door as I pushed back on the door with all my might. My sandals skidded across the pavement as the force of the larger boy's shoves threatened to knock me backwards.

"Run, Ira, run," I yelled. The big boys laughed at my feistiness.

"Ah, leave her alone," said the chipped tooth boy to the others, who complied and refocused their attention on the candy behind the counter.

My face was stubbornly determined as I remained at my post and continued to lean forcefully against the door. Out of the corner of my eye, I could see my brother's heavy frame lumbering farther and farther away from the store, every so often looking behind him. Not until he reached the alley in the next block and disappeared around the corner did I release the tension of my backside against the door and follow the path my brother had taken towards home. Not once did I look back.

◆ ◆ ◆

One day on my way home from school, I met Tina on the playground behind Warrington as we tread over rocks and gravel in the schoolyard. She was in my grade but in a different classroom. Tina was originally from the Northside of Minneapolis. She wore really cool clothes like white go-go boots with tassels on them and bell-bottom pants. Tina's parents were very young, which is probably why she had such up-to-date clothes.

My parents, on the other hand, were not so young. In fact, they were already in their forties. They believed in buying practical clothes like turtleneck sweaters, corduroy pants, stretch pants, and Stride Rite shoes, which were sturdy saddle oxfords that laced up and needed to be tied.

Buying shoes was a fun but serious undertaking in my family. My mom and I would catch the bus downtown to Dayton's Department Store and travel to the fifth floor by escalator or elevator. Once in the shoe section, I would mount a short flight of stairs to a platform with railings. A shoe salesman sat on a stool level with my feet. He first measured them using an elaborate device that measured both the length and width of my feet. He then disappeared through a curtain against the wall into another room. After a few minutes, he would return with a few boxes containing an assortment of shoe styles, which he tried on my feet using a shoehorn.

He then went about the serious business of pressing down on the shoes near my toes to test whether I had enough space around my toes for my feet to grow and inserting his fingers into the shoe along the side of my instep to determine if I had enough room to walk comfortably. I was then allowed to walk down the steps and around the shoe department to try the shoes out and see how they felt on my feet. My mom would look at me as I walked, then call me over to her, so she could repeat what the shoe salesman had already done. Stride Rite shoes were not the cutest shoes in the world, but they were durable. I usually outgrew them long before they ever wore out.

Tina often wore patent leather slip-ons with bows or buckles that matched her trendy outfits. In the wintertime, she had fashionable boots called Kickerinos, which you did not wear shoes under. My boots were rubber and needed to be pulled on over my shoes. Not cool. Another thing I liked about Tina was her bangs. She had long bangs that lay flat on her forehead, which made her look much older than eight.

Tina lived one block north of my house, on Portland, in a red-and-white stucco duplex with her parents, younger sister, and twin baby brothers. When I was not walking to school with the Barrett girls, I would often ring her doorbell in the morning, so we could walk to school together. Because of our differences, I suppose, we became very good friends.

CHAPTER 5

Summer Vacation

♦ ♦ ♦

Every summer, our family went on vacation to visit our out-of-town relatives. We didn't have any relatives in Minneapolis. Even so, I had an array of aunts, uncles, godparents, and play cousins since my parents had plenty of friends. Their close friends took the place of family, and we celebrated birthdays and holidays with them.

But when the summertime rolled around each year, we packed up my dad's car and drove down the highway long distances to see our "real" family. The first stop was the Southside of Chicago, where the majority of my dad's family lived. The Dan Ryan Expressway carried us into a world devoid of whiteness. I peered out of the car window to behold a sea of Blackness, so unlike the world I inhabited in Minnesota.

"Where are the white people?" I remember asking my dad. He laughed out loud but reserved comment.

My childhood impression of Chicago included men with processed hair tied down with silk scarves; children scampering back and forth on porches stacked to the sky; music blasting on speakers, which invited passersby into the record shop under the El tracks that blocked the sunlight on 63rd Street near my great grandmother Mother Dear's house.

I can remember attending the church that my great-grandfather, Ira Monroe Hendon, founded. Morning Star Baptist Church was on the corner of 41st and South Parkway. My grandfather also had a church in the Altgeld Gardens out on 134th Street. My grandparents, T. R. and Thelma Hendon, and their son Edmund lived next door to it. Across the street was a candy store. All over Chicago, buildings were tagged with gang signs according to whose turf they were in (El Rukn, Blackstone Rangers, Gangster Disciples). Because of the high rate of crime, there were barred windows and doors. There was also nonstop movement and activity.

My dad's younger brother, Edmund, was only a few years older than Ira and me. When we went to Chicago, we always had a good time with him. Since their house was across the street from the candy store, we went over there to buy penny candy, potato chips, and pickles as often as possible. One summer, my uncle accidentally shot me in the foot with a BB gun, so I blackmailed him into buying me candy the whole time we were there, or I threatened to spill the beans.

Although they lived in a house next to my grandfather's church, Bethel Baptist, on 134th Street across from Carver Park, most of the housing in Altgeld Gardens consisted of two-story public housing units. There was a lot of crime in the Gardens, so my grandparents had an alarm system, a steel grate on their front and back doors, and chains across the windows. Even so, they still had a problem with burglars. My uncle was a photographer, and apparently, the neighbors knew he owned expensive camera equipment.

Because of the crime, I didn't like Chicago very much. It seemed like a big, mean city to me, and it was. Pudgy was my youngest cousin at that time. He was six years younger than me, and I enjoyed giving him piggyback rides everywhere I went. When we visited Chicago, Pudgy and I were inseparable.

After spending about a week in Chicago, the next stop was Indianapolis, where we visited more of my dad's relatives, including his mother and stepfather, Nano and Daddy Gene, Aunt Minthy and Uncle John. Compared to Chicago, Indianapolis was slower-paced and did not have the feeling of constant danger and excitement Chicago had. My grandparents there had an air conditioner, which was a huge relief on the hot days of summer.

Then it was onward to Ohio where my mom's extended family lived in Cedarville, a small country town. My grandfather had a large garden in the back of the house where he planted and harvested corn, beans, and an assortment of other vegetables, melons, and herbs. On the back porch and in the center of the garden were water pumps with a handle you moved up and down to make the water come out. There were also three sheds in the backyard where my grandpa stored his tools and coal to keep the house heated during cold weather.

Train tracks a block away carried trains that caused the house to shake from them coming and going at all times of the day and night. A long resounding horn alerted men, women, and children to move off the tracks to let the train pass. At night, as I lay in bed, that horn was a lonely sound. I would lie there wondering where the train was heading as it whizzed past in the country night, brightened only by lightning bugs.

A short distance from my grandparents' house, next to the tracks, was a pen containing hogs awaiting freight trains that would transport them to their next destination. My brother and I, city kids hailing from Minneapolis, Minnesota, loved to watch them wallow in the mud, slurp slop, and nurse their piglets. The rails have since been removed, and the pigpen has been replaced by a library, a laundromat, and a pharmacy, which represents progress, I guess, yet I still yearn sometimes for the trains and the hogs.

Back in the day, a rooster's crow awakened us for breakfast. I loved Cedarville for its small-town charm and its feeling of safety and security. My grandparent's clock sat on the living room mantle and chimed at the top of the hour and then again, a half hour later. I remember a donkey-pulled cart making its way up the road along with its driver and the milkman delivering brown glass bottles of Borden's milk.

When not in the garden, my grandfather spent much of his time on the front porch chewing tobacco and spitting tobacco juice into a coffee can with me at his feet on the front steps. When not on the front porch, he could be found in the living room in his big recliner doing the same thing. He seemed to enjoy each day we were there. My grandfather didn't have any teeth, so his food had to be cut up into tiny pieces, and his corn had to be scraped from the cob with a small utensil made specifically for that purpose. He didn't talk much, but he smiled at me often.

One summer when I was six or seven, Grandpa pulled out his pocketknife, made a few moves, and presented me with a freshly cut branch from the tree in the front yard. The branch became my imaginary horse, "Black Beauty," so named after a book my mom was reading to my brother and me that summer. Each day of my time in Ohio, I galloped around the yard on Black Beauty. When vacation was over, my grandpa put her away in the shed for safekeeping until I returned the following summer.

My grandma's memory was going, so whenever she called out to me, she first went down a list of names that included my mom's name, Bernese, and the names of her sisters, Lois and Wylda. I answered to whatever name she landed on since I knew that it was me she was calling. I remember how gently she combed my hair and her black leather high-heeled shoes that laced up.

My cousin Paula grew up in Cedarville, where my maternal grandparents and extended family lived. She was ten years older than me. When our family traveled to Ohio each summer to visit, Paula acted towards me like the older sister I did not have.

Paula was beautiful in appearance. In her background, she had Native American as well as African American heritage on both sides of her family. She had inherited Uncle Paul's beautiful head of hair. His was short and wavy, but Paula's hair was so long, it hung down her back in soft curls. She set it on huge rollers using Dippity Do and then combed it into the fabulous hairstyles of the 1960s, such as French rolls or ponytails with stylish bangs combed across her forehead and bobby pinned into place on the side of her head.

I wanted to be just like her when I became a teenager. Paula was a cheerleader for Cedarville High School. She practiced elaborate routines with her baton on my grandparents' front lawn. She twirled, spun, and tossed her baton high into the air with gusto and then caught it without breaking her marching stride. Whenever we went to Dayton, Ohio, to visit Aunt Lois, Uncle Bob, and their son Bobby Jr., Paula turned all the boys' heads without even trying.

"Hey, Paulette!" I can remember one young man yelling at her from down Orchard Avenue trying to catch her attention but missing the mark by calling her out of her name. As we got out of the car after our trip from Cedarville and headed towards our aunt's house for Sunday dinner, Paula glanced down the street at him but didn't pay him any mind. Teenage boys were always trying to catch her attention, so she just twiddled her fingers in his general direction, tossed her flowing hair, and kept right on walking.

When I was small, Paula would comb my hair into older girl styles, which I loved. She also took me to football games in Cedarville or along with her to visit her friend Treva out in the country. Back behind Central State, a historically Black college located in Wilberforce, Ohio, a few miles from Cedarville, there was a highway that had so many hills and curves, they called it Devil's Backbone. When Paula got her license, she took me for a joyride down Devil's Backbone. The road behind Central State had sharp curves, steep hills, and deep valleys. It was a scary and exciting ride, and it felt good to have an older cousin take me places.

The summer I was ten years old, I sat very still at my grandparents' kitchen table with eager anticipation as Paula used ice cubes wrapped in a washcloth to freeze my earlobes, so she could pierce my ears. After both ears were pierced, she showed me how to keep them clean by pouring peroxide in the bottle top and soaking my earlobes. The peroxide made bubbling sounds as it attacked the bacteria and germs that could possibly cause infection in my newly pierced ears. Wearing earrings made me feel like the big girl I was becoming.

What I enjoyed most about Cedarville were Paula's cousins on her dad's side, the Thompsons. There were eleven children in their family, and we had fun every time I came to visit. Their dad, Uncle Charles, would sometimes give us pop bottles to take to the gas station where we could trade the bottles in for money to buy candy. To feed his brood of eleven children, Uncle Charles kept hunting dogs in a pen behind his house that he used whenever he went hunting wild game, such as possums, raccoons, deer, wild turkeys, and who knows what else. He also kept farm animals on his property—chickens, goats, ducks, and maybe even an occasional pig.

Their mother, Aunt Betty, didn't mind us carrying the two babies, Joyce and Paul, around with us and playing house. We also liked to play records and do the latest dances. I got to live out my fantasy of being part of a large family whenever I came to town.

Because Cedarville was such a small town, the grownups let us come and go as we pleased, so we would walk down to the schoolyard to play on the swings or visit the hogs in the holding pen near the train tracks, or we would simply do nothing, just walk around laughing and talking. Small town life was easygoing and uncomplicated, just what a city girl like me needed sometimes.

Paula eventually met Orville, and they fell in love. Orville was a young man from Yellow Springs, a nearby small town. She and Orville took my brother Ira and me to a drive-in movie one night. Ira and I sat in the front seat of Orville's cream-colored Volkswagen Bug, and Paula and Orville sat in the backseat, so they could smooch. I can remember pretending I was tired and resting my head sideways on the seat so I could spy on them kissing.

Nowadays, whenever I go back to Cedarville to visit, and I look at the rusted pump that is still in the yard behind the house, I can still envision my grandpa in his garden moving slowly down its rows harvesting just the right amount of corn, tomatoes, beans, and potatoes to go with the fried chicken for Sunday dinner. I'll never forget the look of surprise on his face one summer as he cranked the pump's handle, and a swarm of angry bees, which had taken up residence inside, flew from the spigot and stung him. I remember my grandmother sitting at the kitchen table dressing and bandaging his hurt hand.

My mom's older sister, Aunt Lois, and her family lived in the city of Dayton, Ohio, which was about twenty-five miles from Cedarville. Just like Paula, Aunt Lois's son, Bobby Jr., was a teenager when I was a child. He had all the latest records and the best-looking Afro around. Bobby loved to dress. He worked for a company that made cash registers, so he was able to buy a car when he was only seventeen or eighteen years old. Our family always spent a night or two in Dayton whenever we visited Ohio. Bobby would take me for rides in his car, so I could check out the cityscape in Dayton.

Aunt Lois's family lived a couple of blocks away from Bobby's high school, Roosevelt High. From Aunt Lois's front porch, I could hear the high school drum and bugle corps practicing. I would watch them march down Orchard Avenue with the girls twirling their batons and the boys beating the drums and blowing their horns while marching to the beat. The front steps provided me an excellent front-row seat to witness their electrifying choreography and rhythmic movements as their bodies made elaborate and well-executed patterns in the streets of Dayton, Ohio.

In the late sixties, the Black Power Movement was catching fire. I remember Bobby giving me a beaded necklace adorned with a Tiki, which was a carved wooden African mask that symbolized Black pride. He and his friends would sit around in the living room of their home on Orchard Avenue and talk about the plight of Black people. Although I did not understand all that was said, their discussions about racial pride, Black power, and the lyrics of records they played by The Last Poets, which predated rap music but had the same concept—poetry over music—helped to instill within me a sense of pride and a deeper understanding of what it meant to be a Black person in America.

CHAPTER 6

Third Grade

◈ ◈ ◈

Mrs. White, my third-grade teacher, was a strict disciplinarian who lived on the same block as the Barrett sisters. She was youngish and attractive in a teacherly sort of way with dark skin and medium-length hair. Mrs. White dressed conservatively in tailored skirts, form-fitting blouses, and high-heeled shoes. I knew she smoked cigarettes because one time, she invited me into the classroom's storage closet to give me a green sucker for my rare, good behavior, and I could smell cigarettes on her breath.

Mrs. White introduced the class to reading chapter books. Each day she read to us from books by Laura Ingalls Wilder, including *Little House in the Big Woods, Little House on the Prairie,* and *These Happy Golden Years.* I loved hearing about Laura Ingalls and her family's escapades. She also read books to us by E. B. White, like *Charlotte's Web* and *Stuart Little.* Because I liked Wilbur the pig, *Charlotte's Web* was my favorite book at the time.

Mrs. White taught the class how to write in cursive rather than print. She kept a small file box on the windowsill containing index cards for each letter of the alphabet, including both capital and small letters. Each card had arrows indicating how we were supposed to start and finish each character. We were free to get up from our desks to select a card from the index box, so we could practice our handwriting. While she allowed us some freedom in the classroom, Mrs. White was by no means lax when it came to discipline.

When Mrs. White's students stepped out of line, she would whack us with the ruler she always kept nearby or tell the offending party to stand on the side of the classroom and "pump water." This meant we had to put our hands on top of our heads and repeatedly squat down and stand back up until Mrs. White let us go back to our desks. I spent quite a bit of time during my third-grade school year pumping water alongside several of my classmates or being whacked with the ruler. It would be fair to say that collectively my class was a talkative and unruly bunch. Mrs. White did her best to bring us back into line.

Third grade was also the year I learned how to do the Twist, the Dog, and other popular dances of that time. Candy was a girl in my class who taught the rest of the third graders how to do the Dog. She was a pretty, brown-skinned girl with naturally arched eyebrows, sharp features, and a beautiful smile.

One day during recess, she got down on her hands and knees and arched her back up and down in time with the beat of whatever song was in her mind. I stared at Candy in shock and admiration. I wouldn't dare do a dance as nasty as the Dog, but Candy was far more advanced than the rest of us third-grade girls. She had even started to develop breasts, or "titties," as the kids called them. One of my friends told me Candy let her touch one behind the school building. She said it felt like a hard little rock underneath Candy's skin.

On the way home from school one day, I saw a group of kids standing on the outside of Mr. Crown's Barber Shop on 38th Street and 4th Avenue peering through the large plate glass window. Curious, I joined them at the window and looked in.

"Tony Oliva's in the barbershop," a boy with two missing front teeth told me.

"Stop lying," I demanded.

Even I knew Tony Oliva played baseball for the Minnesota Twins. I couldn't believe such a famous man was at the barbershop in our neighborhood.

"I ain't lyin'. He's right there," the boy lisped as he pointed through the window at a dark brown-skinned man sitting in the barber chair.

"I'm fin' to go in there and get his autograph," the toothless boy bragged.

Not to be outdone, I declared, "So am I!"

Usually, girls did not go into the barbershop. The barbershop was officially male territory. But that day, I went in and shyly asked for Tony Oliva's autograph.

On the last day of school, we had a going-away party in our class-room. Warrington, which had ninety-eight percent Black students in 1966, was closing to desegregate the schools in South Minneapolis. All the students at Warrington were going to be bused to five different schools, including Horace Mann, Clinton, Bancroft, Agassiz, and Lyn-dale. I would be going to Bancroft when school started after summer vacation.

Mrs. White let us bring 45 records, so we could dance at the party. I brought *Don't Mess with Bill* by the Marvelettes and *Papa's Got a Brand New Bag* by James Brown. At the party, the students paired off and did one of the latest dances called the Tip. It was a dance modeled after the Temptations' choreography. You stepped on your tiptoes twice on one side and then again twice on the other side while coordinating the syncopated movements of your hands and arms with the foot you were leading with. That day I danced with Candy, who didn't dare do the Dog in front of Mrs. White.

CHAPTER 7

The Polaroid Picture

During the summer of 1973, when I was fifteen years old, my family and I traveled to Indianapolis just as we had done every other summer of my life. Our annual summer vacation began by visiting our relatives on my dad's side of the family, who lived in Chicago and Indianapolis, and then traveling to Ohio to visit my mom's side of the family.

Indianapolis was the home of Nano and Daddy Gene, my grandparents on my dad's side. My favorite little cousin Pudgy, his parents, Norval and Odessa, and his baby brother, Sean, were also visiting Indianapolis with us that summer, along with my dad's sister Auntie Marge. We had driven together in a caravan from Chicago. I can still remember the shoes I had on that day—white webbed sandals with three- to four-inch cork platforms. Nano liked them so much she asked me if she could try them on, and I snapped a picture of her standing in her living room. It was my favorite room in her single-level modern home, mainly because she had air conditioning, which was still somewhat of a luxury in 1973.

Taking family photos was part of our summertime tradition when we visited our extended family, so shortly after we arrived, we all gathered together to sit on the living room floor to take Polaroid pictures. One photo was of Nano, Auntie Marge, Pudgy, Sean, and me. After it was taken, we waited patiently for the minute or so it took to develop. Then the back was peeled off, so the picture could be passed around the room for all the family to see and admire.

When it was finally passed to me, my heart sank as I looked at it. What should have been apparent to me—but was somehow overlooked—could not be denied. Nano, Auntie Marge, Pudgy, and Sean all resembled one another and looked like a family should. Their skin tone was similar in the mid-brown range. Pudgy, Sean, and Auntie Marge were all sporting Afro hairstyles, although Auntie Marge's was more of a curly 'fro with a blue rinse. And there I sat with my pale-yellow skin and freckles with a huge Angela Davis-like natural hairdo.

I am pretty sure that prior to 1973, I realized I looked different from the rest of the family, but for some reason that year, the point was driven painfully home. As the horrifying reality of my adopted familial status sank in, my spirits also sank down to the bottoms of my platform shoes. What was probably apparent to everyone else was brand new to me. I did not look like I belonged in the family.

Where in the past my different looks did not bother me, suddenly they bothered me a great deal. I became angry and sullen and stopped speaking to my little cousin Pudgy, who was six years younger than me. All his life, he had been the object of my adoration. He was used to me playing with him, taking him to the corner store across from our Chicago grandparents' house for candy, and giving him piggyback rides all over the neighborhood. But after seeing the Polaroid picture, I shut down emotionally. I felt like an outsider who didn't look like I belonged to the family, while he fit in perfectly. I shut myself away from him and refused to respond to his attempts to play with me or talk to me.

Of course, Pudgy was too young to understand why I wouldn't talk to him. Plus, I never bothered to explain. If Pudgy entered the room, I would leave. If he came inside, I would go outside. I clamped my jaws tight in an intense frown and ignored him.

At age fifteen, the scab that had protected me from the knowledge that I was adopted was rapidly being scraped away. I could no longer explain away the differences I saw in the mirror that made me appear different from my adoptive family as I could when I was still a child.

"I have light skin and freckles like my mom, and I got my wavy hair from my dad," I would say when schoolmates and friends chattered about which relative they looked like, walked like, or talked like.

But the truth of the matter was, my skin was lighter in complexion than either my mom's or my dad's. As a matter of fact, my dad was very dark-skinned, along with (it seemed to me) the entire population of Chicago's notorious Southside, where I now realized I stood out like an albino in Africa.

Looking at the Polaroid picture that was being circulated around my grandmother's living room brought my simmering pain and rage about being an adopted light-skinned girl to the surface. As a result, I did not want anything to do with Pudgy with his brown skin and physical features that enabled him to fit in perfectly with the rest of the Hendon family. To me, my freckled, beige skin looked obscenely pale in comparison, and my towering Angela Davis-like Afro could not make up for my lack of Afro-centric features.

I simply did not fit in. Filled with self-loathing, I wanted to be all alone. It made no sense for me to continue to pretend to be part of the family gathering that was taking place in Nano's living room. The laughter and conversation continued around me, but I refused to participate. Instead, I just sat there and pouted, wondering, *who am I really?* For the remainder of our time in Indianapolis, I retreated into a shell. I felt just like the proverbial ugly duckling, a swan who felt out of place when she found herself afloat within a family of ducks. I wondered who I really was and how I had come to be in this world.

Looking back, that Polaroid picture was a turning point in my life. It generated within me an unquenchable thirst to have a baby of my own. While sealed birth records kept me from finding my birth parents and extended biological family, at the tender age of fifteen, I decided to have my own child. I wanted to give birth to a blood relative, who would be mine, all mine.

CHAPTER 8

Meeting Blue

The yellow and black Cadillac DeVille turned right off Sheridan Avenue onto Plymouth Avenue and cruised slowly down the street. The driver had one hand on the black-laced, leather-covered steering wheel. His other hand was draped across the armrest, also known as the leaning stool, between the driver's and passenger's seat. As he drove, he leaned hard to the right in the style customary to street players of that era. From the eight-track player situated near the floor in front of the leaning stool blared one of the Ohio Players' recordings, *Black Cat,* which fit the scenario as it was a song about a young man riding in his Cadillac.

Teenagers and young adults strolling along Plymouth Avenue turned and nodded at the well-known and respected young driver as the booming bass reverberated from the speakers of his passing vehicle. Blue flashed his megawatt smile and would nod in return. His brilliant smile revealed perfectly straight, white teeth, his trademark. His nickname, Blue, was never intended to be a compliment. Instead, it was meant to insult the rich black hue of his skin. The words, "You're so black, you're blue," were aimed at him by self-hating children during an impressionable age. But instead of letting the words defeat him, he embraced the nickname, Blue, and he rocked it with pride.

Blue and his siblings were legends on the Northside of Minneapolis. Stairstep brothers and sisters whose ages in 1974 ranged from sixteen to nineteen, the Lockett family was known for their chiseled features, high cheekbones, good looks, soft hair, stylish clothes, long, lithe limbs, and well-executed moves on the dance floor.

I met Blue through one of my best high school friends, DeLady. She became pregnant at age fifteen during the summer we were going into eleventh grade. Her baby's father, Joe, was Blue's cousin. Although I had seen him around, Blue and I did not meet formally until one day in

October of '73 as I was walking down Plymouth Avenue, the main drag of Minneapolis's Northside. There was an assortment of small business-es, stores, and other establishments scattered up and down the street, including First Bank Plymouth, Estes Funeral Chapel, Odell Record Store, and the Way Community Center.

At one point in time, there had been several more businesses, but they were burned down during the race riots of the 1960s. At that time, there had been a strong Jewish presence in the neighborhood; many of the African American churches were once synagogues. Pilot City Health Center, where my mother worked as an obstetrics and gynecolo-gy (OB-GYN) nurse, was housed in a former synagogue.

As I walked past Estes Funeral Home that day, I ran into Blue. He was smiling when I looked up and saw him. The flash of his teeth should have been on a toothpaste commercial.

"Are you over here to see your man?" he asked. "I sure wish it was me."

I looked at him shyly, but inside my heart sang. We spoke for a few minutes then went our separate ways. I thought about Blue the next day at school during typing class and daydreamed about being his girlfriend.

Blue was handsome. I was reminded of the Bible verse, Solomon 1:5: *I am black, but comely . . .* Blue's skin was a deep shade of brown like my dad's. His eyes were beautiful and almond shaped. From the well-pro-nounced hump on the bridge of his nose, I suspected Native American was in his family's gene pool. Blue's coal-black hair would eventually grow long and hang past his shoulders, but at that point in time in 1973, Blue sported an Afro.

The next time I ran into him at a house party, Blue asked me for my phone number, and we started talking on the phone. Before long, he started coming over to visit. He was only seventeen years old, but he was already driving a Cadillac. He worked as an electrical apprentice after school and on weekends to buy gas and keep spending money in his pocket.

What we had most in common was our love of music. He would sometimes borrow my 45s and record albums to tape. I had an exten-sive music collection because I saved my lunch money to spend at Jet

Record Store on the corner of 38th and 4th Avenue South. Whenever we went riding in his car, Blue blasted the latest jams on his eight-track cassette player, like Kool and the Gang's "Jungle Boogie" or the Chi-Lites' "Stoned Out of My Mind."

I looked forward to hearing my doorbell ring and looking out the front window to find Blue standing there. The more time we spent together, the more I liked him.

CHAPTER 9

Fuzzy Warbles

My friend Tina had heard of a nightclub in downtown Minneapolis called Fuzzy Warbles that she wanted to check out.

"How are we gonna get in a nightclub?" I wondered aloud.

"Darla has fake IDs we can use."

Darla was the white girlfriend of Tina's dad. Actually, she was Jewish, which was a form of being white, we guessed. Darla would pick us up that Friday around the corner from Tina's house on 39th and Portland and out of the sight of Tina's mother. She was no joke, and Darla must have known it.

"Don't forget it costs a dollar to get in," Tina reminded me as we parted ways after school. At that time, we were both attending Roosevelt High School. "But the dollar is a cover charge. They give you a ticket to buy a drink."

I had no idea how Tina knew all that about the club, seeing that neither one of us was old enough to get in, but I didn't bother to ask. Tina was seven months older than me, and I was used to her knowing things about life I didn't yet know or understand.

When Friday finally rolled around, I asked my mom if I could go to a party with Tina. After assuring her Darla would take us to the party and pick us up, I was given permission to go. Darla was as good as her word and picked us up around the corner from Tina's house as promised.

Her chubby, cinnamon-toned two-year-old son, Daniel, was in the back seat. According to Tina, Daniel was completely out of control. She said Darla let him do anything his little heart desired, including eating whatever he wanted.

Sure enough, as soon as we got into the car and as if on cue, Daniel said, "Mom, can I have a doughnut?"

"After I drop the girls off, Daniel," Darla promised.

She rummaged around in her purse and handed me her driver's license and passed another fake ID card to Tina. At that time, driver's licenses did not have pictures on them. Her height and weight did not match mine, but I hoped the bouncer wouldn't scrutinize it thoroughly. As we got closer to downtown, Tina handed me a jar of Vaseline.

"Here, Colnese, use some of this on your lips. It will make you look older, like you have on lip gloss."

I put my finger in the jar and rubbed a dab of Vaseline on my lips. Darla pulled up to the corner of 9th and Hennepin and dropped us off in front of the club. By using the fake IDs Darla had lent to us, we slid past the bouncer at the door with ease. Although I had a baby face, my body was well developed to be so young, and Tina looked mature for her age with sexy clothing to match. The bouncer looked at our IDs and waved us through the entrance after the cashier collected our one-dollar cover charge and handed us tickets to get free drinks.

Tina and I approached the bar to place our orders. I had no idea what to get, but I spotted someone seated down the bar drinking something pretty and pink with orange slices and maraschino cherries. I asked the bartender what it was. He told me it was called a Singapore Sling, so that is what I ordered.

It was the last drink either of us paid for that night. The wonderful thing about being teenage girls in a nightclub was that there was an endless supply of middle-aged men who were ready and willing to buy us liquor. The free drinks usually didn't stop until the "last call for alcohol" was called by the disc jockey.

After Tina bought her drink, the two of us found a seat at a small round table. Soon a smiling man chewing a large cigar and sporting a large belly asked if he could join us. The man, who said his name was Curtis, told us he was a Pullman porter on a train. Curtis must have just got paid because his bankroll was fat, and he was generous with it. He chewed on his cigar, nervously making small talk with us. Curtis was pleasant to talk to and didn't seem to mind when we got up from time to time to dance with the younger men. I think he got off from having two attractive young girls at his table.

The dance floor was elevated, so we had to walk up a few steps to get on it. It was enclosed by a black wrought iron railing. The enclosure made it feel as if we were dancing in a mirrored boxing ring. The dance floor was surrounded by mirrors on either side. Marvin Gaye's voice crooned "Let's Get It On" as couples made their way to the dance floor to slow dance. I felt someone tap me on the shoulder.

"Wanna dance?"

I got up and followed the young man to the floor, and soon we were slow dancing. As I wrapped my arms around his shoulders, he draped his arm around my waist, and we moved together in step with the beat. All around us, other couples were doing the same thing—dancing, grinding, and dipping in step with Marvin Gaye's lyrics. I caught a glimpse of us in the mirror as we turned slowly to the music. In that moment, I was hooked on the nightlife. The nightclub scene was a new and exciting world.

After the dance, I went to the bar to get another drink. A big, burly looking dude paid for my drink and sat down next to me as I began to sip on it. The lights came on right then, and the bartender yelled, "Last call for alcohol!" With the lights turned up, people began to make their way to the door and poured out onto the pavement in front of the bar. I followed along with the crowd craning my neck for Tina. I didn't want to miss out on the ride home from Darla, who was supposed to be picking us up at one in the morning when the club closed. The man, who had paid for my drink, followed me out the door and grabbed my arm.

"Come on, let's go."

I looked at him like he was crazy. "Go where?"

"You're coming with me," he demanded. "I bought you a drink, didn't I?"

Out on the street, I got a better look at him. His face was flushed with the effects of too much alcohol. His voice began to get louder and more persistent, his grip on my arm became tighter, and he began to tug on it. I panicked when it finally dawned on me who he was.

I recognized him to be one of the older brothers of a large, notorious Northside family. His face didn't have the most intelligent expression I had ever seen in my life, and his crude demands gave him a caveman-like demeanor. He also seemed like the type of man who would be right at home with grabbing a woman by the hair and dragging her down the street. He appeared to be the type of person that might just start banging on his chest.

Right as I was wondering how I was going to get away from him in one piece, Blue walked up, quickly assessed the situation, and said, "It looks like you need a ride. Come on."

I glanced around nervously to see what was going on with Cave Man. Luckily his attention had been deflected from me to the bouncer, who had heard the loud ruckus. The bouncer glanced down and noticed that homeboy had walked out of the club with a drink in his hand. While the bouncer confronted him about the drink, I fell in step right behind Blue as he led the way down Hennepin Avenue towards the parking lot in the next block. I was silently thanking the Lord that Blue had shown up at the right time to rescue me from the drunken mad man.

When we reached his car, I saw that his sidekick, Gee Rich, was in the driver's seat. We got in the back seat together and rode around town for a while, looking for an after-hours party. Gee Rich asked somebody he pulled up alongside and found out about a party in South Minneapolis on 37th and Stevens at Ronnie Gross's house. On weekends, the house he shared with his girlfriend and their son was transformed into a gambling joint where men shot craps in the upstairs bedroom. Non-gamblers could purchase drinks and fried chicken or fish dinners or just hang out, listen to music, and socialize.

When we got inside, Blue and Gee Rich went upstairs to check out the craps game after ordering a drink for me. I sipped on my drink and eventually followed the crowd outside as the party spilled out onto the front lawn. I was pleasantly surprised to see Tina standing on the stairs leading into the house with a girl I had never seen before but had heard about. Her name was Marita, and she was a mixed girl with bluish-gray eyes and sandy brown curly hair. She was only fourteen or fifteen years old, and word on the street was that she was already turning tricks.

"Man, the bitch been working all night and only made seventeen dollars," her man, Renard, complained loudly to a couple of his friends as Marita got into the back seat of his golden-brown Cadillac.

I recognized one of the guys in the car to be DeAndre. I had seen him around at Phelps Park and at dances at Glenwood-Lyndale Community Center, which was in the Northside projects off Olson Highway. DeAndre was tall, slim, flashy, and always well dressed, usually in a suit. His skin was mahogany brown, and his eyes were round and fringed with thick lashes. He referred to himself as "Diamond DeAndre" because he liked to sport diamond rings and wear gold jewelry.

The young men laughed loudly and slapped one another's palms. I glanced over at Marita to see her reaction to Renard's disrespectful words, but she looked bored and oblivious to what they were saying about her. A few other girls I knew from high school had dropped out to become prostitutes. I saw them as they worked on the "'ho stroll." They sashayed up and down Lake Street, Nicollet Avenue, and Hennepin Avenue, attracting and getting picked up by tricks willing to pay for sex. It may have been a coincidence, but it seemed like the pimping and prostitution in Minneapolis caught on fire and spread rapidly after a movie entitled *The Mack* started being shown at local movie theaters. Then again, it could have been that the movie made me more aware of what was going on around me.

When Tina and I had gone to the movies to check it out, the theater had been full of teenagers and young adults. It was the story of a pimp named Goldie and his whores. The soundtrack by Willie Hutch could be heard blaring out of just about everybody's car. *The Mack* portrayed the lifestyle as being so glamorous that everyone, it seemed, was emulating and reenacting scenes from the movie. What wasn't completely spelled out in the movie was thoroughly covered in books on the topic of pimping by Iceberg Slim and Donald Goines.

Suddenly, I noticed the young men in my neighborhood driving Cadillacs and pimping whores. Many of my friends were being lured into prostitution by the demands of their men and the so-called glamorous life they craved so desperately.

Not long after Marita got into the car with Renard, Blue and Gee Rich came outside to see where I had gone.

"Are you ready to roll?" Blue asked.

"Yeah, hold up a minute."

I walked over to where I saw Tina standing on the front lawn and told her I'd see her later. I then followed them to the car. Gee Rich drove North on Stevens Avenue, then merged onto 35W North, exited onto 94W, heading for the Northside. He drove Blue's car to an address on

4th Street in the projects and got out of the car. Blue said a few parting words to Gee Rich, jumped into the driver's seat, and told me to get up front next to him. He then headed to 11th and Sheridan where he lived with his parents, two sisters, and brother. Blue was second to the youngest.

I was in awe of his sister Jackie, who was nineteen years old at that time and one of the best dressed teenage girls on the Northside. She owned a nice black and yellow two-toned sports car and wore beautiful gold and diamond-studded jewelry. Rumor had it she went out of town and danced in hick towns all over Minnesota to make her loot, but I wasn't sure if that was true or not. Jackie stood out in the crowd as the owner of several full-length furs and an array of clothing that hung just right. In my opinion, she could have given professional models a run for their money with her tall, slender frame, high cheekbones, and pouty lips.

Jasmine, Blue's younger sister's claim to fame was her ability to dance. She and Blue had that in common. He was one of the best dancers in Minneapolis at that time. Blue's brother Apollo was being groomed by an older woman as Minneapolis's next up-and-coming pimp.

As I followed Blue through the back door and past the back porch where his brother Apollo slept, I hoped I wouldn't run into either of his sisters since there was an ongoing rivalry between Northside and Southside girls, who didn't like each other on general principles, mainly possessiveness and jealousy over boys on our respective sides of town.

Luck was on my side. Since it was close to three in the morning, the house was quiet. We crept quietly up the stairs to Blue's room. He turned on his stereo very low. Earth, Wind, and Fire's "Keep Your Head to the Sky" played softly. I looked around the room and liked what I saw. I was the most amazed by his bed, which towered waist high or better above the floor due to an extra two or three mattresses piled on top, and several pillows added for extra comfort.

"Have a seat," he gestured.

I turned around with my back towards the bed, then hoisted myself up. My legs dangled over the edge, but with the bed so high, my feet were nowhere near the floor. Blue climbed up next to me and smoothly wrapped his arms around me while placing his lips on mine for a deep heartfelt soul kiss.

Things quickly heated up between us. Blue was the best kisser I had ever encountered in my nearly sixteen years of life. The best way to describe it is that he took his time and put his heart into everything he did. If his feelings for me during the wee hours of that morning were not real, I couldn't tell by the quality of the kisses he laid on me and the way he touched me. I decided to get even more comfortable and relaxed back against the pillows to receive even more of what Blue had to offer.

"Do you want to spend the night, or don't you love me enough yet?" Blue asked.

Just the way he asked me that question endeared him to me. There was nothing about his tone that implied he had any expectations or that there was any pressure. Unknown to him, he had already captured my heart when he rescued me from danger after the club closed.

"I love you enough," I replied simply.

As far as I was concerned, Blue put the "G" in gentleman. He took me home as the sun was rising and the birds were harmonizing a beautiful melody to let the world know another day was beginning.

CHAPTER 10

Runaway Child

◆ ◆ ◆

Right before my sixteenth birthday, I discovered I was expecting the baby I had wanted for so long, the blood relative I so desperately yearned for. When I told him, Blue was as excited about the pregnancy as I was. His bright smile said it all, and when he pulled me closer to give me a kiss, I could feel his joy and pride about the news I had just shared with him. We had a baby on the way.

Not long after, Blue went to Juvenile Center. I found out when I called his house late one night, and his mother answered the phone. She told me where he was and went on to say much more about his friend, Gee Rich. Mrs. Lockett was very angry at Gee Rich, who she blamed for Blue getting into trouble.

"Ever since he started hanging around with Gee Rich, he's been stealing and staying in trouble," she stormed. "Now he's locked up. I told him about hanging with Gee Rich. He ain't no good."

I listened to Mrs. Lockett as she vented about Blue being in Juvenile Center and her suspicions that Gee Rich had something to do with it. I was happy she was confiding in me, but I was unhappy to learn Blue was locked up. He hadn't been around for a few days, and I had no idea where he was. Now I knew why he had been missing in action; however, being locked up in Juvenile Center was not what I was hoping to hear.

Finally, though, after a few weeks, Blue was released, and I couldn't wait to see him. I was at a Southside party with my friend Mocha. Blue had dropped us off and was going to make a run and then return to the party. As it neared midnight when most Southside teen parties wrapped up, Gee Rich showed up at the party without Blue.

"Hey, girl," he greeted me. "Who's your friend?"

"Where's Blue?" I asked, ignoring his question.

"He told me to make sure you got home safely. He had to take care of something."

"Home? We're not fixin' to go home, are we, Mocha? We came to party!"

"Oh, so your name's Mocha?" Gee Rich looked her up and down. "I'm Gee Rich."

Mocha, my high school friend since tenth grade, nodded her head in greeting. She was pretty. The corners of her mouth were naturally turned up into a perpetual smile. She looked just like a colored baby doll I once had as a child. She was healthy looking and sturdy. Her large Afro was jet black and glossy and didn't look quite real. I knew she was going to make it in life because she could sing. Mocha was already in a band and singing in nightclubs around town.

"Where do you think he is, Gee Rich?" I asked.

"I think he had to pick up his sister Jasmine from a party over North. I know where it's at if we can find a ride over there."

"You know none of these square Southsiders are going anywhere near the Northside," I exclaimed. "I guess we're just going to have to catch a cab. How much money do you have, Mocha?"

"I don't know. About five dollars," she replied, digging around in her pockets.

"All I got is three. What about you, Gee Rich?"

"I'm straight," was his reply. "I got a little something. Just call the cab and stop asking a player to disclose what's in his pockets."

I laughed and shook my head. Gee Rich was forever going on about being a player.

"The party's at Catfish's house, I heard," he continued.

"That sounds like trouble with a capital T. I know Blue's not over there," I declared.

Catfish hung with a group of thugs that called themselves the Undertakers. It was the closest thing to a gang that North Minneapolis had in the mid-seventies. Word on the street was the gang leader, Renard, had set Blue's brother Apollo's car on fire. Just the other day Apollo had gotten into a fight with one of the Undertakers, the light-skinned one named Daryl, about his car being set on fire. The fight broke out at

Odell's Record Store on Plymouth Avenue. With Blue out of Juvenile Center, I knew that the Undertakers would be on edge and expecting retaliation.

"No, there ain't gonna be no beef between Blue and Catfish. Catfish fell out with Renard because he jumped on his sister, Tammy, up at North Commons after the football game, and she's supposedly pregnant by Renard. As a matter of fact, Catfish is supposed to be the one that snitched on Renard and DeAndre when they robbed Key Cadillac," Gee Rich explained. "I heard they both got over five grand apiece."

"Well, I'll stop by there, but if anything jumps off, I'm gone," I reluctantly agreed.

Soon the cab pulled up, and within twenty minutes, we were in front of Catfish's house.

"I don't see very many cars," I noted. "This party must be a dud."

"It's supposed to be a get-together, not an actual party."

Somewhat suspicious, my eyebrows raised, I got out of the cab, and together we walked up the stairs and knocked on the front door. Catfish's pregnant sister, Tammy, answered it. She was what I thought of as a tack-head bitch. She was trifling, nasty looking, and wasn't about anything more than keeping up a bunch of trouble. She looked us up and down but opened the door to let us in.

"Catfish is downstairs," she said, pointing vaguely in the direction of the kitchen. The dishes in the sink looked like the food had dried on them days before. Roaches scattered everywhere when she turned on the kitchen light, so we could find the stairs.

It figures.

I assessed Tammy's shifty eyes and the smirk on her face. Mocha, Gee Rich, and I went downstairs. When we reached the basement, Catfish emerged from the shadows. He could not have had a more fitting nickname.

"I thought there was supposed to be a get-together here," I whispered to Mocha.

"What time is it?" she asked.

Mocha was always watching the clock. Her mother was strict and didn't allow her to be out past eleven-thirty at night.

"I don't know," I replied. "I think Gee Rich brought us over here because he wants to talk to you. It's obvious there ain't no party happening over here."

We followed Catfish through the basement into a small room that had little in it besides a bed, a chair, and a basket full of dirty clothes.

"Y'all want to smoke some reefer?" he asked, digging underneath his pillow and pulling out a baggie full of weed and a package of rolling papers.

"Yeah, roll me up one," Gee Rich nodded.

Catfish removed a bud and some loose marijuana from the bag, crumbled it onto a cigarette paper, rolled it, ran his tongue over it to seal it, put the joint in his mouth, moved it back and forth between his lips to thoroughly seal it, and then lit it. After taking a long drag, he held the joint in the direction of Gee Rich, who took a couple of puffs then handed it to Mocha. She took a polite puff, barely inhaling, and handed it back to Catfish. Mocha knew I didn't smoke weed, so she didn't pass it my way. She didn't really either, except on occasion. Apparently, this night qualified as an occasion.

The two of us had gotten high together at school before, but we had gotten too high, really messed up, and that was the end of that. Mocha had gone home from school that day. She was so high, she said she felt weird. Later Mocha described feeling like she was deep inside herself and couldn't get out. Meanwhile, I had gotten downright paranoid, thinking everyone in school was talking about me, from the students to the teachers. To make matters worse, I couldn't stop worrying about how I looked. During typing class, I couldn't concentrate on learning the home keys because I was too busy trying to figure out how high is up. The harder I tried to grasp the concept of infinity and never-ending space going on and on forever and ever, the more it blew my mind. It was so overwhelming, I finally put my head down on the typewriter in front of me and closed my eyes.

Now that I was pregnant, I had decided not to smoke weed or drink any alcohol. I didn't want my baby to be born with birth defects because of something I did. I wanted my baby to be healthy, which is what compelled me to eat three square meals a day, making sure each meal included portions representing the four food groups. I especially craved bacon, lettuce, tomato, and cheese sandwiches. Eating one of those with a glass of milk gave me a sense of accomplishment that I had succeeded in covering the entire food-group spectrum in one setting.

"Can I talk to you in private?" Gee Rich asked Mocha in a deep voice that let on he was attempting to hold in reefer smoke while getting his point across. "Let's go in here for a minute." Gee Rich gestured towards a curtain that sectioned off another room. Mocha shrugged and followed him through the curtain, leaving me alone with Catfish.

"Why don't you sit over here a little closer?" he suggested, patting the bed next to him. "I ain't gonna bite you."

I wondered why roguish boys like Catfish always promised not to bite, especially since it was so apparent to me that they were nothing but hungry animals.

"Sit over there by you for what? I already got a man."

"Where's your man now? Why you out here by yourself like this here?" Catfish sneered.

I rolled my eyes and retorted, "Because I'm grown, that's why."

"Oh, so you're a smart-ass bitch."

"I got your bitch," I bristled.

Here we go.

"You're out of pocket anyway. You got a man, but you're over here in my face."

A signal went off in my mind flashing, "Danger." A rush of adrenaline brought me to my feet, and I rushed towards the door. Suddenly the lights went out, and Catfish tackled me yelling, "U. T. thing!"

I panicked. Whenever the Undertakers pulled a foul move, they yelled those words. They were known for gang rapes.

Why did I agree to step foot in this death trap? I chastised myself.

My panic sent me into a full-fledged frenzy and gave me the strength to knock Catfish off me and bolt for the door leading to the staircase. I took the steps two at a time, then rushed through the kitchen and hallway towards the front door. When I reached it, I fumbled with the doorknob. To my horror, I discovered the door was locked with a double deadbolt lock. Catfish's sister, Tammy, who had been sitting in the dark in the living room, got up and looked at me blankly.

"Open this damn door!" I demanded, looking over my shoulder into the darkened hallway.

"What's up?" his sister asked, with an amused expression on her face.

"Open this motherfuckin' door, bitch. I swear to God, I ain't got time for your games."

I must have looked and sounded convincing because the door soon swung open, and I hit the street running. I didn't stop until I got to Blue's house a few blocks away. Mrs. Lockett answered the door.

"What you doin' out this late?" she asked with a look of concern as she moved aside to let me in.

"Blue was supposed to pick us up from a party, but he never came back," I explained.

"Well, he's upstairs. You can go on up there," she replied as she locked the door.

When I got up to his room, I found Blue in bed but not asleep. He sat up, surprised to see me over there. After I explained to him what had happened, he got up, pulling on a pair of jeans over his pajama bottoms and slipping on a shirt.

"Let's go." He gestured towards the door.

We got out front and saw Gee Rich and Mocha walking up the street towards us. Blue told Mocha and me to get in the car; then he and Gee Rich stood outside the car talking. As the car door opened, I heard Blue tell Gee Rich, "It'll get handled."

Hearing his words, I felt protected, a feeling that was rare for me. I was usually the one doing the protecting. As Blue slid in under the steering wheel, I looked at him and felt a rush of love and gratitude that he was someone I could run to when wronged.

I don't know if Mocha was scared to go home or what, but she ran away from home that night. Both Mocha and Gee Rich were still in the car when Blue dropped me off at home. I didn't find out Mocha ran away until a few days later when I ran into Gee Rich at the downtown arcade on Hennepin Avenue. He was talking to a sleazy-looking blonde in the doorway when I spotted him.

"Say, hello Joe, do you want to give it a go?" I said, mocking LaBelle's new song, "Lady Marmalade."

When I said it, I was only jive talking, but Gee Rich took it the wrong way. Apparently, he thought I was signifying that the white girl he was with was a hooker, which after thinking about it for a moment, I concluded she probably was, but that wasn't my intent.

"Colnese," Gee Rich began, pulling me to the side, "You shouldn't be signifying like that. That ain't cool. When you see me talking to a lady, you need to give me and her a little more respect."

"Calm down," I responded. "First of all, I wasn't signifying. I was only speaking to you. I wasn't thinking about her then, and I'm still not thinking about her now."

Black dudes in Minneapolis during the 1970s tended to get real funky when they were with white girls. They immediately went into "white damsel in distress" mode. Thankfully, Gee Rich calmed right down.

"Wait here. I'm getting ready to walk this girl to the corner. When I come back, I got something to tell you about your friend."

"Who, Mocha?"

"Hold up. I'll be right back. Don't worry, I'll tell you."

I went up the long, dusty staircase to the arcade to wait. It was a dive arcade. Half of the pinball machines didn't work. I noticed a few shady-looking older guys in their early twenties leaning over the table shooting a game of pool. I loaded a couple of quarters into one of the machines and began to play Space Invaders.

Hennepin Avenue was teeming with pimps recently up from the South looking to get chosen. They hung out in the arcade, stomped up and down the street in their platform shoes, and slid in and out of Moby Dick's where a neon sign boasted you could get "A Whale of a Drink."

I had never been to Moby's, but I had been approached often and much by the up-and-coming pimps. The two at the pool table—one leaning over making a shot, and the other one standing upright rubbing blue chalk on the end of his pool stick—fit the profile: permed hair, one reddish-brown and the other one midnight-black, skinny as rails.

I had observed the pimps along the avenue on nonstop campaigns to get chosen by hookers and paid for their services. "Shake a hand, make a friend," was one of their well-known approaches as women walked past them on the street. I had learned to be polite, but to keep it moving since they could be vicious when rejected. The majority of them were in Minneapolis on a mission to recruit girls to take to work on the "'ho stroll" in New York. Rumor had it there was a street near Times Square known as the Minnesota Strip because so many prostitutes recruited from Minnesota strutted their stuff on it. The ones from the South, who claimed to be from New York, were the most dangerous.

Gorilla pimps, they beat their women with coat hangers, or so it was said. One of my friends, Glenda, had gotten into a car with one named Ocean to smoke a joint. Whatever the joint was laced with knocked her out cold. When she finally came to, she told me she and Ocean were all the way in northern Minnesota in International Falls, on the border of Canada. When they were refused admittance into Canada, Ocean changed directions and headed towards California.

Glenda finally escaped from him as they drove across the country by earning his trust enough to be allowed to go into a gas station to use the restroom by herself. The first couple of times he allowed her to go into a gas station unescorted, she had come back without incident, so he relaxed his guard. The next time she went, she looked out the window and noticed he was distracted, so she asked the attendant to call 911.

I was wary of the New York/Memphis pimps and vowed to never get into a car with one after hearing Glenda's story; however, they were so rampant, it was impossible to completely avoid or ignore them.

I glanced over at the pool table. Right on cue, one of the young men looked my way and winked his eye at me as he moved the toothpick in his mouth from one side to the other. I smiled slightly, nodded my head, then turned back to my pinball game. I wasn't trying to get cussed out, which was highly likely if I did not respond at all.

Gee Rich soon returned. He stood near the pinball machine, watching me fire a machine gun at a galaxy of stars while he explained to me how Mocha had run away from home the night we went to the party together. Further, he told me she had been with him at his friend's place ever since.

"You're kidding!"

"Come on. I'll take you to where she's at," Gee Rich promised.

Together we left the arcade and jumped on the number nine bus at the corner of 6th and Hennepin and headed to South Minneapolis. We got off on 35th Street near the Hosmer Branch Library. It had begun to snow lightly, and it was getting cold outside. We crossed the street, walked half a block, and then went up the back staircase of a four-plex apartment building.

"Who lives here?" I asked.

Gee Rich was busy knocking on the back door and didn't bother to respond. Soon a familiar looking, slender-built teenage girl with fair skin and a dark-brown, well-shaped Afro opened the door.

"Hey, Gee Rich, come on in," she said with a smile.

"Colnese, this is Chirene," Gee Rich introduced us. "Chirene, this is Colnese, Mocha's friend."

"Hey, Colnese, nice to meet you," Chirene responded.

I had seen Chirene a few times before at Fuzzy Warbles. She gestured for us to follow her through the kitchen into the dining room. Mocha was sitting at the dining room table playing a game of Solitaire. She looked surprised but seemed happy to see me.

"Girl, you ran away?" I exclaimed. "For what?"

"My mom never lets me do anything. It was past my curfew, and I was afraid to go home, so I just stayed out."

"Ooh, wee!"

"Do you want to play a game of Tonk?" asked Chirene as she picked up a well-worn deck of cards and began to shuffle.

"Yeah, sure," I replied.

A little boy with large, expressive eyes and pecan brown skin was toddling around the dining room. He sat down hard then got back up on his feet again.

"Is that your baby?" I asked Chirene.

She nodded as she dealt five cards to each of us.

"He's cute. What's his name? How old is he?"

"Terrell's fifteen months. He's small for his age because he was a preemie. He was born when I was only seven months pregnant."

"Come here, Terrell," I said, reaching my arms out towards him. I was surprised when Terrell toddled towards me.

"Well, he's not shy, that's for sure."

I picked the toddler up and sat him on the edge of the table in front of me. He had the most beautiful eyes I had ever seen on a baby boy. I smiled at him brightly.

"Hey, Terrell, where did you get those pretty eyes?"

Terrell looked at me and smiled somewhat bashfully. He stuck his index finger in his mouth and left it there. Instead of his thumb, that was the finger he preferred to suck. My heart melted.

Gee Rich was sitting in the living room with Chirene's man, Miguel, talking "men's talk" while Chirene, Mocha, and I played a few hands of cards. We were having a good time talking and playing, so time flew by. When I heard the ten o'clock news come on, I decided to go home. I was pregnant, tired, and had school in the morning.

"I'll be back tomorrow after school," I promised Mocha. "It was nice meeting you, Chirene. Later, Gee Rich."

Chirene showed me to the back door, opened it for me to exit, and locked it behind me. I walked home alone down the cold, dark streets of South Minneapolis.

CHAPTER 11

Teen Pregnancy

While I was pregnant, my favorite pastime was looking at baby clothes and daydreaming. I fingered the tiny, yellow baby booties and lined them up on the bed underneath the yellow dress and matching cloth-covered rubber pants. I tried to imagine what our baby girl—at least I hoped it was a girl—would look like in it. I went to the chest of drawers and removed a package containing three pairs of pastel-colored infant socks in pink, yellow, and blue, along with a multi-colored receiving blanket. Not wanting to open the socks just yet, I placed the package near the ensemble and imagined how the yellow socks and blanket would complete the outfit I planned for our baby to wear home from the hospital. After gazing longingly at the clothes for a few moments, I returned the baby items to my chest of drawers.

Though I was only four months along in my pregnancy, my chest of drawers was full to overflowing with baby clothes. Some of them I had received from my friend DeLady, whose baby boy, Troy, had already outgrown them. All the rest I had shoplifted from JCPenney with my "five-finger discount." I had become quite skillful at shoplifting during my pregnancy. I began the process by imagining that the baby things belonged to me, which boosted my confidence to then take them out of the store. I had never been caught, although one time, a floorwalker chased me through Powers Department Store and just about caught me. Right as I reached the doorway, he grabbed me by the forearm. I had yanked away from the red-faced white man, crashed through the door, and darted down the street.

Since then, I had pretty much limited my boosting to JCPenney. The baby department was always quiet and usually pretty empty. These factors gave me plenty of time to shop around and carefully select the items I wanted for my baby, whose name I decided would be Ora Lee.

Some of my friends thought Ora Lee was an old-fashioned name, but I liked it anyway. It was an old Southern name.

I hoped my baby would be dark-skinned like Blue. I believed the two of us would produce a cute baby. His physical attributes, such as his dark skin and nice body would hopefully cancel out everything I hated about myself, beginning with my light skin, which seemed to make people treat me differently. Everybody in Blue's family was tall and slim, which I hoped would lower the chances of my baby being "big-boned," "thick," "healthy," or "fat," as some people described me. Blue also had several other good traits, the ones that had initially attracted me to him. He was known all around town for his dancing ability. He was always sharp and could roller skate. He could fight too. In my young mind, that was all that was necessary to make it in the world.

I liked everything about Blue, but if truth be told, I didn't really know him very well. Yes, we hung out at parties and rode around in his car together from one side of town to the other, but he spent most of that time talking to his partners, Gee Rich and Vamp, who were usually in the car with us. With music blasting from the eight-track tape player and reefer smoke thick in the air, it was Blue's world, and, for the time being, I was a part of it.

During the three weeks Blue was locked up in juvenile detention, I had learned a great deal more about him from a thirteen-year-old girl named Thea, who was always over at his house. Thea, I concluded, was a complete mental case. She had a dazed, slow look about her, but at the same time, she seemed to be way ahead of her time.

According to Blue's cousin, Yolanda, Thea was always asking her for advice on how she could entice Blue to go to bed with her. She was a compulsive thief who stole clothes, tapes, and other things to give to Blue. I supposed she was trying to get Blue to be with her, but so far, she hadn't had much success.

I had to admit to myself that Thea was on the right track giving him things since Blue loved money, cars, and clothes. That much I had figured out. I guessed Thea was trying to get tight with me so she could get next to Blue. It proved to me that something about her thinking wasn't quite right. Thea lived with her grandmother, who didn't seem to care what time of the day or night she came home or, for that matter, *if* she even bothered to come home. Thea was always over Blue's house cooking, cleaning, or whatever it took to be there whenever Blue came back through the door.

While most girls acted jealous over the boys they liked, the strange thing about Thea was that the couple of times I showed up at the Lockett's house with Blue, when Thea was there, she seemed to be okay with it. She spoke to both of us and then kept right on cooking, cleaning, or whatever it was she was up to.

I had a jealous streak a mile wide and could not figure out why Thea did not act jealous over our relationship, and for some reason, I didn't feel threatened by Thea's infatuation with Blue. So far, he hadn't given her the time of day, according to his cousin Yolanda. She had lived with the Lockett family ever since she moved to Minneapolis from Houston, Texas ,after her mother passed away. As far as I was concerned, Yolanda knew what she was talking about and had no reason to lie.

Mrs. Lockett liked Thea, too, probably because she helped her around the house so much. She told me she felt sorry for Thea since nobody seemed to care anything about her. Mrs. Lockett was like that. She cared about people, especially the underdog. She liked me, too, but hated that I was pregnant.

"Your po' mama," she moaned when I first broke the news to her. Mrs. Lockett was always lamenting about my "po' mama" whenever I did something particularly outrageous, which was often. Getting pregnant was the worst thing I had done yet, in Mrs. Lockett's opinion. She was from Louisiana and was forever telling me about the South and comparing it to the North.

"Down South, we weren't a bit more thinking about having a baby than the man in the moon," she scolded. "I don't know what's wrong with you Northern girls. I never did want any babies. We were back there in the woods dancing and having a good time. I don't know what's wrong with y'all," she continued, frowning and shaking her head.

No matter what my friends and I did, it never measured up to what Mrs. Lockett and her friends had done in the incomparable South. The only thing not so wonderful about it was the hunger, I surmised. Mrs.

Lockett was always complaining about how hungry she was growing up down there in Louisiana.

The knowledge that Mrs. Lockett would be my baby's grandma, coupled with her kindness and beauty, converged to create a deep bond between Mrs. Lockett and me. In my eyes, she was incredibly beautiful. Like Blue, she had high cheekbones and deep brown, mahogany skin with a splash of cherry undertones. Her eyes curved upward, giving her the appearance of having a smile on her face even when she was serious.

She was the first grown-up I had ever met who could neither read nor write very well. I had a feeling her poor reading ability was due to the substandard school system in the deep South. I had heard quite a few horrendous things about the South as a child of the 1960s during the Civil Rights Movement. Kids down South often had to work, which interfered with their education. Poverty, poor schools, inadequate health care, substandard housing, low-paying jobs, and unfairness and inequality were experienced by African American people in the deep South. This overall lack of equity and equality is what led to the Great Migration to the North during the early twentieth century.

Seeing Mrs. Lockett struggle with reading was my first direct experience with how it played out in real life. I had tried to help her with her reading, but Mrs. Lockett laughingly dismissed my efforts, complaining that I was too impatient. The idea that someone I cared so much about could not do the one thing I got so much pleasure from—reading—created nervous energy within me that translated into frustration.

I was probably impatient because I couldn't remember not being able to read, nor could I even imagine what it must be like not to be able to read or write. That was the one flaw Mrs. Lockett and I could agree on about her down South upbringing. The school system wasn't worth two dead flies when Mrs. Lockett was growing up in the Louisiana woods. Mrs. Lockett was so precious and dear to me, I vowed to dig deep to find some patience somewhere inside of me, so I could help her learn to read. My parents had instilled the belief in me that it is never too late to learn.

As I sat daydreaming over my unborn baby's clothes, I thought about how God actually does work in mysterious ways. He had turned a bad thing—Mrs. Lockett's illiteracy—into a good thing that brought the two of us closer together. With Blue in the Juvenile Center, my pregnancy slowed me down enough to give me plenty of time to help Mrs. Lockett with writing out checks to pay her bills and other things. I didn't have a domestic bone in my body to speak about, so I left the cooking and housework to Thea and busied myself with helping Mrs. Lockett with any reading and writing that needed to be done.

Helping a grown-up made me feel important and mature. Whenever Mrs. Lockett called me to come over and help her, the two of us sat together at the dining room table with paperwork sprawled out in front of us. Mrs. Lockett kept me well entertained with good stories. Even better than the stories about her formative years in the South were the stories about her very own children. I always came away with an earful. Mrs. Lockett told me all about Blue's brother, Apollo, getting turned out to pimping by an old 'ho. Apollo was only eighteen years old, while the woman was a thirty-something-year-old hooker.

"I can't stand that nasty old woman," confided Mrs. Lockett, as she licked a stamp and placed it on the envelope I had just filled out for her. "Apollo was hard-working and doing good before she got her nasty hands on him. I think she been sucking on his thing."

My mouth dropped open in shock. The tidbit of information was almost too juicy for words. "You're kidding!" I exclaimed.

"I wish I was kidding," she sniffed. "Down South, we didn't do no nasty mess like that. These women up here sure is nasty! She been sucking on his thing and driving him crazy."

I would have been embarrassed about the subject if it were my own mother discussing something as shocking as the idea of oral sex. But since it was Mrs. Lockett, it made the topic all the more interesting and solidified our bond. I had never discussed such a thing with an adult. My girlfriends and I had covered it briefly, just enough to declare that we would never, as long as we lived, do such a thing as nasty as that. While I wasn't completely convinced someone could go crazy because of oral sex, I concluded that since Mrs. Lockett believed it and said it with such conviction, it must be true. The next time I saw Apollo, I made a mental note to watch him and see if he exhibited any strange behavior.

Apollo didn't care too much for me. I wasn't sure why. There was really no reason for it, as far as I was concerned, but I could tell he was somewhat chilly towards me and maintained his distance. It could be the Southside-Northside thing, which normally didn't apply between men and women, or it could simply be his disdain for squares. I was considered square according to the rules of the game Apollo now lived by. If you weren't out there on the street corner, in a massage parlor, twirling around a pole, or someplace else selling your behind, you were a square. I didn't care. I would stay square, and too bad if Apollo didn't like it.

"Uh-huh," Mrs. Lockett continued. "You know Apollo's been going with Viola for the longest time. They were getting along just fine. Then here comes this nasty heifer, and all hell breaks loose. Here she comes giving him money, sucking his thing, and making him lazy. He ain't gonna be good for nothing. If she keeps on sucking on his thing like she been doing, she's gonna take his nature from him."

I digested this tidbit of information while sealing an envelope. If truth be told, I didn't care much about Viola losing Apollo to the old 'ho. Viola and her Northside friends couldn't stand my Southside friends and me because of the Northside-Southside rivalry. Northside girls were very possessive over the Northside boys. My going with Blue was a violation of the unwritten law that existed between the two sides of town. I had gotten into fights before because Northside girls felt they owned all Northside boys, but I had fought and proved that I could hold my own, so we had called a reluctant truce. Once folks knew you would fight, you gained a reputation for not being scared to fight. Thus, you were left alone.

◈ ◈ ◈

I was proud to be having a baby by Blue. The Locketts were a popular family on the Northside. Because the four siblings were close in age, their house was the teenage neighborhood hangout. As an adopted person, I felt ungrounded and free-floating because of my lack of biological connections. I believed my baby's family ties to the Lockett family would somehow extend to me and ground me to their firm foundation.

I transferred to Holmes School for teen mothers in Southeast Minneapolis near the University of Minnesota campus. The good thing about going to Holmes was that a bus picked me up at the door every morning and took me to the door of the school. Riding in the school bus and picking up the other pregnant teens made for an interesting bus ride and took me to parts of the city I had never been to before. We stopped at a huge mansion on Park Avenue where we picked up white girls staying temporarily at the Lutheran Social Services Home for Unwed Mothers. The majority of the girls staying there were placing their babies for adoption. After delivering their babies, they would return home.

Next, we rolled through the Franklin Avenue neighborhood in South Minneapolis and picked up a few pregnant Indian girls, as Native Americans were referred to during that time period. The bus even picked up a Chinese girl who lived not far from Roosevelt High School. Most of the Black and mixed girls who attended Holmes School lived in North Minneapolis, but they rode a different bus.

The school was small and cozy. There was a comfortable couch in the hallway by the locker where I spent quite a bit of quality time reclining and reading an assortment of paperback books from a nearby book rack. I loved to lie on the couch and daydream about my soon-to-be baby girl. I read the pamphlets on pregnancy and childbirth that I received from Lutheran Deaconess Hospital, where I went once a month for my prenatal visits at the clinic. I liked to see how my baby was developing from the pictures in the pamphlet, which showed sketches of the developing fetus's progress. Nearby, hot water gurgled and hissed in the school's radiators, keeping the school nice and toasty warm throughout the winter.

I often left school before it was over for the day and caught the city bus to visit my friend Mocha, who was still on the run and staying over at Chirene's house. We spent our time eating Jimmy Dean sausage sandwiches, drinking Kool-Aid so thick with sugar it had the consistency of juice, playing cards, and yakking it up.

Chirene's best friend Kayla had a little girl by Gee Rich named Coco. She was two years old. When Chirene and Kayla went out at night to party, I often babysat Terrell and Coco. One night after the clubs closed,

Blue showed up over Chirene's house to see me. For some reason, I felt shy around him that night, but I was happy to see him. Everyone else's life was going on as usual, but pregnancy had slowed my life way down. One of the reasons I didn't go out anymore was because I was outgrowing my party clothes. I wasn't showing enough yet to justify wearing maternity clothes, so I really didn't have anything decent to wear to the club. Plus, I didn't want to drink while I was pregnant because I didn't want to harm my baby. In my book, drinking and clubbing went hand in hand, so for the time being, I was content to stay in and babysit.

One afternoon DeLady and I were walking down Fourth Avenue after I had started showing. Blue was driving down the avenue with some friends. When he saw me, he jumped out of his car and came over to where we were standing on the sidewalk. Right in front of everyone, he rubbed my pregnant belly and announced to his friends proudly, "We're having us a nine-pounder!"

CHAPTER 12

Stillbirth

◆ ◆ ◆

One day in early May 1974, I walked to a track meet at South High School with my friends, DeLady and Carmen, a distance of roughly three miles. After the track meet was over, we were hungry, so we walked to Burger King on 34th and Nicollet for a burger and fries. After eating, we parted company and went home in opposite directions.

When the pains first started, I had just settled down to watch Perry Mason. Every night at ten o'clock, I watched the show, a murder mystery centered in a courtroom. The first cramp took me by surprise but left quickly. The next one came roughly thirty minutes later and lasted longer than the first. By the time Perry Mason won the court case—as usual—I was doubled up on the floor in the center of the kitchen. I wondered if all the walking I had done that day caused me to go into labor or whether it had been jumping up and down at the track meet. My mom advised me to get on my hands and knees and do pelvic rocks.

"You're probably having Braxton Hicks contractions," she told me. "They're quite common during the third trimester of pregnancy."

So I got on my hands and knees and rocked like mad, but the intense pains continued to come and go long after my mom and dad had gone to bed for the night. By three in the morning, there was no break between cramps. One would no sooner leave than the other would begin. Whenever I felt the tightening sensation in my lower abdomen, I moaned, "Oh, no," and got into position to do some more rocking. After a particularly severe cramp, I felt nauseous and stumbled down the hall from my bedroom to the bathroom. After I threw up, I felt a little better. My mom came into the bathroom as I sat on the side of the tub.

"Are you still having pains?"

"Uh-huh, but I feel a little better,"

"It was probably that hamburger you ate tonight. It might have been a little tainted."

"Yep," I agreed hopefully, as I got up from sitting on the edge of the tub to head back to my room and back to bed.

My mom also went back into her room and got into bed. About thirty seconds later, I felt my stomach begin to tighten up again. It was so intense that I rolled out of bed onto the floor this time. I rolled back and forth, holding my stomach. Soon I was back on my feet, racing back into the bathroom. The urgency to have a bowel movement was overwhelming, so I sat on the toilet, hoping that whatever virus was causing me to have so much pain would expel itself so I could get some sleep. Instead, I began to give birth. When I felt the pressure from the baby's head pushing its way out, I fell to the floor with my hands between my legs, trying to keep it in.

"Mom, my baby's coming out," I screamed.

My mom woke my dad up, and together they rushed me to Lutheran Deaconess Hospital. My father ran two or three stoplights racing through the darkened Minneapolis streets to get me to the hospital, but it was all in vain, as far as I was concerned. My baby was born dead anyway.

Moments after I was admitted and wheeled into the delivery room, my baby shot out of my body so fast that the nurse almost didn't catch her. The tiny baby dangling at the end of the umbilical cord was silent. The nurse, who had turned away to wash her hands, saw that the birth had taken place and moved quickly to scoop the baby up into her arms.

There were several hard, cold surfaces in the delivery room—a steel-gray metal sink, the metal countertop, and the stirrups my feet rested in. Even the delivery table was hard and cold. But what was most hard and cold was my baby's lifeless body. The light in the room even felt harsh and unnaturally bright.

"Can I see my baby?" I asked the young nurse after she cut the umbilical cord, wrapped the tiny form in a towel, and laid her down in an Isolette.

The nurse lifted the tiny baby from the Isolette, brought her over to me, and held her up for me to inspect. I gazed sadly at the lifeless infant wrapped in the white hospital towel. An intense wave of euphoria and an overwhelming sense of sorrow hit me at the same time. As I looked at my baby, hot tears ran down the sides of my face. Her lifeless body was dark against the white towel the nurse had wrapped her in. Her face was tiny, and her diminutive hands were perfectly shaped. Her mouth was open, and her eyes were closed.

The baby's skin was dark brown, almost black just like Blue's, except for her diminutive hands, which were almost as light in color as my tan skin. I noted that the baby's arms were long like her father's, but her parted lips were exactly like mine. Her top lip was thin and bow-shaped, while her bottom lip was somewhat fuller—my brother described them as cat lips. A damp mat of black curly hair encircled her face.

I was amazed to finally behold the sight of my baby girl, but my feelings were conflicted. Although she was dead, I finally had a blood relative. I could see my likeness, and it made me happy yet filled me with grief at the same time. As I turned away, a tear rolled from the corner of my eye, made its way down my freckled cheek, and disappeared into my thick bushy Afro. The nurse took the baby away, and I was left alone in the recovery room to struggle with my conflicting emotions.

I decided to call Chirene. I needed to tell somebody what had happened. I had spent nearly every day of my pregnancy over at Chirene's apartment, so I knew she would care about me losing my baby, and I was right. Even with it being close to four in the morning, Chirene caught a cab to the hospital to see me. After I told her what had happened, she asked to see the baby.

When the nurse came back in to push on my stomach to check the blood flow, I asked her, "Can I see my baby again?"

The nurse looked at me sadly and shook her head no.

"Why not?"

"Your baby is gone off the floor now. Get some sleep."

The nurse patted my arm sympathetically and left the room. Chirene and I talked a little longer. Soon she told me she had to get back home, so she called a cab and left the hospital. I appreciated Chirene getting out of her bed to come to see me when I really needed a friend.

After she left, I reflected on the day's events that had ended with my baby being stillborn.

I slept fitfully that night. I could not get the tiny image of my firstborn out of my mind. I shared a room with a woman who had undergone a hysterectomy earlier in the day. Her moaning and groaning throughout the night echoed my internal conflict and helped to drown out the sound of the newborns crying in the nursery down the hall. I closed my eyes and stared at the tiny black baby etched in my mind until sleep blotted out my grief.

Every so often, a nurse would come in, push down on my stomach to check the blood flow, and continue her rounds. With the baby gone, my stomach looked soft and mushy, not at all like it had before. It was a couple of shades darker, and a dark brown line ran down the middle of it and disappeared from my sight. The nurse who was poking on my stomach at the time was a Mexican woman around thirty-five years old, I guessed.

"How far along were you?" she asked while sticking a thermometer between my lips.

"Twenty-eight weeks," was my muffled answer.

"Twenty-eight weeks? A lady down the hall had her baby at twenty-seven weeks, and her baby lived. It's a little boy." The nurse removed the thermometer and gazed intently at the mercury before shaking it up and down a few times. "Your temperature's normal. Give me your arm so I can check your pressure."

I offered the nurse my right arm. I turned my face away from the nurse to hide my sudden tears. The pressure from the cuff on my arm grew tighter and tighter, reminding me of how my stomach had tightened into a painful knot and then relaxed over and over again until I thought I couldn't stand it anymore. The pain had finally ended with my baby almost being born in the toilet.

There was no insurance, so there was no money for a headstone. I decided to have my baby cremated since I couldn't bear to think of her buried in an unmarked grave. That would have made her seem more lost to me than she was already.

As an adopted person, I sometimes felt like a lost child who couldn't find her way back home. Having a baby of my own was the only way I knew to recapture a piece of myself. My true identify was lost when I was relinquished for adoption. In my mind, giving birth to a baby of my own was a way of creating a birth family since I knew of no way to find them. I had tried but was blocked at every turn. Just like every attempt I made to discover my lost identity had failed, so my body had failed me, too, by failing to nurture and protect my baby until she was strong enough to thrive on her own.

Although I had no control over life and death, I could control where my baby's final resting place would be. I would see to it that my baby would not be lost in time and space. Mr. Estes, the only Black mortician in town, handled the cremation. I liked Mr. Estes, a no-nonsense, dignified Black man who knew how to handle folks with compassion and courtesy when they were grieving. He had a perpetual look of consolation on his face. Come to think of it, I could not recall ever seeing him smile. I guessed all the years of ministering to the grief-stricken had wiped the smile right off his face.

I appreciated Mr. Estes's serious expression. The concern I saw in his eyes paid homage to the blues I was feeling. I surely did not need anybody smiling all up in my face when my world and everything in it that mattered had caved in. I believed my baby was in good hands with Mr. Estes. I pictured her ashes blowing in the wind. Imagining my baby's spirit taking flight was my only consolation.

I called the Lockett household the night of the stillbirth and told Mrs. Lockett what had happened. The next day Jasmine and Yolanda came to visit me in the hospital. They brought with them the piggy bank Mrs. Lockett had been saving pennies and other coins in for our baby, who was now dead. Through the gray fog of my sadness, I noticed that the baby's bank was not a piggy bank after all, but instead was a gorilla bank. The gorilla was made of plaster and had a mop of black hair glued to the top of its head. He was so ugly, I'm certain he would have scared my baby had she lived, but I loved Mrs. Lockett even more than before for caring enough to take her precious time to put her pennies aside for our baby. I could imagine her dropping coins into the gorilla bank one by one with a heart filled with love and kindness throughout the months I had been pregnant. It was an unexpected surprise, letting me know my baby had been welcomed into her heart.

A curious type of pain coming and going only to return
  again
And then when I thought I could stand no more, I felt the
  pressure of my first baby's head
Sheening through the dark through red stoplights to the
  hospital,
The ride seemingly lasting forever
Dark empty and quiet hallways invaded by me
Being pushed in a wheelchair by a faceless figure in white
Looking into the glare of the light in the delivery room
Patiently waiting while the cord that bound she & me
  together
For so many months was cut
Arms and legs restrained
Only my face was able to move as I looked into the face
Of my tiny brown baby with black curly hair
Her mouth was parted but no sound escaped
She was dead/on/arrival
Rolling back to my room with empty stomach & empty
  arms
The sun slowly rising
On the day her father refused to come see me when I needed
  him most

CHAPTER 13

All Alone in Love

◆ ◆ ◆

The couples on the dance floor bumped hips in perfect rhythm. They bumped standing up, they bumped squatting down, sometimes they alternated from bumping hips to bumping knees or thighs, but they never missed a beat. The Commodores' popular record *The Bump* blared from the jukebox.

It was 1974, and the Filling Station was jumpin'! There were wall-to-wall Black folks drinking, smoking, talking stuff, and having a good time. The band, Philadelphia Story and the Sweet Taste of Sin, had taken a break, and the jukebox was working overtime. For the most part, the Filling Station was a player's bar. Pimps, prostitutes, gamblers, and drug dealers spent their time and money there every weekend.

But then, so did everyone else: Pretenders, wannabes, used-to-be's, and wayward teenagers trying to grow up too fast hung out there, too. The legal drinking age was eighteen, but my friends and I would dress up, smear lip gloss or Vaseline on our lips, and slide in unnoticed. On rare occasions, we were asked to produce fake IDs, compliments of Darla, Tina's daddy's girlfriend.

In the ladies' room, I dipped my finger into a pot of wine-colored lip gloss. Staring into the small mirrored compact, I applied the gloss to my lips. After holding a match to the tip of my black eyebrow pencil to soften it, I drew a line on my bottom eyelid. From one of the bathroom stalls, I could smell the pungent odor of reefer, but my mind was not on getting high. My mind was on one thing and one thing only. Blue, my deceased baby's father, was in the club. I had only seen him once since our baby was stillborn. My mom had done her best to try to keep me away from him. I guess she was trying to keep me from getting pregnant again.

Although I was in the hospital for four days, Blue had not come to see me. I have no idea what we would have said to one another if he had shown up. It was probably just as well. I was too empty physically, mentally, and emotionally to carry on a conversation with him about the loss of our baby girl. When I finally saw him a week later, he told me the reason he hadn't come to see me was because he wanted to hurt the doctors for not saving his baby, so he thought it would be better to stay away.

Blue kept trying to see me even though I could never get out of the house. I had mixed feelings about him not coming to the hospital to see me. I still had feelings for him, but the pressure from my mother to break up with him was unrelenting.

"I wouldn't have the time of day for a boy who didn't show me any more consideration than that," she had told me each and every time I asked her if Blue had called.

The last time I'd told Blue I couldn't get out of the house to see him, he hadn't called back anymore. I had been too grief-stricken at the time to care very much, one way or the other, but now that I had seen him at the Filling Station, I wanted him back. I also wanted my baby back. The two of them were tied together in my mind, and I knew the only way to get my baby back was through him. I took one last sip of my Sloe Gin and 7-Up and left the bathroom. After scanning the nightclub for a few moments, I found Blue leaning against the bar.

He was a handsome sight. His ebony skin was pulled tight across his high cheekbones and prominent Native American nose. A shock of blue-black permed hair curled away from his face and hung downward towards his shoulders. His slanted almond-shaped eyes seemed to smile even when he was serious. African and Native American features combined to make him look both proud and regal. I could see the flash of his straight white teeth from where I stood, which contrasted and complimented his dark brown skin as he talked to a man standing to his right.

My thick, wavy hair had been hot combed and curled. I had brushed it to one side, securing it in place with bobby pins. The resulting hairstyle was a cascade of deep mahogany ringlets framing the right side of my face with baby blue and white flowers pinned behind my left ear Pointer Sisters' style. I approached Blue with a smile on my face.

"Hey, you sure are looking good tonight," I told him.

"Get away from me!"

"What?"

The force of the back of Blue's hand across my cheek came as a complete surprise, and I stumbled backwards against the bar. He followed the first blow with a second and then disappeared into the crowd. I was stunned, but before I could figure out what had happened, Blue's older sister Jackie, who had seen what happened from across the bar, came over to me and helped me into the bathroom.

"He don't have no right puttin' his hands on you," Jackie said angrily. "Don't take that off of him."

I stared into the mirror. One side of my face was puffy. Angrily, I wiped tears from my eyes.

"I hate him! I'm gonna hurt him," I cried out in pain and anger.

"Come on, I'll give you a ride home. I don't know what makes a man think he can hit on a woman. You haven't done anything to him. What's his problem? I'm telling you, he's my brother and I love him, but you don't have to take abuse. Come on, let's go. Don't say anything to him if you run into him on the way out of here. Just ignore him."

Jackie grabbed me firmly by my upper arm and ushered me through the crowd. The bar was about to close, and some of the people were leaving. Others were making their way to the bar in response to the bartender's cries.

"Last call for alcohol! Last call for alcohol! It's hotel-motel time. You ain't got to go home, but you got to get out of here!"

Jackie and I had to go through what some people called the "no-pay side," past the pool tables to get to the side door leading to the parking lot. Blue leaned against the jukebox, pool stick in hand, awaiting his turn. His opponent pointed his stick in the direction of the left corner pocket and then slammed the eight ball across the table. As I walked past, Blue's eyes never left the pool table.

"I'm not going home," I told Jackie once we got to her car. "You can drop me off at the after-hours joint."

"Where's it at tonight?"

"On 33rd and Portland. Do you want to go with me?"

"You know I don't party on the Southside. There ain't nothing over South for me. I'm trying to catch up with some folks on the Northside."

"Oh, well, that's all right then. I guess there ain't nothing for me on the Northside. Not anymore, as least."

This was the nicest Jackie had ever been to me. Previously, she had acted as though she held me in the same contempt and low esteem as my Southside counterparts. Initially, Blue's sisters and cousin had not been receptive to our relationship, but after I lost the baby, Jasmine, Yolanda, and now Jackie had warmed up to me and had begun to show me some love.

I stared out the window as we rolled down the darkened streets of Minneapolis. What had started as anger quickly morphed into anguish. *First my baby, and now Blue. Who or what will I lose next?* When we reached 33rd and Portland, I jumped out of the car.

"Thanks, Jackie, I'll catch you later."

"All right then, Colnese. See you."

Jackie's yellow and black sports car sped away as I headed towards the after-hours party. Cars were lined up on both sides of Portland Avenue, as well as up and down 33rd Street. It was a warm summer evening in July, and several people were standing outside in front of the large, white house where the after-hours party was being held.

"Hey, Scorpio."

I turned towards the direction of the voice. It couldn't be anybody but J. B., a man in his mid-forties who liked me. Sure enough, J. B. was sitting in his car, a red and white Cadillac El Dorado pimpmobile. The top of the car was padded with the back window cut into the shape of a diamond.

"Come here, Scorpio, I got something for you."

I opened up the passenger door and slid in.

"What's up, J. B.?"

I was used to being the object of an older man's desire. I knew how to play them at a distance and not get too involved, but at the same time not hurt their feelings and bruise their sensitive egos. Older men were always good for a drink or a few dollars. Some of my friends actually turned tricks with older men, but I prided myself on being a master at talking them out of their cash and favors.

"I got a little blow. Have you ever snorted any?"

"No, but I'm game to try some."

"What happened to your face?"

"Me and Blue got into it down at the club."

"This'll straighten you out." J. B. dipped a tiny coke spoon into the mound of cocaine, which was centered on the inside of a fifty-dollar bill, and held it up to my left nostril. I pinched my right nostril shut and took a large snort. J. B. dipped the coke spoon again and gave me another blast up the other nostril. A feeling of well-being enveloped me, and my emotional and physical pain transformed into euphoria. I began to loosen up some.

"Would you like something to drink?" he asked.

"Yeah, get me a brandy and Coke."

J. B. went into the house and soon came back carrying two drinks. I sipped on my drink and grooved to the music on J. B.'s tape deck.

"Look, are you going to stay here, or do you want me to drop you off at home? I got to go pick my women up. They get off at two o'clock."

J. B.'s women worked at Maggie's sauna.

"You can take me home. Can I get another toot of that blow?"

"Sure, Scorpio." J. B. gave me another one-on-one, a toot of blow up each nostril, and then drove me home.

"Good night, Scorpio."

"Good night, J. B."

I got out of the car and walked slowly to the back door of our house. I was careful not to wake up my mom and dad whenever I came in late. They had grown used to my late hours and had long ago ceased trying to enforce a curfew even though I was only sixteen. The couple of times they had locked me in the house, I had climbed out the window of my bedroom. Now I more or less came and went as I pleased.

For the remainder of my sixteenth summer, I ran wild. I was all about nightclubs, after-hours parties, cocaine, and alcohol. I was young, single, and free. No job, no school, no responsibility. Nothing to do but party all night, sleep all day, and then start all over again. Blue wouldn't have anything to do with me, and this hurt me deeply. Every time I tried to talk to him, he brushed me off. His rejection and the loss of my baby were more painful than anything I had ever experienced.

I got high on anything I could get my hands on to blot out the pain and to get up enough nerve to talk to him. Uppers, downers, Valiums, pain pills, it didn't matter. I would take anything except acid. I didn't want to go on a trip I couldn't come back from. I wanted more than anything for Blue to tell me why he wouldn't even talk to me. Coping with grief, rejection, and loss was slowly driving me crazy.

I had started hanging around with Blue's sister Jasmine, so I was over the Lockett's house all the time. Jasmine had developed a crush on Anthony, my friend Diallo's brother. Diallo had been my grade school crush when I was in second grade at Warrington Elementary School. At that time, he went by his given name, Randy, but had since changed it to Diallo, an African name, when he was in junior high school.

Being in Diallo's company once again brought back fond memories of our grade school days at Warrington when he was my boyfriend. Diallo and I had rekindled our relationship once again when we were in the eighth grade. At the time, I was attending Breck, a private college preparatory school, so I seldom saw him in person, but we talked on the phone just about every night.

Jasmine and I spent a great deal of time visiting Diallo's house during the summer of 1974 as Jasmine and Anthony's courtship caught afire. Diallo's mother was having complications from her diabetes, so Jasmine and I often visited her at Mount Sinai Hospital, where she was being treated after having a stroke. Spending time at Diallo's house with Jasmine helped me to keep my mind off Blue and the loss of our baby somewhat, but not completely. I often ran into him when I visited Jasmine at the Lockett's house, but he just ignored me.

My depression was growing deeper and deeper, and I was self-medicating as often as possible. Downers like Valium were my drug of choice since they relaxed me and blunted my emotions. If I took them with alcohol, it was the perfect mix.

One night at an after-hours party on 38th Street and 5th Avenue, Marita and I were in the bathroom applying make-up and combing our hair when somebody started banging on the door.

"Wait a damn minute," hollered Marita through the door.

When we finally came out of the bathroom, a dude named Robert pushed past us and rushed into the bathroom.

"What were you all doing in there, feeling on each other?" he yelled rudely.

"None of your damn business," I answered, pausing in the doorway.

My hand was resting on the door jamb near the hinges, and my fingers had not quite cleared the door. When Robert slammed the door shut, my fingers were smashed between the door and the frame, causing the door to bounce back open. Robert turned around to see what had prevented the door from shutting all the way, and I held my hand up for him to see.

"Look what you did," I said calmly.

The impact of the door slamming shut had caused the fingernails of my left middle and ring fingers to come off. Streams of blood poured from my hand onto the floor, but I had taken so many pain pills and downers mixed with alcohol, I couldn't feel any pain.

"Oh, baby, I'm sorry. Let me get you a towel."

Robert looked around the bathroom, but there were no towels to be found. He paid the house woman, Ree, two dollars for a towel, which I used to wrap around my injured hand. I left the party shortly afterwards. The party was on the next block within walking distance from my house. As I walked home in the wee hours of the morning, the sun rose on a brand new day.

CHAPTER 14

Anger

◆◆ ◆◆ ◆

Things were not going right for me, and I didn't know exactly who to take it out on, so I took it out on the world. I would fight at the drop of a dime, and I often did. It didn't take much to trigger my anger, and the relief I felt letting it out was much better than keeping it bottled up inside.

That summer I returned to work for my second year at Phyllis Wheatley Community Center's day camp, Camp Katharine Parsons. Each day we loaded up the school bus with campers and counselors and drove out to the campsite in Watertown, Minnesota, about thirty miles away from the Twin Cities. The 106-acre camp was situated on the edge of Oak Lake. Many of the campers from the past summer had returned. Many of the junior and senior camp counselors I had worked with the previous year had also returned. I looked forward to spending time at camp with the friends and coworkers I had worked with the summer before. They included DarCia, Kitt, Brenda, Archie, Roosevelt (Cookie), Melvin, Pat, Janice, and Juan. There were also a few new additions to the Camp Parsons crew, including Clive.

Clive was an interesting character. He always wore a leather jacket and a crocheted red, black, and green floppy hat no matter how hot it got outside. He had a huge boom box that he carried everywhere he went. Sometimes after camp, rather than catching the bus back to the Southside, I would instead visit my friend Kayla, who lived in the Banneker apartments up the hill from Phyllis Wheatley Community Center. Clive's uncle lived across the court in another of the apartment complex's buildings. He was always bragging about the drinks his uncle knew how to fix.

"Man, I'm telling you," Clive exclaimed, "My uncle's drinks will get you messed up!"

One day I decided to take him up on it. After camp, we headed to Clive's uncle's house for one of his famous drinks. He mixed it up in a large plastic tumbler. I had never drunk that much of anything except Kool-Aid. I took a sip, and it was powerful stuff, but I drank it down anyway. Then Clive and I went outside and sat on a grassy hill.

True to Clive's word, the drink messed me up. I had never been so drunk in my life. I liked to drink, but I definitely did not like to be drunk, at least not to the point of staggering. As long as we were seated, I had a good time with Clive laughing and talking, but when I tried to get up, that's when I knew I was in over my head. The world was spinning and whirling around. I took two steps and fell back down on the grassy slope. Clive asked me to come back inside, but I knew I had to get somewhere fast.

"No, I'm going to go over to my friend's house," I slurred.

"You're not walking over there by yourself," was Clive's reply, revealing a chivalrous side that, in my sober state of mind, I wasn't even aware of. "I'll walk you over there."

Although I knocked and knocked, Kayla didn't answer the door.

"She might be over her auntie's house," I mumbled drunkenly and began to stagger down the hall in the general direction of the building's exit.

"Where does her auntie live?" asked Clive.

"Over there on Barnes Place," I pointed the way, and the two of us took off walking, me staggering and Clive helping me along to the best of his ability.

Once we got to the large pink house, I got a little nervous, that is, if nervousness was even possible in such a drunken state. I wasn't so drunk that I didn't realize Kayla's Aunt Bessie would cuss me out for banging on her door in the middle of the night drunk. I knew that a cussing out was guaranteed if I showed up at the door drunk along with a teenage boy. It was rare for a grown woman to approve of fastness or anything that resembled it, so I played it drunkenly safe and bid Clive a good night.

"I'll see you tomorrow at camp," I said a little too loudly.

"Are you sure you're going to be all right?" Clive asked. "How do you know she's at home?"

"She's here," I assured him before leaning over the banister and throwing up into the bushes. The light by the back door came on, and Clive took that as a hint to disappear down the alley we had walked through.

Aunt Bessie took one look at me, instantly knew the whole story, and showed me to the couch. She then went upstairs and came back down with a pillow and blanket. Without another word, I passed out on Aunt Bessie's couch.

◆ ◈ ◇

The friendship between Clive and I continued to deepen throughout the summer, but it never got to the romantic stage. I was still grieving over Blue, so I didn't look at other guys in that way. I appreciated his companionship, but he wanted more, or so it seemed. Clive showed the way he felt about me by teasing me. As the summer camp season ended, his teasing escalated to a higher level until one day it finally struck a nerve.

Rather than spend the day out at Camp Parsons, we took the campers to a picnic and outing at Carver Park, a nature reserve. There were wood chip-covered trails through the nature reserve on which the counselors and campers hiked behind a Carver Park nature guide. Clive, as usual, was trying to get a rise out of me, but I wasn't in a playing mood. I was a moody person to begin with, but since my baby's stillbirth, my emotional highs and lows were out of control.

Clive pushed me and took off down the trail expecting me to chase him like I normally would. Instead, I kept walking. Next, he picked up a tree toad and tried to startle me with it, but I wasn't afraid of tree toads, so I simply rolled my eyes.

"Fat bitch," he taunted me.

"Yo' mama," was my half-hearted reply.

"Your baby died of gonorrhea," he retorted.

Although it was bright daylight outside, his hateful words caused the forest around us to go black with little white spots. The sound of birds and crickets was snuffed out and replaced by a thin ringing in my suddenly deaf ears. The rush of adrenaline that shot through my veins felt like hot grease. Not wanting to let the campers see me cry, I turned and ran to the camp bus. Hot, angry tears ran down my face. I slowed down when I got close to the bus and began looking for a large stick, vowing to myself that I would either make him retract those words or die trying.

I pushed up against the school bus door with my shoulder, and it opened. I went to the back of the bus and laid in wait until Clive and the campers finally returned. Clive sat two seats in front of me. As soon as his butt touched the seat, I shot up from where I was sitting with the stick and went to work on his head. I pounded Clive's head with that stick like there was no tomorrow. Later my friends told me that Eric, the bus driver, seemingly flew over the seats, as well as the campers and other counselors, to get between Clive and me. Mrs. Walters, the camp director, grabbed me and Eric grabbed Clive, who was still in a state of shock and hadn't fully recovered. Mrs. Walters wrenched the stick out of my grasp, and I collapsed back down into my seat. I put my head down on the seat in front of me and sobbed.

"Get off the bus, young lady," demanded Mrs. Walters. I tried to pull myself together, but before I could regain my composure, Mrs. Walters grabbed my arm and jerked it like I was four or five years old instead of sixteen.

I had had enough. "Get your hands off me, bitch," I yelled. Mrs. Walters' eyes got big as saucers, and she slapped my face as hard as she could. Needless to say, that was my last day at Camp Parsons.

CHAPTER 15

Detroit

◈ ◈ ◈

Blue's sister Jasmine and I were still hanging around together, so I spent a lot of time at the Lockett's house with her. Blue still didn't want anything to do with me, but I was somewhat content just to be near him and his family. Occasionally, I caught a glimpse of his comings and goings through the back door of the house.

Mrs. Lockett had decided to go visit her Aunt Ethel in Detroit. She took Jasmine and me along with her. We caught the Greyhound bus to Chicago, where we transferred to another bus heading to Detroit. Jasmine and I filled up with junk food from the vending machines along the way, so we weren't very hungry once we arrived in a cab from the bus station to Aunt Ethel's house on the West Side of Detroit. She lived on the second floor of a large brick duplex, and her daughter lived on the first floor.

When we had dragged the last of our suitcases up the stairs to Aunt Ethel's place, we were greeted by a breakfast spread on the dining room table fit for kings and queens. Aunt Ethel had prepared a huge platter full of scrambled eggs, sausage, thick slices of bacon, hot buttered toast, and a large bowl full of grits. There was also a pitcher of orange juice on the table, and coffee was perking in the kitchen. Jasmine and I picked at our food and then excused ourselves to go out onto the screened-in porch, which was where we would sleep during the visit.

That night, Jasmine's male cousin visited us on the porch and sat up talking to Jasmine and me half the night. I must have drifted off because before I knew it, the sun was rising on a new day of adventure and discovery in Detroit, Michigan.

I had some cousins on the East Side of Detroit, known as the rough and tough side of the city off Mack and Garland Avenues. That was where my cousin Mary Jane lived. Mary Jane's brother, Butch, had been murdered in one of Detroit's ongoing notorious acts of violence. In 1974 when we visited, Motor City's heyday was over, and poverty and crime were rampant. When we left the West Side to go visit my relatives on the East Side, Jasmine's Aunt Ethel gave us words of advice.

"Don't look at nobody, and don't talk to nobody. If somebody hollers at you from a car, keep on walking. Above all, don't get in nobody's car."

Aunt Ethel's list went on and on. In truth, when we arrived on the East Side, it resembled the West Side with its big stately brick homes. In my opinion, a ghetto was a ghetto no matter what side of town it was on. There were different class levels, poverty rates, and unemployment rates, but in my experience, there were good and bad people no matter where you went. Racism and oppression created conditions that caused some people to prey on others, which increased crime and violence rates in low-income neighborhoods, but I had learned to watch my back no matter where I was.

Minneapolis didn't really have what amounted to a ghetto that ranked on the scale with Detroit or Chicago because the population of African Americans in the Twin Cities was comparatively small. Traveling to other cities with large Black populations fascinated me because Minneapolis had always been behind the times with music and dances. KUXL, our radio soul station, went off the air when the sun went down, and dances were out of style by the time they reached the Twin Cities. Whenever someone from Minneapolis traveled out of town, they always brought back the latest dances and music.

Mary Jane's daughter, LaChaun, had a mouth on her that would not quit, and she was only six years old. The last time I saw her, she was only two years old and was already bold and talkative.

"Black power, soul sister!" she'd say with her two-year-old fist raised in a black power salute.

The older folks in the family, including my dad, just looked at LaChaun and shook their heads. She was too much. Since the last time I had been to Detroit when I was thirteen years old, Mary Jane had given birth to another little girl, Tammy. She was the prettiest little girl I had seen in quite a while. She had dark brown skin, which was customary on my dad's side of the family, and long, wavy, jet-black hair. She was a doll.

Mary Jane decided to take Jasmine and me out on the town, so we got dressed up that weekend and went to Jazz West on Detroit's West Side and another night club. The Detroit Emeralds were on the bill that night. After the club, Jasmine and I spent the night at Mary Jane's house. We tried to squeeze into LaChaun's bed with her, but it was too small, so I wound up sleeping on the couch.

The next day we decided to walk to the store, and we took LaChaun with us. On the way to the store, LaChaun said with conviction, "You can't be my cousin. You don't never buy me nothing. You don't never take me nowhere. Anyway, you're white."

Jasmine got a kick out of LaChaun and her sassy mouth, so she fell out laughing, but I didn't think it was funny.

CHAPTER 16

Von

◈ ◈ ◈

One night as I was hanging out having a few drinks on the no-pay side
of the Filling Station, I was introduced to Von, a fly guy from East St.
Louis, Illinois, who was new to the Twin Cities. I was introduced to
him by his homeboy, William, someone I knew from the neighborhood.
When Von smiled, all I saw was a flash of light reflecting from his gold-
trimmed front teeth. He was decked out from head to toe in a three-
piece suit, and his hair was permed and finger waved. A diamond pinkie
ring adorned his hand.

He told me his name was Von. I later learned that his name was
LeVorn, but it sounded like he was saying Von because of his southern
accent. Von looked real good to me, and I definitely liked his style. He
had plenty of Southern swag. After being dissed all summer by Blue, I
welcomed his attention. Von ordered me a drink and got a shot of Hen-
nessy for himself. I sat on the barstool next to him and did my best to
follow the line of conversation. His strong Southern accent made it difficult for me to understand everything he was saying, so I just nodded
and smiled, and we got along just fine.

When the bar's lights flashed at a quarter to one letting the patrons
know that soon it would be "hotel-motel time," Von picked up his keys
from the bar with a flourish and gestured with his head for me to follow
him, which I did. We went around the building to the parking lot. When
we reached his vehicle, he held open the passenger door of his forest
green Cadillac—complete with a leopard skin ragtop and TV anten-
nas—for me to get in. We headed to a duplex on the corner of 39th and
4th Avenue. I didn't think it would hurt to stay and visit awhile since he
was staying just two blocks from where I lived. I could walk home, if
need be, I reasoned.

Lining the street in front of the duplex on 4th Avenue and along 39th Street were Cadillacs of nearly every color in the rainbow. They were lemon yellow, hot pink, baby blue, jet black, and two-toned brown and white. Von, his brothers, and a few cousins and friends had come to the Twin Cities together from East St. Louis, Illinois. Most of them drove Cadillacs, but there was also an Electra 225, otherwise known as a deuce and a quarter, which belonged to Bruh, William's ace boon coon.

Von and I went inside, and I stayed with him until the break of dawn. Von was sprawled out asleep as I dressed quickly and got the hell out of there for my early-morning stroll home. I was still feeling slightly tipsy from the night before, so I climbed into bed and slept a few hours until I smelled breakfast cooking and heard my dad getting ready for church. I felt a strong urge to go to church with him. Spending the night with Von, a twenty-six-year-old man to my sweet sixteen, felt scandalous even to me. I had crossed a line that had not been crossed by me.

Through the haze of my hangover, I reminisced back over the course of the summer, all the way up to the night before, and could not think of a better place for me to be than seated next to my dad at Zion Baptist Church. When my dad and I arrived at church, I suddenly felt sick to my stomach, so I told him to go into church without me.

"Dad, I'll meet you in the sanctuary."

My dad nodded his head in agreement and continued up the outside staircase towards the church entrance. Meanwhile, I bent over behind a tree in front of the church and threw up. The hangover had me feeling sick and queasy. I felt as though I was experiencing firsthand exactly how it felt to live the life of a sinner.

With my head still throbbing, I made my way up the church's front steps, opened the door, and slipped inside to join my dad on the pew where he regularly sat each Sunday. Sitting next to him in church that day brought back childhood memories of going to Sunday school and church each and every Sunday.

CHAPTER 17

Sunday Mornings

✦ ✦ ✦

My brother Ira and I had perfect attendance at St. Peter's AME Church Sunday school. All the children gathered in the church's basement and sat on folding chairs where we sang hymns accompanied by Leslie, the Sunday school pianist. After listening to announcements and a message delivered by the superintendent of the Sunday school, either Mr. or Mrs. Chivers, we were dismissed by age group to go to our respective Sunday school classes.

Each class was held in a classroom partitioned from the common area by an accordion-pleated curtain of olive-green vinyl. Ora Newman was my Sunday school teacher. She taught us Bible stories and passed out small cards to each of us that had a colorful picture with a corresponding Bible story underneath, which she read to us and asked us questions about.

I liked Ora. She was a pretty, brown-skinned woman with a nice smile and a small gap between her two front teeth. One of them was occasionally smudged with coral lipstick, which I thought was a beautiful contrast to her pearly-white teeth. Midway through our Sunday school class, Ora served us a snack of graham crackers and grape Kool-Aid in small, multihued tin cups of purple, gold, blue, and green. We then colored pictures with Biblical themes, such as Noah's Ark, Moses and the Ten Commandments, and, of course, the Last Supper.

The Sunday school crayons were kept in a straw basket, which Ora dumped in the middle of the table, so we could choose the ones we wanted to color with. Most of the crayons were broken and well used with rounded rather than pointed tips. At the end of Sunday school, Ora would gather them up and put them back in the basket for use next time.

We also sang songs: "This Little Light of Mine," "Jesus Loves Me," and "How Great Thou Art!" As a child, it was comforting for me to know that God has the whole world in His hands. The meaning of those song lyrics is comforting to this day. I enjoyed Sunday school and simply loved going over to Ora and her husband Oscar's house afterwards for pancakes on the days we didn't go to church with our dad. Ora and Oscar were friends of our family. They didn't have any children of their own, so whenever we visited their house, we received their undivided attention.

Either Ora or Oscar would cook our pancakes on the griddle in the middle of their stovetop between the burners. I remember how the batter would sizzle when it was poured onto the hot metal surface oiled with a dab of Crisco. When the batter began to bubble up in the center, the pancakes would be flipped over to the other side to brown before using a spatula to pile them onto our plates with a side of bacon or sausage. The pancakes always turned out perfect. They were medium brown with tan splotches throughout, a pat of melted butter in the center, and maple syrup dripping off the sides of the stack just like the picture on the pancake box.

As a preschooler, I can also remember sitting on my swing set, looking up at the sky and singing, "All night, all day, angels watching over me, my Lord." I liked the idea of angels watching over me. My mother taught my brother and me to say our blessings before each meal, and every night before we went to bed, we got down on our knees to say our prayers.

My mom and dad were of different protestant denominations. She was brought up in the African Methodist Episcopal church, and my dad was a staunch Baptist. Both his father and grandfather were Baptist ministers. "Baptist born and Baptist bred, and when I die, I'm Baptist dead," was his claim to fame. Therefore, we attended Sunday school at St. Peter's AME Church each Sunday morning at nine-thirty, and then it was off to Zion Baptist Church for the eleven o'clock service with our dad.

I enjoyed the Baptist service because of all the passion expressed by the saints of God. The spirit flowed from the time the choir marched in two by two in their maroon and gold satin choir robes singing old Negro spirituals through the emotional sermons delivered by Reverend

Holloway (and later by his successor, Pastor Curtis Herron), right up to when the doors of the church were opened, so new members could join, and the Benediction signaled that church service was over.

When the service was especially moving, the sisters would "get happy." They would clap their hands, throw them in the air, shout Hallelujah, shed tears of joy or pain, and sometimes even pass out when the goodness of God overcame them. When the spirit moved, the ushers would go into high gear fanning the saints, giving them tissues to wipe their eyes, and covering their legs with holy cloth when they were "slain by the spirit" to preserve their dignity. We children were all eyes and ears when the sisters in the church got happy!

The church brethren did not express themselves spiritually in quite the same manner. In particular, the deacons of the church were a stern group of dignified men who kept their emotions in check. Occasionally, you might spot one of them removing a spotless white handkerchief from his suitcoat pocket and dabbing his eyes a bit if the sermon or music happened to touch a spiritual nerve.

Rather than express their spirituality in a display of emotionalism, as the sisters were inclined to do, the righteousness of the brothers in Christ was displayed in their day-to-day lives. They demonstrated their commitment to the Lord by being staunch and upright Christian men, who were the heads of their households and the pillars of our community. As a rule, they were reliable men who kept their word. There was comfort in knowing their yeses meant yes and their noes meant no. Looking back, I realize I was extremely blessed to have a dad who was cut from the cloth of Christian values and spiritual beliefs.

Learning about God's greatness as a child was a good thing because it made me feel safe and secure. It helped to know in times of trouble that "trouble don't last always" and that God, who loves us dearly, sits high on the throne of grace, ready, willing, and able to help us when we are in need.

When I was pregnant by Blue and began to show, I stopped going to church. My mother didn't think it looked right for me to be sitting in church pregnant and unmarried at sixteen years old. But on that day, hungover or not, it felt right to be sitting in church next to my dad. I was slipping deeper and deeper into darkness, and I knew it, but from my childhood Sunday school lessons and all the time I had spent sitting on the pews of Zion Baptist Church, I had not forgotten where to go when I needed help.

> *I will lift up mine eyes unto the hills, from whence cometh*
> *my help.*
> *My help cometh from the Lord, which made Heaven and*
> *earth.*
>
> *—Psalms 121*

CHAPTER 18

Indiana Bound

◆ ◆ ◆

For the rest of the summer, I hung out on Cadillac Corner with Von and his family. Occasionally, two of my friends also hung out there with me. The men they were involved with were friends or relatives of the East St. Louis crew. I had heard rumors that they were turning tricks on Lake Street. It wasn't that hard to believe. All the tell-tale signs were there: the long wigs, the extra makeup, the short dresses, the daily jaunt up 4th Avenue heading towards the 'ho stroll. I never asked them about it, though. After all, I had problems of my own.

One day, as I was seated on the front steps sharing a bottle of wine with Von and we watched his brothers polishing their Cadillacs in the summer sun, I was scandalized to see my mom and dad pull up to the corner. My dad's blinker was on as he waited to turn right onto 4th Avenue. I saw my mom point me out to him, so it was too late to attempt to disappear inside the house. I had already been sighted. My dad rolled down the window and gestured for me to come over to the car. Without asking any questions, he told me to get into the car.

"Where are you going?" I asked.

"Just get in," my dad repeated.

My parents must have put two and two together and come up with four pertaining to the flashy men surrounding me in the sunlight. Their gold teeth, permed hair, and rainbow-hued Cadillacs parked up and down the street told a story I didn't fully understand, but apparently, my parents did. I didn't see any way around it, so reluctantly, I said goodbye to Von, walked over to the car, and got in.

Within the next two weeks, the verdict had come down. I was going to live with my dad's relatives in Indianapolis. The powers-that-be had deemed me to be out of control and in need of a different, more wholesome environment. My dad's cousin Luther visited Minneapolis, checked out my vibes and lifestyle, and concluded that he could turn my life around.

"Let her come stay with Lorraine and me for a while," he had advised my parents. "We'll straighten her out."

My parents, who were at their wits' end on how to deal with me, their wayward daughter, swallowed the bait—hook, line, and sinker. They readily gave in to the idea of someone stepping up to the plate to help them stop my downward spiral. If anyone had the potential to do it, they firmly believed that Cousin Luther did.

Unlike my dad's humble and unassuming ways, Luther had a strong and domineering personality. He was a no-nonsense-man-about-town. He owned and successfully operated two businesses—a travel company and an accounting firm—which he ran just like he did everything and everyone else in his life, with an iron fist. Apparently, he viewed conquering my wayward spirit as one more challenge he would take on and succeed in doing so.

Luther had very little patience for people who could not handle the affairs that had been placed into their hands. He undoubtedly saw my dad's inability to control his daughter as an example of someone who was not handling his affairs properly. Therefore, Luther had decided that he and his wife Lorraine would accept the challenge to take me under their wings and straighten me out.

I immediately warmed up to the idea of moving to Indianapolis to finish high school. I had an adventurous spirit and looked upon the move as a brand new and exciting adventure in my life. Minneapolis had played out, in my opinion. It was time to move on to potentially bigger and better things.

As I packed my clothes, I thought about the prospect of leaving Minneapolis. I felt remorseful about having to say goodbye to my new love, Von. He had rescued me from my grief and depression. I didn't see our ten-year age difference as a problem. As a matter of fact, Von and his brothers gave me a sense of what it felt like to be part of a large extended family, and I would miss them.

Not long before my move to Indiana, Von told me he was going back to East Saint Louis to pawn his diamond rings because he needed money.

With him leaving Minneapolis, it was probably as good a time as any for me to leave town, too. As my father's Catalina sheened towards Chicago, I thought about Von. I would miss him, his style, his golden smile, and the good times we shared on Cadillac Corner that summer. As the telephone poles raced by, the wires dipping up and down between them, my mind raced ahead to Indianapolis. I wondered what the city held in store for me.

CHAPTER 19

Nap Town

❖ ❖ ❖

It didn't take long for the honeymoon of being in a new town to end. One morning I was confronted before school by Luther.

"Pee in this jar," demanded Luther as he thrust an empty peanut butter jar at me.

"Pee in that jar for what?" I wanted to know.

"You were on your period when you got here, but you haven't had a period since. I want you to pee in this jar so I can find out if you're pregnant."

I stared at Luther like he had lost his mind. I searched his face for signs that he was playing a game with me early in the morning, but his face had a determined look on it that I had seen before.

"I already went to the bathroom," I lied.

"When?"

"I got up in the middle of the night and went." I was determined not to pee on demand in anybody's jar, including Luther's.

I wondered how he knew I was on my period when I arrived in Indianapolis. My father had never concerned himself with such personal female affairs back home in Minneapolis, but then again, dealing with Cousin Luther was an entirely new ball game.

"You didn't get up in the middle of the night to go to the bathroom, or I would have heard you."

"Yes, I did, but if you want me to, I'll try to go again."

I took the jar and headed into the bathroom. I knew better than to outwardly defy Luther. A few minutes later, I emerged from the bathroom with the empty jar in hand.

"I couldn't go," I explained, holding it out to him.

Luther refused to take it.

"No, you keep it. I want you to pee in that jar tomorrow morning."

Having laid down the law, Luther stalked away. The next morning, I got up early and crept into the bathroom. I carefully climbed into the bathtub and positioned myself over the drain. I peed as quietly as possible and then tiptoed back into my room and got back into bed. A few minutes later, Luther was at the bedroom door pounding as if his very life depended on it.

"Where's that jar? Get up and go pee in the jar."

I got up and grabbed the jar from the dresser where I had left it the day before. Once more, I couldn't produce any pee for him. When I handed the empty jar to him, he became furious.

"I don't know what kind of game you think you're playing, but one way or the other, you're going to pee in this jar! Don't think you're going to come down here and get pregnant and make me look bad."

I couldn't understand his logic. How on earth could my pregnancy make Luther look bad? If anything, I would be the one looking bad. I decided to keep my thoughts to myself since Luther looked dangerously close to going off.

"You're trying to make me look bad, aren't you, girl? They said you were hardheaded, but I had no idea," he said, shaking his head. "Go get ready for school, but tomorrow I want some pee in this jar."

Luther stormed down the hall, and I went about the business of getting ready for another school day.

Later that day, I went to the paper shack and called a friend.

"Hey, girl."

"Colnese, is that you?"

"Yeah, girl, it's me."

"What's up? How do you like it in Indiana?"

"It's all right. My dad's cousin is tripping, though. He thinks I'm pregnant."

"Pregnant? Are you?"

"If I am, he jinxed me. Do you know that man actually wakes me up in the morning to take a pregnancy test?"

"You're kidding."

"I wish I was kidding."

"What are you going to do?"

"If I'm pregnant, I sure as hell ain't having it."

"Who's baby?"

"Mine for now. Wire me $50, would you?"

"You getting rid of it?"

"I want to be prepared for the worst-case scenario."

"Yeah, okay then, I'll send it. When you gonna pay me back?"

"How in the hell am I supposed to know? I don't have no money. Maybe I can get my mom to give it to you."

"Why don't you just ask your mom for the money?"

"I don't want her to be worrying about me all the way down here with a crazy man who thinks I'm pregnant."

"Well, let me know how everything turns out. What code word should I use."

"Use 'baby,' what else?"

"Girl, you're crazy as hell. Well, I better let you go. I know it's long distance."

"When are you going to send it?"

"I don't get paid until Friday. I'll send it then."

"Okay, later."

"Yeah, later."

I had to be prepared. I knew I couldn't stall Luther forever with his jar in the morning.

◆ ◈ ◦

Luther refused to give me a key to the house. When asked, he told me that his children had never had keys to the house, so as far as he was concerned, I didn't need a key either. Instead, every day after school, I went to Luther's oldest daughter Luretha's beauty shop and stayed there until eight or nine at night when the shop closed.

If truth be told, I didn't mind sitting in the shop. There was always a whirlwind of action going on with people getting their hair done or just coming in to talk as they went about their daily activities. Luretha was very popular in Indianapolis, so the shop was always packed.

One of the things I liked about the shop was that there was always something good to eat since Luretha and the other ladies were forever sending out for food. There was a Church's Chicken right across the street. If I was hungry and there was nothing else good to eat, I'd go get some chicken wings, douse them with hot sauce, and have a chicken-eating good time.

Broad Ripple High School let out at one thirty in the afternoon, and I usually arrived at the shop a little after two o'clock. After finishing my homework, I took long walks down 38th Street to see what I could see. Being used to Minneapolis's small Black population, Indianapolis's Black community seemed endless. I wanted to explore every last block, so I walked and looked and walked and looked some more.

My mom had told me before I left Minneapolis that once I got settled in, she would send me some money to buy a bike to ride. When I asked Luther about it, he joked, "A bike? You're hell on your feet. What do you need with a bike?"

I had to agree with him. I felt confined when indoors and yearned for the freedom of the street. Wandering the streets of Indianapolis helped quench an inner longing that drove me to explore block after endless block. What I was searching for, I didn't exactly know. Sometimes I felt as though whatever I was searching for was right around the next corner, but I had yet to find it up to that point. I also knew if I stayed in the house or at the shop, I might miss something, some unnamed action or adventure. So I roamed the streets in search of an answer to the unspoken question burning deep within me and for the unnamed something that would fill up the emptiness within my soul.

Although I enjoyed my time at the shop, I didn't like the fact that Cousin Luther did not trust me with a key. Back at home I had been entrusted with a key since I was in elementary school. Not having a key to unlock the house I now called home was only one of the ways in which my life had taken a giant step backwards by moving to Indianapolis. The legal drinking age was twenty-one in Indianapolis, so my nightclubbing and partying days had come to a screeching halt.

Whereas the girls in Minneapolis that I hung around with were already into the nightlife and after-hours scene, the girls in Indianapolis seemed way slower than my Minneapolis friends. Most of them looked at me with mistrust in their eyes. I was a new girl on their turf, one more girl to contend with in the never-ending tug of war over the fellows, which placed me in a catch-22 position. Where most of the girls were unfriendly towards me, the majority of the boys were quite the opposite. In fact, they were very friendly. The more guys I made friends with, the less the girls liked me. For the most part, I didn't care. I spent much of my time standing on the corner of 40th and Boulevard Street with a few of the neighborhood guys drinking wine, which for some reason was called "oil" in Nap Town. It wasn't long before they nicknamed me "Iron Throat" because I could out-drink them all.

The wine I drank made me feel warm and happy inside. In my early teens, I had developed a love for wine. I loved the warm feeling that spread through my body and the buzz I felt as the result of my drinking it. As a shy girl, I loved the lowering of my inhibitions.

When it started getting cold outside, we sometimes went into the paper shack to drink. Because Larry, who lived across the street from Luther, had a paper route, he had a key to the shack. I liked the paper shack because there was a phone in there. When I got homesick, I used it to call my friends in Minneapolis long distance. Although hanging around exclusively with the young men was all right for the most part, there were times that I longed for a girlfriend to talk things over with. It was during those times that I got especially homesick for my friends in Minneapolis.

One of the guys I hung around with was only fifteen. His name was Brian, and I sometimes walked to the bus stop with him in the morning. He worked in Luretha's shop after school sweeping up and running errands, so I was connected to Brian in a different way than I was to my wine-drinking friends.

Brian liked me, although I didn't know it at first. He never said anything to me to let me know he liked me, and I had never given him any reason to think he had a chance with me. Brian was cute—his hair was as red as his skin—but he was not mature enough for me, at least not in my eyes he wasn't. I found out the hard way Brian liked me.

"You've been around here kissing Brian," accused Luretha one day during a lull in customers at the shop.

"Brian?" I was shocked.

"Don't play that innocent role with me. You know you kissed Brian because Brian told me."

"Brian's a liar if he told you that because I haven't kissed him. He ain't nothin' but a kid to me. What would I look like kissing him?"

"I don't know. You tell me."

I was close to tears. I didn't like the idea of Brian lying on me, nor did I like Luretha believing it and throwing it up in my face. I didn't say any more about it to Luretha, but inwardly I vowed to stay away from Brian with his lying self.

I went outside and sat on the steps of the shop. The sun was going down, and the sky was a beautiful mixture of pink, orange, and aqua blue. I could hear Luretha inside laughing and talking with her customers, and suddenly I felt very lonely. Luretha was supposed to be my cousin, but she had believed Brian over me. Conversely, Brian was supposed to be my friend, but he had lied on me. All my real friends were back home, and I missed them. I missed walking down the hallways of my school in Minneapolis and knowing everybody by name.

At Broad Ripple, I walked alone for the most part. Two ninth grade girls, Carole and Bobbie, had gone out of their way to befriend me, but they were the only ones to do so. They had been best friends since grade school, and although they did everything they could to make me feel included, I missed having a best friend of my own.

I sat on the steps a long time, looking at the sky and thinking of my friends and family back in Minneapolis. The sky slowly turned deep blue and then black. One star twinkled red and white. I brightened up a little. It was the same star that my friend Shirlynn and I had searched the sky for every night as we sat together at Phelps Park the summer before. I wondered if Shirlynn was back home looking at it right now. Somehow the idea that my friend was looking at the same star made me feel less lonely and closer to home.

One by one, Luretha's customers left the shop. Finally, Luretha, too, came out of the shop and announced that she was ready to go. I followed her to the car and got in. Together we rode home in silence.

CHAPTER 20

Bees in My Bonnet

✦ ✦ ✦

Cousin Luther was convinced I was crazy. When I told him and Cousin Lorraine about some of my adventures in Minneapolis, he shook his head and said, "Girl, you got bees in your bonnet."

I wasn't quite sure what he meant because every last thing I told them about was the truth. When I had told him and Cousin Lorraine about my stillborn baby girl, he told me I had bees in my bonnet. One day I cooked myself some breakfast. I made bacon, eggs, and toast and poured syrup over the toast. I also poured myself a large glass of milk and a small glass of orange juice.

"I shouldn't have put syrup on the toast," I confided to Cousin Lorraine, who was sitting at the table reading the paper as I took a bite of bacon.

"Why on earth not?"

"Well, it would have been a very nutritious and healthy breakfast without the syrup sloshing around in my stomach on top of everything."

Cousin Lorraine gave me a sideways glance, shook her head, and returned her attention to the paper. Without asking, I knew what Cousin Lorraine was thinking.

That girl has bees in her bonnet.

Cousin Luther and I were engaged in an ongoing battle for power and control. The score was usually even. For every point I scored, Cousin Luther countered it with a sophisticated move of his own. Every so often, however, Cousin Luther would gain a couple of points, mainly because he didn't play fair. He read my mail, intercepted my phone calls, and changed the rules almost daily.

One of the ways he kept my adventurous spirit and wanderlust under control was to lock me in the house. His house had double deadbolt locks, so if he and Cousin Lorraine had to go someplace, rather than risk leaving me in the house alone, unattended, and free to leave, he would lock me in. There was a sliding glass door in the kitchen that did not have a double dead bolt lock. Instead, it led into the backyard where the dogs were kept.

One day Luther and Lorraine had been gone for a particularly long time, and I wanted to go to the store. I went down to the kitchen and stood in front of the sliding glass door. I had only been in Indianapolis for two months, but by this time, Cousin Luther had gotten to the point where he knew just how much my freedom meant to me. On the door was a sign that said, "Mavis is out."

Mavis was Cousin Luther's German Shepherd. They also had Lacy, Cousin Lorraine's golden retriever. Although I was scared of both dogs, I wasn't as scared of Lacy as I was of Mavis. Lacy was a punk, in my opinion, but Mavis was nuts. All she did all day long was prance from one side of the yard to the other, barking like crazy.

I thought back to the time Mavis had tricked me into letting her into the house and then turned on me. One day when I was lying on the floor in front of the sliding glass door listening to the radio, Mavis had come to the door and "smiled" at me—at least it looked to me like she was smiling. Her mouth was open, her tongue hung out, and she had a happy look in her eyes.

I went to the door and greeted Mavis through the glass. Mavis started wriggling all over. She jumped up and put her paws on the glass and wriggled and panted even harder. I slid the door open about an inch to see if Mavis would bark. Mavis stuck her nose between the crack and then sniffed and pawed the opening and whined a little bit.

I looked around to see what Mavis was whining about and spotted the dog's weather-beaten and chewed-up toy dog bone in the corner of the kitchen. I was all for making friends with Mavis—after all, the dog was often all that stood between me and freedom—so I opened the door wide enough for Mavis to come in and get her bone.

Mavis bounded into the house, headed straight for the corner of the kitchen, and grabbed the bone. She trotted past me and appeared to be on her way back outside when she suddenly stopped, dropped the bone, and started barking like crazy. In a flying leap, I jumped up on the kitchen counter. Mavis stood her ground in the middle of the floor and barked and bared her teeth. I looked at Mavis with contempt.

You are so two-faced! Here I am trying to do you a favor, and you act a fool.

I didn't dare say anything out loud for fear that Mavis would spring on me. Mavis kept me up on the counter for another five minutes before Lorraine finally heard the commotion and came downstairs to free me from my captor.

As I looked out into the yard, I remembered that scene with Mavis and knew that the dog was not to be trusted because, after all, she belonged to Cousin Luther. That said it all, as far as I was concerned. From where I stood, I couldn't see either of the dogs. A fenced-in dog pen was at the back of the yard near the alley. The gate hung open, letting me know that the dogs were somewhere out in the yard. Most likely, they were on one side of the house or the other. If they were on the left side, I could break for the right side where there was a gate leading to the front yard and freedom. If they were on the right side, I would run right into them and probably be eaten alive.

I decided to play it cool and wait them out. After a few minutes at my post, I spotted Lacy trotting across the yard from the right side of the house with Mavis close behind. I measured the distance between the dogs and the gate. Quietly I slid the door open and stepped outside. Lacy glanced at me. I remained motionless. After a second or two, Lacy continued across the yard, and I decided to run for it. I made a mad dash for the gate, hurling my body against it. I hurriedly unlatched it and tumbled through to the other side.

Behind me I could hear Mavis' and Lacy's frenzied barking behind me. I kicked the gate shut seconds before the dogs reached my point of departure. Mavis bounded towards the fence, leaping upwards and against it. Her forepaws locked around the top of the fence while her back paws scrambled in a frantic attempt to hoist her body up and over the top. Too short to reach the top of the fence, Lacy sat back on her haunches and echoed Mavis's frenzied barks. I didn't slow my pace until I made it safely through the front gate and down the three steps to the sidewalk and freedom.

CHAPTER 21

Kicked to the Curb with No Return

When I rounded the corner on my way back home from the store, I saw two cars in front of the house and knew that Luther and Lorraine had beat me home. I could see that the front door was open. Luther met me at the door. He stepped aside so I could walk in and then ambushed me from the side, knocking me into the lamp. I took off running. Luther tried to grab me, but I yanked away from him, knocking over the end table and lamp in the process.

There was a staircase in the center of the house right in front of the doorway. On one side of the staircase was the living room and dining room, and on the other side was a hallway that led to a bedroom and bathroom. The kitchen and family room could be accessed from either side of the staircase, so you could follow a path all the way through the house and wind up back at the staircase. Luther chased me through the house and back around to the front door. Cousin Lorraine tried to head me off, but I broke through the human barricade and ran outside. I took the stairs two at a time, but Luther caught up with me when I reached the sidewalk and tackled me. He grabbed me under my arms.

"Grab her feet," he gasped to Lorraine, who was close behind us in hot pursuit.

I kicked my feet, struggled, and yelled at the top of my lungs. Cousin Lorraine grabbed my legs while Cousin Luther continued his firm grip on my arms. I thrashed and fought for all I was worth. I felt the material of my wool maroon coat rip as I struggled to get away. Across the street, I could see porch lights come on as the neighbors came outside to get a ringside view.

"Call the police!" I yelled as I continued to put up a serious fight to get away from them. But the neighbors just stood there and looked at the scene unfolding in front of them.

I could be killed out here, and these fools wouldn't do a thing to help me, I thought irritably.

Luther and Lorraine inched towards the house with me flailing around between them. The two of them breathed in short gasps as they struggled to carry me inside.

"Let her go," gasped Lorraine as she let go of my feet. "I'm not going to have a heart attack over her and her crazy self."

A defeated Luther let go of my arms. I rolled away from them, jumped to my feet, and trotted across the street.

"Don't come back here no time soon," hollered Luther after me. "If you can't abide by the rules of my house, then you don't need to be here."

I had no plans of returning any time soon, so I headed towards my grandmother's house. Nano lived on 37th and Graceland, a few blocks over and a few blocks down from Cousin Luther. As I walked down the darkening Indianapolis streets, I thought about what had just taken place.

Luther didn't have any business putting his hands on me, as far as I was concerned. That was where I drew the line. Anyone who crossed that line had hell to pay, and I didn't care who they were supposed to be. I wasn't anybody's wild animal, who needed to be broken in. I was a human being with rights, and one of those rights was not to be struck in anger by anyone who felt inclined to do so.

The lights were on in my grandmother's living room. I rang the doorbell, and soon Nano opened the door. Daddy Gene stood close behind her.

"Come on in, Colnese. Luther just called and told us all about what happened."

"Don't be inviting her in here," said Daddy Gene. "We don't need to borrow nobody else's problems."

"Well, look at her. Her clothes are all ripped and everything. She can at least come in and change into something," pleaded my grandmother.

"She can come in for a minute but make it quick like."

I backed away from the house. "No, that's all right."

"Call me if you need anything," called Nano from the door. "We just don't want any trouble. You know how Luther can be."

"Yeah, okay," I said aloud.

I know how he can be, but I would never leave my granddaughter out-side on the street for Luther or nobody else. I bet if I was their "real" granddaughter, they would let me in.

Being adopted was something I did not like to think about, but it would sneak into my consciousness every so often, no matter how hard I tried to beat it back into the shadows of my mind. When I was around extended family like Cousin Luther and other relatives, it was difficult to ignore the obvious. I was adopted and did not look like I belonged to the family, which made me question whether or not I was truly accepted as a part of the family. It was as simple as that.

When I was pregnant with my baby, I was trying to create a birth family for myself, and even that had failed. Now I was living in a strange town with people who were related to me, but I still felt like an outsider. And now I really was an outsider. Literally outside, as a matter of fact, with no place to go.

I headed down 38th Street. Maybe I could go over to Carole's house. It wasn't that late, only around nine thirty at night. Carole lived a cou-ple of streets over. I brightened up a little as I remembered I did have a friend to turn to. I rang the doorbell, and Carole's father came to the door. He looked a little surprised that I had come over so late, but he let me in anyway.

"Hey, Colnese!" Carole exclaimed. She seemed genuinely happy to see me. "Where are you headed this late?"

"Oh, I was just coming from my grandmother's house and decided to see what was up with you," I answered truthfully.

"Oh, nothing. I was just getting ready to wash my hair."

As if on cue, Carole's mother appeared at the kitchen door with a towel and a bottle of shampoo.

"How are you, Colnese? Carole's told us so much about you. You're from Minne-an-apolis, aren't you?"

I noticed that lots of Indiana folks pronounced the name of my home-town like it rhymed with Indianapolis.

"Yes, ma'am."

"So how are you enjoying your stay down in these parts?"

"Just fine, ma'am."

I was beginning to lose my nerve. Carole's family seemed so close, and Carole was so well protected. I didn't know how to begin to tell them I was put out. They would probably think I was a bad influence on their daughter, and I didn't have enough friends in town to risk losing one of them.

"Well, I'd better be going. I just stopped by to holler at you. See you at school tomorrow, Carole. Nice meeting you folks."

"Yes, it was nice meeting you."

Carole's father showed me to the door.

Just as suddenly as I had arrived, I was right back outside on the street. I heard the door slam shut, and I turned around to look at the house. The light shining through the windows looked so inviting. I imagined that Carole's father had probably repositioned himself on the couch in front of the television, and Carole's mother was probably sitting next to him waiting to help Carole rinse the shampoo out of her hair—a normal family on a Sunday evening getting ready for the week ahead. I pulled myself away from the front of the house and began walking. It was a little chilly outside, but not too bad. When I reached 40th and Boulevard, I ran into two of the guys I sometimes hung out on the corner with, Randall and Jason. I soon found out that they were put out, too.

"What are you put out for?" I asked.

"My old man is crazy," answered Jason absently.

"Nothing, just because," was Randall's reply. "How about you?"

"No reason. I just walked to the store," I answered.

"Man, folks sure do be trippin'," Jason said, gazing off in the distance. "Well, ain't no sense in standing around here. The liquor store is closed."

"Where is there to go in Nap Town on a Sunday night?" wondered Randall.

"I guess we'll find out," I volunteered.

The three of us started walking up Boulevard Avenue towards 38th Street in the direction I had just come from. When we passed Carole's house, I didn't give it a second glance. Being put out didn't seem quite so bad now that I had company.

"I know what we can do," volunteered Jason.

"What's that?"

"Let's go get my brother's car."

"Man, your brother will kill you," exclaimed Randall.

"He's over his girl's spot. How's he gonna know?"

"It's your brother and your life. Count me in. I'm game."

"Where'd he park it?" I asked.

"It's over there on Graceland behind my auntie's house."

"That's way down there. Ain't that about seven blocks from here?"

"You got it."

In no great hurry, we moved slowly down the street. The night loomed in front of us, larger than life. We had several more hours to kill before the break of dawn and no reason to rush headlong into the unknown. Night was no stranger to me. I had walked the streets many late nights coming home from after-hours parties or friends' houses. I liked nothing better than the sound of birds chirping in the trees right before dawn. Unlike many girls my age, I knew no fear. Each threatening situation I encountered, I tackled head-on. It didn't occur to me that I could avoid danger by taking the proper precautions.

Walking down the street in the middle of the night with two young men in their prime posed no threat to me. The predators I had encountered along the way sensed the lack of fear within me. Unsure of what generated my boldness, for the most part, they left me alone. On the other hand, if they were looking for trouble, they found it in me.

Randall and Jason accepted my presence without question. Although my female status precluded me from being one of the boys per se, in the short time they'd known me, I'd shown them that I could hold my own and was not to be disrespected. When we reached the back yard of Jason's aunt's house, they worked quickly and quietly to hot-wire the car. The old model Oldsmobile sputtered to life, and we were on our way.

"Man, I'm hungry," grumbled Randall. "Let's go get us some White Castle's."

"I'm hip," I agreed. "I could go for some burgers myself. What, you got some money?"

"Don't I always?"

"Hell, no!" was my quick comeback.

We all shared a good laugh as Jason pointed the car towards 38th Street. We were rolling, but not for long. Flashing red lights came upon us from the back, and Jason was forced to pull the car over to the curb.

"Damn, it's Johnny Law. Ain't this a bitch!"

"Get out of the car with your hands up," one of the police officers yelled into a megaphone.

We slid from the car with our hands raised above their heads. We knew better than to make any sudden moves. We did not want to make the police any more paranoid than their jobs had already made them.

"Put your hands on top of the car," intoned the voice.

I put my hands on top of the car and stared into the blinding light. One of the police officers approached the car.

"Whose car is this?" he wanted to know.

"My brother's," answered Jason.

"Do you want to produce your driver's license?"

Jason reached slowly into his pocket and pulled it out.

"Do you have the registration for the car?"

"Yes, sir, it's in the glove compartment."

The other police officer opened the passenger door and began rummaging through the glove compartment. He deposited a stack of road maps, a screwdriver, and a wad of paper napkins on the hood of the car.

"Is this vehicle insured?"

"Yes, sir."

"Do you have proof of that insurance in your possession?"

"It should be in the glove compartment."

The police officer had removed everything from the glove compartment but had not come up with either the vehicle registration or the insurance papers.

"Since you are unable to produce the registration for this vehicle or proof of the fact that this vehicle is, in fact, insured, we are going to have to tow it. You're free to go."

"Damn," muttered Jason under his breath.

"What was that, son?"

"Nothing, sir."

"All right, then. You all have a good night."

I couldn't believe the bad luck that we were having.

"Can you believe this mess?" I asked.

"Man!" exclaimed Randall. "Now, where in the hell are we gonna go?"

"Man, don't even worry about it. My uncle lives right around the corner."

"You uncle ain't gonna let us in, especially since we got Colnese with us. How does that look?"

"He don't have to let us in. They never lock the side door, and it leads right down to the basement."

"Do they have any dogs?" I asked as the images of Mavis and Lacy suddenly came to mind.

"Nah, they used to, but it died. It was a Doberman. Man, that dog was so bad, he could tear up any dog in this whole city! My uncle used to feed him gunpowder to make him mean."

"Man, I remember that dog," retorted Randall. "That dog wasn't nothing. My pop's dog woulda tore your uncle's dog's head off."

"Get out of here," answered Jason, his face twisted up in disgust. "Your uncle's dog wasn't nothin' but a punk! Everybody knows that."

"I bet neither one of them dogs could whup Mavis," I contributed.

"Mavis?" Randall looked at Jason and began to laugh.

"Mavis?" Jason looked back at Randall with widened eyes and an open mouth, and then suddenly, he grabbed his stomach and doubled over laughing. "Who the hell is Mavis?" he asked in a strangled voice.

"My cousin's dog," I answered indignantly. "Mavis is the baddest dog of them all!"

"The baddest of them all?" Jason collapsed to the ground, and was rolling around laughing. Randall leaned against a traffic pole to hold himself up.

"Wha . . . wha . . . what kind of name is that for a dog?" Jason could hardly catch his breath.

"Shut up," I demanded. "You don't know what you're talking about." I couldn't believe I was actually defending the crazy dog.

"Man, where's a bathroom?" asked Randall, trying to control his laughter. "I done laughed so hard I'm about to pee on myself."

"White Castle is just up the street," I replied, more than ready to change the subject.

As the three of us made our way towards White Castle, Randall would nudge Jason every so often, and they would both double up in laughter again. I looked at them with disdain and shook my head. They reminded me of my brother and his friends. Once they got going laughing about something funny, it was hard to sober them up.

Finally, we made it to White Castle. After we had all relieved ourselves and downed some burgers and fries, we headed over to Jason's uncle's house. Just like Jason had described, the side door opened to a staircase that led downstairs. The door to the kitchen was about four steps up. A sliver of light could be seen at the bottom of the closed door. Quietly we crept down the stairs and into the basement.

"Where are we going to sleep?" I whispered.

Walking quietly, Jason passed through the open laundry area and opened a door midway across the basement. He motioned for us to follow him. We entered a large unfinished room. There was an old ping pong table in the middle of the room and a couple of folding chairs lining the walls.

"Just a minute, y'all, I'll be right back."

Jason left the room, and in a matter of seconds, had returned with an arm full of blankets. He passed them out to Randall and me.

"Make yourselves at home."

I took the blanket from him, spread it out on the floor, and stretched out.

"I need something to cover up with," I said.

Randall thrust his blanket towards me. "Go ahead."

I scooted over to the edge of the blanket. "There's room enough for all of us. We'll just use the other blankets to cover up with."

"You got to be crazy!" exclaimed Jason. "I ain't sleeping next to no hard legs. I'm cool where I am."

Jason had wrapped his blanket around himself like a cocoon and laid down a few feet away.

"Whatever," I replied.

Randall dropped down on the blanket next to me, spreading his blanket across the two of us, and turned his back to me.

"Who's going to turn out the light?"

"Damn!" Jason got back up, pulled on a chain that hung almost to the floor, and it was dark. A little light was visible near the room's door from the stairway light.

I could hear someone walking on the floor above us, and I could feel the cold concrete of the basement floor through the thin blanket underneath me.

Life is a trip. When I woke up this morning, nobody could have told me I would be lying on a cold concrete floor with two guys that I hardly know. You just never know what's going to happen next.

I lay there listening to Jason's and Randall's heavy breathing and thinking about the condition of my life until sleep quieted the voices in my mind.

◈ ◈ ◈

Somebody was shaking me, so I opened my eyes.

"Come on, get up. We got to get out of here." Jason was standing above me. Randall was nowhere to be seen. "Let's go."

"Yeah, all right, I'm getting up." I got up off the floor and stretched. "Where's Randall?"

"He's in the bathroom," he said, pointing to a door in the corner of the room that I hadn't seen the night before.

"What time is it?"

"I don't know, maybe five or six."

Randall came out of the bathroom. "You need to use it?"

I nodded and went through the door. The small room contained only a toilet. Much to my relief, a roll of toilet paper was on the floor next to it. After a night on the cold floor, I was in no mood to drip dry.

"Hurry up out of there," I heard Jason say from the other side of the door. "We got to go. Don't flush the toilet either. It makes too much noise."

"Yeah, okay, okay, I'm coming."

When I emerged from the small room, Jason and Randall were waiting by the stairs for me. We hurried up the stairs and outside, where the sun was beginning to rise in the east. Together we walked down to 38th Street and turned towards Boulevard, the street where we had come together the night before. When we reached the corner store, we separated.

"Well, I guess this is where we go our separate ways," I announced.

"Yeah, see you around," said Randall, bracing himself against the wind and heading down the street.

"In a minute." Jason threw his hands up, stuffed them in his jacket pockets, and strode away.

I started walking towards what I had called home for the past few months. When I reached the corner, I was surprised to see my parent's Catalina parked in front. I had never been so happy to see anything in all my life. Tears of relief welled up in my eyes. I was being rescued. I looked up at the sky. The moon was still visible, but it was beginning to get lighter and lighter as the sun slowly rose higher in the sky.

"Good morning, God," I whispered.

CHAPTER 22

Home Sweet Home

◆ ◈ ◈

I was on my way home. We were midway through Wisconsin, and Indiana was far, far behind us. Home welled up in my chest and got bigger and bigger until I felt as if it were going to jump right out of my mouth. Riding in the back seat of the car, I could hardly contain myself. I thought about seeing my friends again and couldn't wait to get home.

Although I knew I had been homesick, I hadn't realized how much until the prospect of going home had suddenly become a reality. I found out later that Luther had called my mom and dad and demanded that they come and get me right that minute, so they had driven all night long and arrived minutes before I'd rounded the corner the following morning.

All that was behind me now. The sun was beginning to go down. The sky in front of us was hot pink and yellow, surrounded by a deepening blue. The highway that seemed to stretch endlessly in front of us was bordered by clumps of pine trees nestled between stretches of farmland. I dozed off and on to make the time pass more quickly and kept my mind on home until I saw the twinkling lights of Saint Paul loom in front of us like an oasis in the desert.

I soon found that in three short months, Minneapolis had changed. Everywhere I went, my friends were talking about who had chosen who and who was paying who. At first, I didn't know what they were talking about, but in time I figured out that prostitution was the biggest game in town.

Von had returned to Minneapolis while I was in Indianapolis, and he and other members of the Evans family had blown up in the pimp game. The next time I saw him, Von was leaving a nightclub in a full-length mink coat and matching mink hat with a blonde on each arm. He and his brothers were considered to be in the big league, and I could see that he was way out of my league. They were so big, in fact, that the Evans family eventually came under the scrutiny of the FBI. Von and his brothers would go down in history as the biggest pimp ring to ever hit the Twin Cities.

"I know you heard that Alana chose Blue," Tina said excitedly on the phone. "I saw her workin' downtown on Hennepin last night. I heard she's accepting fives and tens. Blue told her don't turn down no money."

I couldn't believe my ears or my eyes. It seemed as though everywhere I looked, I saw the girlfriends I had grown up with strolling down Lake Street or Hennepin Avenue trying to catch tricks; either that or jumping on the Greyhound bus to go to some hick town and dance with next to no clothes on, just a G-string and pasties. The day after I got back into town, I went over to Blue's house to hear with my own ears what he was up to.

"You need to come on and get with me. We'll live like kings and queens," he had crooned. "But you got to pay me—give up some of them dollar bills—to be with me."

I wanted nothing more than to be with him, but I couldn't see myself laying up with the nasty-looking tricks that canvassed Lake Street trying to spend "twenty bucks" with any and everyone who happened by. Furthermore, Blue had been my boyfriend with no money involved. Why should I suddenly have to give him money now? I soon found out that he had turned even more cold-blooded in the months I had been gone. A couple of times when I had gone to visit him late at night after the parties were over, he flat out told me not to come over there unless I had some money.

I was tempted to prove myself, so I snatched thirty-five dollars or so from a drunk man one night on Hennepin and gave it to Blue. I had been on my way out of Othello's, formerly known as Fuzzy Warbles, when a drunk came up behind me and put his arm around me. I allowed his arm to stay where it was as we continued down the street together. Right before we reached the alleyway, I grabbed his hand that was wrapped around my waist, and with my other hand I dipped into his pocket, grabbed a fist full of dollar bills and took off running. At first, the trick was close behind me, but I darted down the alley and lost him after I rounded the corner heading back towards Hennepin. I spotted a car idling at a traffic light, ran up to it, and jumped in just as the light turned green.

"What's going on?" asked the surprised driver.

"Hey, baby, could you give me a lift over North? I'll make it worth your while."

"Oh, yeah?"

"Yeah, I sure will. Just drive the car," I said, looking nervously over my shoulder. I talked stuff to the man all the way over North about the fun we were going to have once we got there, but when he stopped at a light near my destination, I jumped out.

"Hey, wait a minute, where are you going?" I turned around and saw the man's angry face illuminated by the streetlight. I laughed and disappeared between two houses.

When I offered it to him, Blue took the money, folded it up, and put it into a shoebox full of money. I sat down expectantly, hoping that the money I had offered up had somehow resealed our bond. I looked at the box again with a little uncertainty. My money looked small and insignificant alongside the wads of tens and twenties within the box. Blue repositioned himself atop his bed that consisted of a box spring and three mattresses where he could look down from his throne upon his kingdom—the basement room of his family's home.

"I usually don't accept nothing less than a hundred dollars a night, but you're still learning, so I'll let it slide this time, but don't bring me no more chump change."

"Chump change?" To me, who had never held anything but a summer job making no more than fifty dollars a week, coming up with thirty-five dollars in one night was a lot of money.

Blue didn't bother to answer. "Look here. I'll talk to you later. I got to go make a run," he said, getting up and motioning me towards the stairs that led up to the back door and outside.

I looked at him in shock. I had given him all my money, and he was putting me out of his house. I walked slowly over to the stairs. I couldn't believe it. I felt like a trick myself. Suddenly a flash of anger jolted me to my senses.

"Yeah, all right, punk."

I took the stairs two at a time, but Blue still caught up with me before I could make it out the back door. His open palm connected with the side of my head, knocking it into the door jamb. I ignored the pain as I concentrated on getting the door open. Blue grabbed for me, but I was able to break away from his grasp. I flew down the back steps and out towards the alley. I glanced behind me to see if he was still coming, but he had turned around and gone back inside.

"You punk ass bitch," I yelled, breathing heavily. "I hope you die and rot in hell!"

It was past one in the morning, and the buses had stopped running for the night. I angrily wiped my tears and began the long walk home, desperately hoping I would catch another ride along the way.

CHAPTER 23

Psych Ward

Because the time I spent in Indianapolis had failed to snap me out of my downward spiral, my parents decided that a stint in St. Mary's psych ward might do me some good. When they sat me down to present the topic to me, I was apathetic. There was nothing happening outside of the hospital to make me desire to remain unhospitalized, so much to my parents' surprise, I did not rebel against the idea. In fact, I was even a tad bit interested in the prospect of spending some time in the psych ward.

Mental illness had always interested me. I started a psychology course in high school but had skipped class so much I failed it. Since then, I had read the textbook from my failed high school psychology class practically from cover to cover. I was intrigued by human behavior and the wide spectrum of mental illnesses and personality disorders described in the textbook. Beginning with Trash Can Annie, I had seen my fair share of abnormal behavior and wanted to know more about the root causes of it. I wondered what caused people to go crazy. Because I was very much in touch with reality, I was pretty certain I was not crazy. It was just that reality wasn't all that satisfying to me at that point in time. I doubted that the psych ward would snap me out of my depression, but it was something to do.

On the day I was scheduled to check in, I packed a few clothes in an overnight case and rode with my mom and dad to the hospital. The psych ward was located on the fifth floor of St. Mary's Hospital. While my mom and dad completed the paperwork, I was given a brief tour of the ward. I was pleasantly surprised to find that the lounge had a pool table. I decided to practice up during my stay to impress the pool players at the Filling Station when I returned to the nightclub scene.

I was then shown to my room where I met my roommate, a seriously overweight white woman with long brown hair. After meeting her, I returned to the front lobby to bid my parents goodbye. I felt guilty about being in the hospital because of what I imagined the cost of my hospitalization would be, but I couldn't talk them out of it, so I decided to give it a try.

The first evening was uneventful. They had group therapy where the residents formed a circle on the floor and talked about their issues. No one drew me into the discussion, so I sat there quietly and listened. One man stuttered badly when the subject of his mother's upcoming visit was introduced. I was impressed by the severity of the turmoil he was experiencing as his face turned a deep shade of red while he stammered, stuttered, and attempted to spit out coherent words for all he was worth. I wondered what his mother had done to him during his childhood to cause him to go completely berserk at the thought of her.

There was only one other Black person on the psych ward. I met him the following day in the activities room while I practiced my game of pool. He had just come back from electroshock therapy. I recognized him as the father of some little kids who lived near the end of my block. I wanted to ask him why he needed shock treatments, but I didn't. I reasoned that if he wanted to talk about it, he would eventually. Maybe during group therapy that night, I hoped. I was very curious to find out whether or not it hurt and whether they really put popsicle sticks in your mouth during the procedure, so you wouldn't swallow your tongue.

I spent a significant portion of the day either on the phone or waiting to use the phone. When I returned to my room, I found my roommate trying to strangle herself with a long shoelace. I called the nurse, who came in and intervened. While I had no reason to doubt the sincerity of my roommate's desire to end her life, I did find her weapon of choice to be suspect. As large as she was, she would most certainly need something a bit more substantial than a shoelace.

Later that afternoon, I spent some time working on the Minnesota Multiphasic Personality Inventory. Its purpose was to find out exactly how "crazy" I actually was. After I finished that, I went to the lounge area where many of the residents were playing cards. I saw the guy from the night before and couldn't resist asking him about his mother. His face turned a deep shade of purple, and he began to stutter. His card mates glared at me. I tried my best to look innocent but concerned.

I wondered when I would finally see the psychiatrist. I had seen him walking through the ward, but he had yet to even interview me. Because there were so many people on the ward who had serious mental illnesses, I supposed I was not his top priority. I could relate to that, but I also thought about the money that my mom and dad were forking over for me to talk on the phone and play pool, all of which I could do, or arrange to do, at home.

When the third day arrived and nothing new had happened, I decided it was time to vacate the premises. On a deep level, I realized that even being on a psych ward couldn't fix what was wrong with me. I knew that not knowing my true identity and having no way to find out who I was is what ailed me. Plus, I missed the streets and yearned to know what had happened out there in the real world since I had been away, so I worked on planning my escape.

I had noticed that although it was a locked ward, the elevators in front of the nurses' station were unmonitored, for the most part. I needed to walk past the elevator to get to the activity room, and as luck would have it, the elevator doors opened up right as I was walking by. A group of visitors was leaving the floor, and I followed them onto the elevator, hospital wristband, bare feet, and all. The group glanced nervously at me, and I realized I was going to have to make a quick move once the elevator doors opened, or else I would find myself right back on the psych ward.

As I exited through the revolving door of the hospital on the main floor, I was relieved to see a cab parked right in front. I jumped in and told the cabbie to take me to my friend Kayla's house on Banneker Avenue on the Northside, and off we went. My psych ward experience was a wrap.

CHAPTER 24

Baby's First Birthday

◆ ◆ ◆

On my baby's first birthday, my depression deepened. Nobody remembered or mentioned the baby who had failed to thrive a year earlier. I sat on a barstool at the Cozy Bar and drank one drink after the other. In between drinks, I staggered to the bathroom to snort some cocaine to snap myself out of my drunkenness. I shared some of the blow with my friend Tina, who came out of one of the stalls.

"Let's go down to Cassius," suggested Tina between toots of blow. "I got this sap out there that's been buying me drinks all night. He'll sport you as long as you're with me."

"Fine with me," I replied. "I ain't doing nothin' no way."

As we came out of the bathroom, we ran into Marita, who was backed up against the bar. Another girl named Cherie was all up in her face.

"You high yellow bitch, I'll kick your ass," Cherie threatened.

Marita rolled her eyes but didn't say anything. I could tell she didn't want to fight. Cherie could tell Marita didn't want to fight either, but she kept on pressing the issue. I had noticed that a lot of girls picked on Marita mainly because she wasn't a fighter. A man pulled on Cherie's arm playfully and distracted her attention by whispering something in her ear. As Cherie leaned into the man to listen to what was on his mind, Marita slipped into the ladies' room. Tina and I followed right behind her.

"What's her problem?" asked Tina.

"Oh, she's tripping," answered Marita brushing her hair.

"You shouldn't let her talk to you that way," I insisted. "Who's she calling a yellow bitch as yellow as she is?"

I had a chip on my shoulder, and it didn't take much to set it off. "I got her yellow bitch," I declared and then turned around and walked out of the bathroom. About halfway up the bar, I found Cherie with her back to me, still talking to the same man.

"Who are you calling a high yellow bitch?" I asked with one hand on my hip, my chin jutting out towards Cherie.

"I wasn't talking to you, so it ain't none of your damn business," she retorted.

"Well, I heard you were talking about me!" I stepped in closer.

"You better get up out of my face," said Cherie with a snarl.

I jumped back a step and then punched Cherie dead in her mouth with a left hook. The fight was on. We fought from one side of the bar to the other. I had a fist full of Cherie's hair, and Cherie had a fist full of mine. The fight was deadlocked. In our struggle, we leaned over a small partition separating an elevated area of tables from the dance floor below. We panted into each other's faces as we clung to one another. I inched backward over the partition and felt myself falling onto the dance floor below while pulling Cherie along over the partition and downwards along with me. After we landed on the dance floor, we tussled around on the floor for a few seconds before being pulled apart by the bouncer and a couple of other men, one of whom was the man Tina had been drinking with.

"You all got to get up out of this bar," hollered the bouncer. "Get on out of here!"

"Trick baby," I yelled at Cherie as Tina and I exited from the side door.

"Who is she calling a trick baby?" asked Cherie's mother, who worked as a cook at the bar and had emerged from the kitchen during the scuffle.

"Let's get out of here," said Tina. "You must be crazy! You know all her kin people work up in this bar."

"No, she's the one that's crazy. She's all the time trying to start something with somebody."

By that time, I had totally forgotten that it wasn't originally my fight. I felt righteous indignation and had made it my fight because I couldn't stand to see anybody get picked on. I knew my intolerance for bullying stemmed back to my childhood when I had to protect my brother Ira from the bad boys that picked on him daily and regularly chased him home from school. Our parents had taught Ira that he was not supposed to fight, but somehow, they had forgotten to teach me the same lesson.

◀◀ ◀ ◀

After we made it to Cassius Bar, Tina and I settled onto our barstools and ordered drinks and hamburgers. Cassius Burgers were known to be the best burgers in the city. In my opinion, it was the combination of grilled onions, a heavy coating of grease, and the bar's atmosphere that made the hamburgers taste so good.

Once our food arrived, I took a bite, chewed awhile, and then said philosophically, "You got to feed liquor."

"That's right," agreed Tina tearing into hers. "If you don't feed liquor, you'll wish you did!"

We both laughed. Our sponsor that evening was a man who appeared to be in his early fifties. He stood a ways down the bar talking to some friends. Occasionally he'd glance down the bar in our direction. If our drinks were low, he'd signal the bartender to rack us up fresh ones.

"Here comes Tilson," whispered Tina.

One of Minneapolis's renowned pimps made his way down the narrow aisle that separated the bar from the tables lining the wall. Through the mirror, I followed his progress. He had on a beige trench coat held together with a belt tied in a knot at his waistline.

"I don't think he has anything on under there," I said, nudging my friend. Tilson's legs were bare under the coat, and he had on a pair of clogs.

"If I didn't know any better, I'd swear he was gay," declared Tina, as Tilson opened his coat to reveal he was wearing nothing but a pair of bikini underwear.

"Well, I guess you do know better," I snickered.

"Shut up, girl, you're crazy."

Tina made it her business to sample the goods of the big pimps in town. If a pimp drove a Cadillac, Tina's mission was to ride in it at least once before a charge was put on her. Sooner or later, the question of money would come up—usually in the form of a sarcastic comment about how Tina liked riding in Cadillacs but didn't like paying the note—and she would fade right out of the picture.

Although she was an exotic dancer, who was very much in demand, Tina prided herself on not paying a pimp. Her reputation was known, but that didn't stop the pimps from trying to break down her resistance. Each one seemed to think that he would be the one to send her to work and have her bring the money home to "daddy." So far, each one of them had failed miserably. Tina went to work all right, but instead of bringing the money home to whichever "daddy" was in her life at the given time, she instead filled her closets with assorted shoes, purses, leather coats, and other niceties.

I liked her style. She was flamboyant, and as one pimp had so accurately put it, she decorated herself. She had an assortment of exotic wigs that she got from the Chinese wig shop, which she decked out with flowers, bows, and even cherries. Tina's clothes were flashy, and she liked to dress. She especially liked shoes, and she would pay top dollar for an unusual pair.

"Come in the bathroom with me and get a toot of this blow," I suggested.

"You ain't said nothin' but a word," said Tina getting up from the bar and heading towards the bathroom with me. Tina and I closed ourselves in one of the two stalls where we each took a one-on-one hit of cocaine.

"Watch that hole, would you?" I asked, looking worriedly at a hole in the corner of the stall near the base of the wall. Whenever I used the bathroom at Cassius Bar, I kept my eye on the hole in fear that a rat or mouse would dart out of it.

"Girl, you may not be afraid of many things, but you sure can't stand the idea of a rat or a mouse," said Tina laughing.

"You got that right," I agreed.

The bar was in an old part of downtown about a block from the train station. I believed rats and mice liked to make their homes near the tracks, an idea I got as a child when I saw an enormous rat waddling along the tracks in Ohio when visiting my grandparents in Cedarville. Marita told me that one time she saw a mouse scampering around the assorted bottles of liquor behind the bar.

"Girl, let's get out of here. This bar is a death trap."

It was true. More than one person I knew had lost their life in Cassius Bar and Grill, but that didn't stop anyone from going there. Cassius was a world in and of itself full of atmosphere. Pimps, hustlers, thieves, addicts, dealers, and other nightlife characters made it their special haven. I heard in its early years it had been a classy establishment for the city's Black elite, but the passage of time had greatly changed its clientele base. During the day, it was still a meeting place for white businessmen, who enjoyed Cassius Burgers as much as their nighttime counterparts, but early evening brought about a sinister change to the bar's atmosphere.

"Yeah, I'm about ready to roll," agreed Tina. "Let's make this move."

When we emerged from the ladies' room, Tina beckoned to the man whose name we did not know because it didn't matter to us. He was just another older man who desired young women and would spend his money to prove it. The man bid his cronies farewell, and we headed out the back door to the parking lot.

"Where're you headed?" asked Tina after we had gotten into the car.

"Drop me off over at Blue's," I answered.

It took a whole lot of liquor for me to get up enough courage to talk to Blue. The liquor somehow emboldened me while it dulled the pain of his inevitable rejection. I knocked on the back door. Blue's brother, Apollo, unlocked it and disappeared into the kitchen. I went down the steps that led to Blue's room. I had so much on my mind. I wanted to talk to him about our lost baby and about the past year we had spent apart. Blue was adjusting the knobs on his stereo. He looked up as I came down the stairs.

"You might as well turn right back around and go on back upstairs," he snarled.

"I just want to talk to you for a minute."

"We ain't got nothing to talk about."

I sat down on the steps. "Can't we just talk for a few minutes? I promise I'll leave after that."

"Nah," he said, turning back to the stereo.

The question that had been plaguing me for the past year came to the surface. "But why don't you want to talk to me?" I asked desperately.

"Because you ain't shit. Now, go on back upstairs."

I got up from where I was seated and went slowly back upstairs. The light was on in the kitchen, but the rest of the house was dark. I could hear the muted sound of the stereo playing in Blue's basement room. I sat down at the kitchen table and thought about what he had said to me.

Blue's words, "You ain't shit," echoed in my mind.

He's right. I ain't shit.

The devil whispering in my ear caused my thoughts to swirl around in my head and reminded me that I hadn't finished school, didn't have a job, and hell, even my own mother hadn't wanted me at birth.

Blue's right. I ain't shit.

The cocaine was beginning to wear off. The depressant effect of the alcohol coupled with the crash from the cocaine withdrawal sent me plunging downward into an emotional tailspin. All of my usual feistiness and defiance had disappeared, and I stared at the floor in defeat and despair.

My baby was dead, and my boyfriend didn't want me anymore unless I sold my body. I didn't want to do that. I didn't have whatever it was that it took to do that. I didn't fit into the fast crowd, but at the same time, I didn't have a job, wasn't in school, and didn't have any identifiable goals in life, so I didn't fit into the square crowd either. I landed on what seemed to be a logical conclusion.

I'm better off dead.

I gave in to the forces that had been working on me for a long, long time. I got up, went into the bathroom, and searched the medicine cabinet for a razor blade. Once I found it, I went back into the kitchen. Not wanting to bleed all over Mrs. Lockett's kitchen floor, I retrieved a milk carton out of the trash can, placed it between my legs, and began slitting my wrists.

Every time my blood would start to clot, I would slice another gash in my wrist. The cocaine that was still in my system prevented me from feeling the pain of the razor blade. The lack of pain made it possible for me to detach myself somewhat from the scene. As I sat there waiting to die, I had visions of what the next day would bring.

I pictured the Lockett family getting up in the morning and finding me dead on the kitchen floor. Blue would be sorry then, I concluded,

satisfied that he would finally pay for the emotional pain he had inflicted upon me. I hoped his penance would be unceasing grief and anguish
related to my untimely demise.

The fourth razor cut on my right wrist began to clot causing my blood
to slow its departure from my body, so I started cutting my left wrist. As
I held both wrists over the open milk carton, Blue's mother appeared in
the doorway.

"What are you doing up so late?" Mrs. Lockett asked me, as kind
as ever. "Why don't you go in there and get in bed with Jasmine or
Yolanda?"

"No, I'm all right."

Mrs. Lockett's eyes dropped down to the milk carton held firmly between my legs and began screaming.

"Oh, my God, oh my God!"

The sleeping household came to life. I heard the pounding of feet
coming from different directions in the four-bedroom, two-story house.

"Call the ambulance," Mrs. Lockett commanded. "Oh, Lord!"

I did not respond to any of the commotion going on around me. I
sat in the kitchen chair, resting my arms on the milk carton until the
ambulance attendants finally arrived. One of them removed the carton
from my hands and wrapped my wrists loosely with gauze. I silently
followed the young white men to the ambulance and got in. The ambulance breezed down Olson Highway en route to the Hennepin County
Medical Center. The light was on in the ambulance, so I could not see
through the windows outside. After a while, I felt the ambulance make
a couple of turns and then stop.

The emergency room was busy as usual. The chairs lining the walls
were full of people, but I did not join them in their endless wait for relief
from whatever was ailing them. Having arrived by ambulance, I had
top priority, so I was seen by medical personnel immediately. As they
wheeled me away to an empty cubicle, I could see Mrs. Lockett talking
animatedly to my mom and dad, who had appeared in the emergency
room.

I was in the emergency room for a few hours. The stitches being sewn
painstakingly into my arms by the intern seemed to take forever, which

gave me time to think about the night's events. The effects of the drugs and alcohol had worn off, and I became annoyed by the tugging sensation on my wrists as the earnest young intern worked intently on repairing the damage to them through the remainder of the night.

I could see the light of day beginning to filter into the hospital through the Venetian blinds. I stared at the ceiling of the emergency room. The Novocain was beginning to wear off. The pricks of the needle and the sensation of needle and thread winding their way through my flesh and back out again let me know I was still alive.

> *A curious type of pain in my heart had refused to leave me*
> *for a year.*
> *My daughter's birthday, but no cake and ice cream smeared*
> *on the face*
> *of a little brown baby with black curly hair.*
> *Her father refused to see me when I needed him once again.*
> *One light on in the dark quiet house with me sitting staring*
> *at the slow drip of the faucet.*
> *Depression after being after me all year long finally over-*
> *came me and seeped slowly*
> *through my mind until I couldn't think for the weight of it.*
> *The razor blade slicing gashes in my wrists seemed to have*
> *a mind of its own,*
> *For all I could do was stare at the slow drip of the red mud*
> *coming out*
> *of my arms and into the milk carton.*
> *Laying on the table in the emergency ward of General*
> *Hospital*
> *Noting how time consuming having forty-six stitches is.*
> *Riding home watching the sun slowly rise on the day*
> *I realized I wasn't dead,*
> *just my mind and the relationship between me and No*
> *Name's father.*

On the day immediately after my suicide attempt, I felt more alive than I ever had before. I felt renewed. The violets seemed to have budded overnight. The scent of blooming lilacs sweetened the air. The sun shone majestically in the sky, and the shouts of playing children filled the air as I walked up 4th Avenue on that beautiful spring day.

I gazed upwards. God had saved my life, this much I knew, but for what purpose? I was still no better off than I had been the day before. My baby was still dead. I was still adopted and didn't know who I really was or how I had come to be. I still did not have a job or any hopes of securing one, but nevertheless, I was happy to be alive.

Tina had called me earlier to tell me off for trying to kill myself. The grapevine was alive and well. The word had spread that quickly.

"Girl, I told my dad what you did, and he said, 'If Colnese would have succeeded in killing herself, true enough, we would have shed tears, but at some point, we would have had to go on with our lives. The scars on her wrists are going to last a lifetime. They are not going to go away. So tell her that for me.'"

I listened intently. I knew my friend was concerned, but what Tina and her dad didn't know was that I had already made up my mind that from that point on if anyone hurt me or did me wrong, I would no longer turn the anger inward on myself. No more suicide for me. I promised myself that in the future, whenever I was wronged, I would strike back.

CHAPTER 25

Bar Fight

◆ ◆ ◆

DeLady and I sat at the bar on the no-pay side of the Filling Station, sipping our drinks and checking out the men at the pool tables.

"Here comes trouble," announced DeLady.

I glanced in the direction DeLady was looking and saw Leora, Effie, and Johnetta make their way into the bar. The three sisters were decked out from head to toe in black and red. Effie's red and black brim was pulled down low over one eye. Red button earrings glowed brightly against her dark brown skin. Effie's red fingernails were so long they curled over. Leora, the oldest sister and ringleader, led the way. The scowl on her face warned others to fall back and move out of her way. Their baby sister Johnetta looked like a Black Barbie doll with her hair pulled back into a tight ponytail at the crown of her head, which fell just below her shoulders.

I admired them but kept my distance. The sisters were known to be as mean as snakes, and they started trouble wherever they went. I couldn't understand why three women who always looked so nice got into as many fights as they did. Leora started most of the fights over her man, Thurston.

Tina told me about the night she had accepted a ride home from a party with him. As they stopped at a stop sign, Leora came out of nowhere, snatched the door of the car open, climbed right over Thurston, and proceeded to scratch up Tina's face. Very few women would give Thurston the time of day because he could not or would not control his woman. I suspected he was probably on a perpetual ego trip from being the focal point of so many fights around town.

"I'll be back, girl," I told DeLady, as I headed towards the pay side of the bar to see the band. When I returned a short time later, DeLady was yelling across the bar at Leora. Suddenly she picked up a glass and hurled it in Leora's direction. It smashed against the wall and fell to the floor. Leora grabbed a beer bottle and darted around the bar towards DeLady. Two bouncers grabbed her and escorted her, kicking, screaming, and cussing right out the front door. Another bouncer grabbed DeLady by the arm and escorted her towards the back of the Filling Station. I pushed through the crowd and followed them out the back door.

As we started to make our way through the parking lot, we saw a small entourage rounding the corner of the building. Leora led the way with a knife glinting in the dark and raised high above her head. Her sisters were half walking and half trotting behind her. When Leora caught up with DeLady, she grabbed her by her long hair, raised the knife in the air, and swung. DeLady caught her wrist, and they began to tussle.

My attention was drawn away from their fight by the sight of Effie, Johnetta, and another woman I didn't know running towards the fight in progress. Realizing that they were getting ready to jump in and not stopping to think, I rushed Johnetta and pushed her backwards. Caught off guard, Johnetta stumbled, quickly regained her balance, and turned towards me. Out of the corner of my eye, I saw Effie and the other woman charging at me. All three of them seemed to have forgotten all about Leora and DeLady's fight. My instincts and adrenaline kicked in.

I can't let them get me on the ground.

As the trio converged upon me, I concentrated on staying on my feet. I had a fist full of someone's hair. I let go and pushed hard against the woman's shoulders causing her to stumble backwards a step or two. Another one charged in, and my fists flew wildly. As I turned my head to the right, I noticed a dot of blood on my black and white polka dot pants suit. I wasn't sure if it had come from me or someone else.

I didn't know how much longer I could hold them off before they ambushed me and brought me down. I knew if they got me on the ground, it was all over. They would stomp me and probably kick my teeth out, which was something to be avoided at all costs. A large crowd made a circle around us as they watched the action. Out of the corner of my eye, I saw that DeLady was still duking it out with Leora.

"Break this shit up," I heard a man's voice yell. "The police are coming."

"Yeah, break it up," said another man, who I recognized as one of the bar's owners.

I felt someone's arms pulling me back. At the same time, I saw a large man named Nate grab two of the other girls, one by the arm and one around the waist.

Leora was cussing and spitting and still yelling as Bruh ushered De-Lady and me into his car. His woman, my close friend Pam, jumped in the front seat, and Bruh cranked it up. I asked Bruh to stop by my house before we went to the after-hours party on Cadillac Corner. I ran inside and came back out with a large butcher knife stuffed down the front of my pants.

The night was hot, and I patrolled the front of the party, keeping my eye out for any signs of Leora and the pack. Von was manning the door of the after-hours party, so I saw him only briefly. Everyone who came to the party from the Filling Station had seen the fight. Because Leora and her sisters had a reputation, and since I had gotten into a fight with them and lived to tell about it, I felt my street credibility and respect go up a few notches.

I stayed at the party long enough for anyone interested to know that I had stood my ground. After about an hour on patrol, I walked the two blocks back home and went to bed. It had been a stressful night.

CHAPTER 26

Godmother

My friend Shirlynn and I were bored. There was nothing new or exciting happening at Phelps Park across the street from her house. Shirlynn and I hung out together daily during the summer of 1975 when we were seventeen years old.

"Let's walk up to Mr. Nooky's," suggested Shirlynn.

Mr. Nooky's was a corner store owned by a man we considered to be the neighborhood child molester. There was hardly a girl around who Mr. Nooky hadn't made some type of move on. Some of his overtures were subtle, some not so subtle. One time when I was twelve years old, I paid for a ten cents bag of sunflower seeds with a dollar, and Mr. Nooky had dropped the change down my blouse. He was nasty.

But because Mr. Nooky's store was within walking distance on the busy corner of 38th Street and 4th Avenue, a corner we passed on our way to and from school, there seemed to be no way to avoid him. The girls in the neighborhood were careful not to enter the store unless they were in twos or threes or unless his wife was working. She was the best watchdog we could have ever hoped for. But by the way she treated the young girls who came into the store, anyone would have thought it was the children coming on to Mr. Nooky and not the other way around. As Shirlynn and I neared the store, we saw Tyrone, a friend of ours, standing on the front steps of a yellow house.

"Do you all want to see my baby?"

"You don't have a baby," charged Shirlynn.

Tyrone was only fifteen years old. He acted gossipy and girlish, which led us to believe he might be headed in a whole 'nother direction than the direction that would produce a baby at the tender young age of fifteen.

"Come and see," he said, beckoning us up the stairs towards the house.

Shirlynn and I followed him into the large yellow house set on a low hill. Lying on a burnt orange sectional couch swaddled in a receiving blanket was the smallest and prettiest baby I had ever seen. Her small nostrils flared perfectly, and her lips were pursed just so. Wisps of soft auburn hair curled around her golden-brown face.

"Ooh, she's so pretty," I cooed. "Can I hold her?"

"Yeah, but be careful with her head, though," Tyrone cautioned.

"Who are you talking to? I know how to hold a baby."

I scooped the tiny baby off the couch, laying her face up on my lap. With her head nestled just above my knees, her entire body fit perfectly.

"What's her name?" asked Shirlynn.

"Keisha," Tyrone replied.

I stroked the baby's tiny hand, and Keisha rewarded me by grabbing hold of my finger and holding it tight. Her eyes opened, and her dark brown eyes searched my face. I was amazed by the intensity of the infant's gaze.

"Let me hold her," demanded Shirlynn.

I shifted the baby from my lap to Shirlynn's outstretched arms and looked around the living room. Sitting on top of a what-not shelf was a framed photograph of a man in a black and white suit, holding a pistol. He wore a black brim broken down on one side, shading his left eye. At the bottom corner of the picture frame was a small photo of a boy who looked to be around six years old. He also wore a black and white suit but sported a white brim. He, too, held a pistol in his hand. His foot rested on the back of a chair, and he bent over in a mirror image of the man in the larger photograph. They were obviously father and son.

"Who is that?" I asked, impressed with the gangster era pose.

"That's Thurston and his son, Leon," answered Tyrone.

"Thurston and his son Leon?" I parroted while leaning closer to the photograph.

Sure enough, Thurston, the love of Leora's life, stared back at me from the frame. Panicked, my eyes scanned the entire what-not shelf. Lo and behold, on the bottom shelf, there was a framed picture of Leora, live and in living color, decked out from head to toe in, yes, black and red.

"Is this Leora's house?" I asked Tyrone incredulously.

"Uh-huh."

"Is this Leora's baby?"

"Yep," Tyrone confirmed nonchalantly.

"Come on, Shirlynn, let's get out of here."

I grabbed the baby from Shirlynn and thrust her into Tyrone's arms.

"What's up?" a surprised Tyrone asked me while Shirlynn looked at me quizzically.

"Me and Leora don't get along! We got into a fight at the Filling Station last summer. If she came home right now and caught me in her living room holding her baby . . ."

I hit the screen door and exited with the quickness with Shirlynn close behind me. The door slammed shut behind us.

"Tyrone must be crazy," I complained as Shirlynn and I continued our journey to Mr. Nooky's. "He's trippin'. He must have heard about our fight at the Filling Station last year. It was the talk of the town at the time."

"Maybe not," replied the ever-optimistic Shirlynn. She was very good-natured and found it hard to believe that some people had evil ulterior motives.

"I don't know, but I sure am glad Leora didn't come back home while we were there."

We went into the store and made our purchases, unmolested for a change by Mr. Nooky. We were headed back to the park when Leora flung her screen door open and flew outside. She stampeded down the hill of her front yard towards the sidewalk where Shirlynn and I were walking.

"Why, you funky bitch! Don't you ever bring your nasty ass in my house and hold my baby again. Do you hear me?"

Leora pointed her long fingernail into my face. I was amazed by how short and tiny she was up close. It must be the platform shoes she wore to the clubs that made her appear taller, I reasoned, while watching Leora closely for any imminent signs of danger or random attack.

Leora continued on a rather lengthy tirade about what she would do to me and how she would do it if I ever stepped foot on her property again. All the while, she paced back and forth and looked every bit of being able to back up her threats. I rested my weight on one leg, folded my arms across my mid-section, and listened.

Once Leora slowed down her tirade long enough for me to get a word in edgewise, I replied, "I'm sorry, I would feel the same way if I came home and found out you had been in my house. But I didn't know it was your house or your baby until I was already inside. As soon as I found out about it, I left, didn't I, Shirlynn?"

Shirlynn nodded her head in agreement. "Uh-huh, she sure did."

Leora looked at both of us in surprise. She had obviously come out of the house prepared for a fight. At the very least, she expected me to argue with her and cuss back at her. But from the way I looked at it, wrong was wrong. I had to admit to myself that being inside of Leora's house—a sworn enemy—was a violation of the street code and could definitely be interpreted as disrespect.

"You didn't know it was my house? Whose house did you think it was?"

"Tyrone told us to come in and see his baby," Shirlynn contributed her two cents to the drama that was unfolding in front of her.

Leora jerked her head back towards the house, but Tyrone had conveniently disappeared from the front porch and was out of sight.

"Well, ain't that a bitch?" exclaimed Leora. "Of all the people I know, you're the last person I want near my baby."

"Your baby sure is pretty," Shirlynn said sincerely.

"She sure is," I agreed. "I just didn't know she was yours, but she is cute. How old is she?"

"Three weeks old, but anyway, I was pissed. I thought you had a lot of nerve coming up in my house after you got into a fight with my sisters. And by the way, where's that bitch DeLady?"

That question kicked off a long conversation between us that began with our rehashing the fateful night of our fight at the Filling Station and the events preceding it. Apparently, there had been a previous negative encounter between Leora and DeLady at a Northside party.

"Actually, I really don't have nothing against you, Colnese," Leora declared after about fifteen minutes of animated dialogue, with each of us telling our side of the story. "That's between you and my sisters, but I can't stand that bitch DeLady, and she better not ever come down 4th Avenue this far. If she got business down this way, she better take a detour!"

The dimple in Leora's face deepened as she pursed her lips for added emphasis. The stress on her face began to relax a little. I had unintentionally diffused the situation by humbling myself enough to apologize. On the porch, we could hear a small cry.

"Do you all want to come and sit on the porch while I feed my baby?"

"Yeah, okay. We're not doing anything," I responded.

"Just hanging out," Shirlynn added.

We followed Leora up the steps to the porch door, and for the second time that day, we went inside. After a while, sitting there on Leora's front porch felt like the most natural thing in the world to me, and by three in the morning, it felt as though we had been friends forever. After giving Keisha her feeding, Leora casually passed her to me when she got up to go check on her two other children, who by then had fallen asleep on the couch in front of the TV set.

Holding the tiny baby reminded me of my long-lost daughter, and when Leora returned, I told her all about my pregnancy and stillbirth. We compared labor and delivery experiences and shared stories about the loves of our lives, Thurston and Blue. By the time the sun came up, I had even shown Leora the razor blade marks on my wrists, and Leora had shown Shirlynn and me one of her strip-tease dance moves where she rapidly flexed the cheeks of her behind while gyrating her hips. Shirlynn and I nodded our appreciation of her dance moves and expertise. While she was dancing, her three-year-old daughter, Tasha, came out onto the porch blinking sleepily. She stood there and listened while we swapped life experiences.

"I don't hide nothin' from my kids," Leora explained.

Around five in the morning, Shirlynn and I called it a night and headed home.

"Y'all come back any time, you hear?" Leora told us as we left.

"Okay, we will," we agreed.

As we walked home together, we discussed the turn of the day's events and were in awe about how quickly a former enemy of mine had become a person we liked—a lot! We felt honored that a grown woman had taken us into her confidence and talked to us like we were also women in our twenties with households to run and children to take care of. Although Shirlynn had older sisters, she said they had never been as candid with her as Leora had been that night. I didn't even have an older sister, so I was especially appreciative of Leora's seemingly infinite wisdom.

Over the rest of the summer, Shirlynn and I found ourselves over Leora's house more and more often. There was only one rule: Don't look at her man and don't talk to her man. That was simple enough since the two of us were scared to death of him. The few times he had swaggered through the door while we were there, with a scowl on his face mean enough to scare anyone with good sense, had been enough for us. We didn't even want to look at him, let alone talk to him. So with that one rule understood, the three of us became fast friends.

I became more and more attached to little Keisha, who was helping me get over the loss of my baby. One day I bagged up all the baby clothes that were still packed away in my chest of drawers and carried them over to Leora's house, who was quite naturally surprised and pleased about all the baby things being gifted to Keisha.

One day I overheard Leora tell some friends who dropped by, "That's Keisha's godmother," and I was touched. I picked Keisha up from where she was lying on a blanket on the floor, chewing a rattle, and kissed her on the cheek. Keisha grabbed my forefinger and squeezed it tight. I sat down on the couch and cradled the baby in my arms. Out on the front porch, I could hear Leora entertaining her company. The sounds of the women's voices and laughter rose above the TV that was always on, but I had no desire to join them. I was content right where I was with the warmth of Keisha's breath on my neck and her firm grasp on my finger.

CHAPTER 27

Life Changes

The summer was coming to an end, and the park had finally played out. Even the nightly craps games were tired. Nobody won enough money to get excited about, and nobody lost enough money to get into a fight. Shirlynn and I had even ceased our nightly habit of sitting at the park and looking up at the stars. Our special red and white star had been hiding from us lately. Shirlynn's mother was talking about putting her out on her eighteenth birthday, which was August twenty-ninth and right around the corner, so we had more important things to think about right here on earth. Besides, Shirlynn was in love.

His name was Ezell, and he lived in North Minneapolis. He caught the bus over South almost daily to hang around the Southsiders—well, at least the Southside girls. Northside boys tended to intimidate the Southside boys, so they mainly stood back and watched helplessly while one girl after another fell head over heels for some Northsider.

Ezell was bowlegged, which made him look downright tasty in a pair of jeans, especially his patchwork denim jeans or his two-tone jeans. Capping off his look was a tight muscle shirt that, of course, showed off his muscular shoulders and arms. Ezell talked real slow. He had a slight Southern accent, which drove Shirlynn wild. They never said very much to one another in person, but Shirlynn usually walked him to the bus stop to catch the last bus over North, and then he would kiss her goodbye and promise to call her when he got home.

"What I really need is a job," Shirlynn declared one night as we sat on the swings at Phelps Park after dark.

"I hear you," I agreed. "I'm tired of being broke, and in a few months, I'll be too old to steal anymore."

I had become a master shoplifter. Shirlynn used to be, but she stopped when her brother Junebug went to prison. At that point, her father put his foot down and dared anyone else in the family to go astray. After a few unannounced raids on her closet by her dad, who was checking for stolen clothes and threatening to turn her over to the juvenile authorities, Shirlynn gave up her life of crime.

I, however, had yet to turn over a new leaf. I prided myself on my shoplifting skills. I began by psyching myself up and convincing myself that the goods really and truly belonged to me, and then I would go to work. I had a large tan leather purse, which was taller than it was wide, so I could pack several articles of clothing in it while not attracting attention to myself.

In comparison, there was a group of girls I knew that carried what looked like duffel bags shoplifting with them. I couldn't understand how they continued to get away with it because they might as well have had a sign around their necks that read, "Watch me, I'm a thief."

I usually placed the articles of clothing I wanted to boost in a central location. Then moving quickly, I would remove them from their hangers, roll them up, and stuff them in my purse, which was always unzipped and ready for action. I would then keep it moving. When my purse was full, I would head to a locker either in the basement of the Forum Cafeteria or in the Radisson Arcade to unload my loot and then start all over again.

I had only been busted one time, and that was when I had become too confident and gotten careless. I had been at Dayton's department store at ten thirty in the morning to fill out a job application. I then had time to kill between filling out the application and coming back for a job interview at one o'clock. On my way out of the store, I spotted a pretty, red plastic bracelet that would go perfectly with the flowered skirt and red midriff blouse I had stolen earlier in the week. The look I was trying to achieve was the Pointer Sisters' style. They were known for wearing colorful old-fashioned dresses, button earrings, and flowers in their hair.

Without missing a beat, I picked up the bracelet, stuffed it into my pocket, and then stepped onto the down escalator. There was a Black man in front of me who sort of resembled Lionel Ritchie of the Commodores. His skin was light brown, and he had brown curly hair that was three or four inches long. I paid him no attention as I reached into my pants pocket to admire the red bracelet once more. When the escalator reached ground level, the man was waiting for me at the bottom of the revolving staircase. He approached me and grabbed me by the arm.

"Come with me. You're under arrest for shoplifting."

I looked up at him coyly and smiled because at first I thought he was hitting on me. But when he failed to return my smile and instead tightened his grip on my arm, I knew he was store security, which caused me to lose control of my bladder and pee on myself.

"I have to go to the bathroom," I stammered as he led me through the store.

"You'll just have to wait," he said gruffly.

I felt hot pee running down the legs of my jeans. *What a sellout,* I thought resentfully.

Of all the low-down, unexpected things to happen to me, this was the lowest of them all—a Black floorwalker. I knew to watch out for the white floorwalkers. I recognized them instantly by their obvious methods of catching would-be shoplifters. They stalked Black teenagers wherever we went and would appear and re-appear on the opposite side of whatever rack of clothing we happened to be browsing through.

I sat on the black chair that he had ordered me to sit on in urine-soaked jeans until the police arrived to take me to the Hennepin County Juvenile Center. I followed the police officers through the store and out of Dayton's 8th Street exit into the waiting squad car. I was more concerned about how my mother would react than I was about being caught shoplifting.

Once at the Juvenile Center, I waited on a hard, wooden bench for my mother to come pick me up. When she finally arrived, she was tight-lipped and had little to say. She even allowed me to exit the cab downtown. I waved goodbye to my mom, who I knew would return to work at Pilot City Health Center, and then headed to the locker where I had stored some stolen items earlier that day. I recounted the story to Shirlynn as we sat on the swings at Phelps Park that night.

"Your luck is getting bad, girl. It's time for you to find a job before you end up getting sent up," advised Shirlynn, shaking her head.

"Where am I going to get a job? Who's going to hire me? I sure don't have no experience."

"I heard they were hiring over at Northwest Linen on Olson Highway. You don't need no experience."

"Doing what?"

"It's a laundry service. All you have to do is feed sheets and pillow-cases and towels and stuff through a big machine that irons them. My sister's friend used to work there."

"Want to catch the bus over there with me tomorrow?"

"Yeah, okay, I don't have nothing else to do. Maybe we can both get a job there."

"All right then, I'll see you tomorrow, Shirlynn."

I started up the hill home to face the music but suddenly turned around again.

"Shirlynn, would you walk with me to the top of the hill? I have to tell you something."

Shirlynn glanced up at the darkening sky. "If we hurry. You know I don't like walking alone after dark."

I knew indeed. Too many times Shirlynn had made me stand at the top of the hill and watch her as she raced down the hill as fast as she could, attempting to stay a step ahead of her fear of the dark.

"Yeah, yeah, yeah. You know I got your back," I reassured her.

As we walked up the hill between Park and Oakland Avenues, I tried to think of a way to tell my friend something I had never told another living soul, my deepest, darkest secret. When we reached the top of the hill, I still had not opened my mouth.

"Okay, here we are. What did you have to tell me?" asked Shirlynn good-naturedly.

"Shirlynn, I've never told anybody this before, and I hope you don't tell nobody else."

My eyes searched Shirlynn's face for a hint she could be trusted with the secret I believed would make me explode if I didn't tell somebody.

"No, I won't tell nobody," Shirlynn replied in an alarmed tone of voice. "What is it?"

"Shirlynn, I'm adopted."

"Adopted? I didn't know that!"

We stood on the corner at the top of the hill in silence for a long time before either of us spoke again. I am certain my face reflected the pain and shame I felt about my very own mother not keeping me. In the neighborhood where I had lived all my life, most of the families did not have much money. In the majority of households, the father was long gone. I could sense envy from some because my mother and father were still both present, and each had a job.

Growing up in a family with two breadwinners among so many families who relied heavily on the welfare system set me apart. More money meant more privileges, such as dance lessons, music lessons, and a different outfit to wear to school each day. Even in families where both parents were present, there were generally many more children to feed and clothe than the two children that made up my own family, so the money earned had to stretch much farther.

Where other families' burdens were on display—you can't hide poverty—mine were hidden from sight. I guarded the secret of my adoption like some people guarded precious gems. I had nightmares of people pointing their fingers, laughing at me, and taunting me with harmful words. "Ha, ha, your own mother didn't want you," which would hurt primarily because that was what I believed to be true.

So now I hung my head in shame, wondering how the truth I had revealed would affect my status in a community where family meant everything. Even the poorest children could boast of a family network that loved and cherished them, a belief that could be quickly put to the test. Whenever a family member was picked on, brothers, sisters, aunties, uncles, and cousins would converge from all over the neighborhood to show their love by beating down the offending party or at the very least by threatening the offending party with consequences and repercussions.

I did not belong to such a unified family network. Feeling like the odd-man-out in the neighborhood, I worried that revealing my secret would set me even farther apart from the norm. While some neighborhood families may have been poor, against all odds, they kept their children. I finally looked up and into Shirlynn's face and saw revealed in her expression the empathy she felt for me and the burden my secret had caused me.

"Why do Black people have so many problems?" Shirlynn asked simply.

Not knowing, I just shrugged my shoulders and shook my head in wonder. When we finally said our goodbyes and parted company for the night, I stood and watched as Shirlynn raced towards home, where her own family totaled nine brothers and sisters. A few of them had moved out and were already living on their own. Shirlynn also had several nieces and nephews, who often spent the night at the family's large white stucco home. When Shirlynn reached the bottom of the hill and disappeared from sight, I turned and headed for home.

I was surprised when neither my mother nor my father had much to say about the shoplifting incident. They both looked tired and disgusted. My father, sitting at the kitchen table reading the paper, wouldn't even look at me, so I decided to go to bed. After all, the next day would be a big job-hunting day.

The following day, I was the last person to get hired. Northwest Linen only had two job openings, and another girl and I got them. Shirlynn was a little disappointed she had not been hired but being good-natured, she didn't stay down too long about much of anything.

"Let's stop by Ezell's house before we catch the bus back over South," she suggested. Ezell lived in the projects not too far from where we were.

"No, girl, I got to get home and change out of these clothes and come back over here by three. Can you believe that he wants me to start working this afternoon?"

"He wants you to start already? Shoot, I wanted to see Ezell, but I guess I can see him tomorrow."

"He's probably not home anyway. You know he's probably at the park looking for you."

"Yeah, you might be right. Well, anyway, here comes the bus. We better run and catch it. You know how slow these Northside buses run." Shirlynn and I took off running towards the bus stop.

That night I learned the true meaning of work. In my estimation, it must have been as hot as hell in the laundry room, where I stood alongside a gang of other people running towels and other linens through the machine. The lady on the other side of the machine, who caught the laundry I was feeding into it once it came out on the other side, wore a towel around her neck to catch the sweat. She also had a wet washcloth pressed against her forehead. Together we stood on our feet and worked steadily for two hours at a time until the whistle blew, when we were able to take a fifteen-minute break.

My shift was from three in the afternoon until eleven at night. The last break for the night was at nine thirty when I followed the rest of my fellow laborers outside to catch the breeze and smoke cigarettes. I didn't smoke, but I joined the group anyway. Anything was better than staying inside that sweatbox.

As we stood outside in the parking lot, a couple of cars jetted past us down Olson Highway at top speed. A few moments later, I could hear the crash of metal in the distance and knew there had been an accident. The workers talked excitedly among themselves until the whistle blew, speculating about what had happened. As the door slammed behind us, signaling two more hours of hard labor, I could hear sirens in the night. It was a lonely sound.

◈ ◈ ◈

I never went back to that job again. Ezell was dead. Shirlynn called me in the middle of the night to tell me. I couldn't believe it. Shirlynn couldn't believe it either, but it was true.

Shirlynn had called Ezell's house around twelve-thirty in the morning after he failed to show up at the park. When she'd asked to speak to him, his sister Joy told her, "Ezell's dead," and hung up the phone.

Later Shirlynn found out Ezell and his brother, Theo, had been racing down Olson Highway, hit the curb, and crashed into a tree. It was rumored that Theo, who was blind, had been in the driver's seat steering, and Ezell had been in the passenger seat shifting the gears. This could not be confirmed immediately because both of them had been thrown from the car, and now his brother was in the hospital in a coma hovering near death. I had never seen my friend so deep-down depressed. Shirlynn just couldn't seem to shake it, not even after the funeral had come and gone.

"The world's coming to an end," the minister had intoned at the funeral. "You all need to get your lives together and get saved. Salvation is the only way."

The message had deeply affected Shirlynn.

"Do you really think the world is coming to an end?" she asked. "If it is, I want to get saved. I sure don't want to burn in hell."

"I don't know," I answered absently.

I really hadn't thought about it before, and now that I was thinking about it, I didn't have a strong opinion either way. In certain ways, life was still so new to me I just could not conceptualize the world coming to an end. There were so many things I had not yet experienced, so I quickly dismissed the concept of the world coming to an end. I knew my friend was very curious about what happens in the hereafter because of Ezell. As far as hell was concerned, Curtis Mayfield had recorded a song with these lyrics, "If there's a hell below, we're all gonna go," and I believed him.

"There's a revival Friday night at the Church of God in Christ. Do you want to go?" Shirlynn asked.

"Ain't there supposed to be a party Friday night?"

"Yeah, I think so, but I'd rather go to church."

"Okay, I'll go with you. It's not like they don't have a party every weekend."

That Friday night at church, Shirlynn got saved. The minister asked anyone who wanted salvation to come to the front during altar call. Shirlynn went forward and accepted Jesus Christ as her personal savior.

CHAPTER 28

On My Own

I was sleeping later and later in the day. My mom was getting sick and tired of calling home from work and finding me still in bed. One evening she came into my room and handed me a copy of the *Spokesman-Recorder*, the Twin Cities Black newspaper.

"Look here," she said, pointing to the want-ads. "They're hiring child-care aides over at Northside Child Development Center. You love children—why don't you go over there and apply?"

I looked at the ad, which featured a part-time position from noon until six in the evening. Well, those working hours certainly wouldn't interfere with my nocturnal activities or my sleep. I decided I would at least apply for the job.

Who knows? I might even get lucky.

"Okay. I'll go over there tomorrow."

I jumped up, ran out the door, and headed over to my friend Shirlynn's house to tell her, but as usual, she wasn't home. She was spending more and more time at church and less time with me. Even when she was home, which was rarely, she had little or no time to spend with me.

"I'm not supposed to hang around with unsaved people," she eventually explained.

Shirlynn had joined Evangelist Crusaders, a sanctified church, and spent much of her time passing out religious tracts and trying to convince sinners that their souls needed saving. She had recently found a job at Control Data and was making pretty good money. Her mother was frustrated because, in her opinion, Shirlynn was giving all her money to the church.

"Shirlynn's brainwashed," she told me. "I have a good mind to go down to that church and give the preacher a piece of my mind."

It was the fourth day in a row I had gone to visit, but Shirlynn wasn't home.

"She won't have anything to do with me anymore," I complained to Shirlynn's mother, who was sitting outside in their backyard on the patio. "I don't know why. I never tried to get her in trouble or anything."

"I know you didn't, baby. Just give Shirlynn some time. Maybe this is a phase she's going through."

"I hope so," I said as I turned around and slowly headed up the hill from Shirlynn's house towards mine, two blocks away.

I felt very lonely without Shirlynn to hang around with every day, but not lonely enough to join the Evangelist Crusaders Church. I was brought up in a Baptist church, which was different from Shirlynn's sanctified church. I often wondered if something was wrong with my spirit because the couple of times I visited Shirlynn's church, everyone got filled with the Holy Ghost except me.

All around me, believers were speaking in tongues and praising God while I stood there fervently praying and hoping for the spirit of the Lord to rain down on me, too. My inability to speak in tongues made me feel out of place and unworthy. I wound up feeling much lonelier in church—a place I believed should offer a sense of belonging and peace of mind—than I did roaming the streets by myself. While walking home from Shirlynn's house, I thought about the possibility of landing the job at Northside Child Development Center. I sincerely hoped I would be lucky and get hired because there was nothing else to do.

The next day I went to the childcare center and filled out an application. It was challenging to fill in the blanks since the only previous work experience I had was as a junior counselor at Camp Parsons, a program of Phyllis Wheatley Community Center, for two summers when I was fifteen and sixteen years old. *At least it was with children*, I reasoned, as I filled in the section on work history with a flourish.

Suddenly, I also remembered volunteering at St. Peters AME Church when I was fourteen years old as a childcare assistant in their nursery school after I got out of school each day. I filled that in under the section on volunteer and community service. When I was finished filling out the application, I handed it to the receptionist, who told me to come back the following Wednesday for an interview.

That Wednesday, I was offered the job, which I happily accepted. The director, Beverly, provided me with a tour of the center. I noted that nearly all the children and staff were Black apart from two Hispanic women, who turned out to be mother and daughter, and a few Native American children. There were also a few white staff members, including the nurse, a cook, and the kindergarten teacher.

As I was leaving the center, I saw a group of toddlers line up and waddle out of the lunchroom. I stood there fascinated as they followed one another in a haphazard line. Every so often, one of them would plop down on the floor and sit there until one of the aides helped the baby back up on their feet.

While passing the restroom, I saw several toddlers taking turns standing on a stepstool and washing their hands. It was with extreme care that one would pass the bar of soap to the next one in line after finishing with it. I watched with interest as a two-year-old little girl turned the soap over and over again in her hands and then rinsed thoroughly under the stream of water gushing from the faucet. She then dried her hands with a brown paper towel with equal concentration and care.

Next, Beverly showed me the classroom where I would be working. It was nap time, and the preschool children tossed and turned on their cots. One or two of them were actually asleep, but the rest took turns popping their heads up from their cots to scan the room and then quickly put them back down again. One little girl saw me as I peeked into the room, and her grin showed a space where two teeth used to be. I smiled back. *I'm going to like it here*, I thought, as I exited the building and headed to the bus stop for the long ride home.

Two months after I started working at Northside Child Development Center, I found an apartment for a hundred and thirty dollars a month and moved out on my own. The apartment was on Blaisdell Avenue. It was a one-bedroom apartment in an older building. One of its distinguishing features was a built-in breakfast nook. Blaisdell Avenue was one block off Nicollet Avenue's "'ho stroll." Living so close to the stroll had its definite advantages, one of them being that I picked up extra money babysitting while mothers worked the streets. Every now and then, a hooker would ask me if she could turn tricks out of my

144 ◈ ◈ COLNESE M. HENDON

apartment, which I always turned down. My living space was sacred to me and was not something I wanted to open to tricks.

Living so close to the track also had its disadvantages. The tricks—usually white men—thought every woman walking down the street was for sale, which infuriated me. I took great pleasure in turning down their solicitations. My typical response to an inquiry of "Twenty bucks?" lip-synced from a moving vehicle was my middle finger. One night while walking home from the Tom Thumb convenience store, which was situated next to a sauna across the alley from my apartment building, a trick asked me, "How much would you charge to beat me?" while nervously flicking his tongue in and out of his mouth.

"That wouldn't be a good idea," was my response. "I'm afraid if I started beating you, I might beat you to death!"

Even though it was dark outside, I could see the man's cheeks turn flaming red as he quickly rolled up his window and sped off. Because of the roving tricks and other predators in the neighborhood, I didn't particularly like living alone. Sometimes it was scary, and I didn't believe I could trust anybody.

Two months after I moved into the apartment, I came home from work to find that someone had broken into my apartment and had stolen my portable color television set. The thief had gotten in through what had once been an icebox, a small closet that could be accessed from the outer hallway into the apartment. Too late I figured out that the only thing preventing anyone who wanted to enter my apartment uninvited was a latched cupboard door in the kitchen, which the thief had broken through.

From the very small entry, I concluded the person who had broken in had to be extremely skinny to slide through a space less than a square foot in diameter. After taking inventory of who had been in my apartment, I suspected the culprit was a friend of Shirlynn's boyfriend named Ace. I couldn't prove it, so there was nothing I could do about it except seethe with anger.

While having my own apartment had turned out to be less fun and more responsibility than I had anticipated, my job at Northside Child Development Center continued to be the highlight of my life. Working in the daycare center was just what the doctor ordered. I worked hard to keep the children in my classroom entertained, sometimes even spending my meager earnings to buy glitter and glue for art projects, jump ropes, coloring books, and other things to entertain the preschoolers with. They rewarded me with their love. When I arrived at the childcare center at noon during their naptime, I would hear their little voices, "Teacher's here!"

Excited whispers would ripple up and down the rows of supposed-to-be-sleeping preschoolers. The head teacher would roll her eyes. I suppose she was annoyed that all her hard work getting them to settle down for a nap had been disrupted. I would sit on the floor between the cots and give back rubs to the more disruptive children to settle them down once more.

When the room was quiet once again, I would sit at the head table and plan the afternoon activity session for the four-year-old group, which I led. Sometimes it would be an art project; other times, it would be a story or a learning activity, such as teaching the children how to print their names on lined paper. They particularly liked learning how to print various words, and they would give me seemingly endless requests about words they wanted to learn.

"Teacher, show me how to write my baby sister's name," or "Teacher, write horse.'"

One day a little girl named Erica stumped me for the first time since I had been working there.

"Teacher, show me how to write, 'My mom died.'"

I paused while I thought hard about how to best respond to her request.

"Why do you want to know how to write that?" I asked.

"Because she did die," Erica explained, "And I don't have anything that says so."

I was at a loss for words. I had noticed Erica was picked up each day by her grandmother, one of her aunts, or her great-grandmother, Gee Gee, but I had not known until that moment it was because Erica's mother had died. I wondered what it felt like to be a little girl dealing with such a huge loss. I imagined having the words defining the tragedy she had experienced written down on paper might somehow make her loss easier to bear.

I also wondered how her grandmother would respond if Erica came home from preschool that day and showed her a piece of paper with those words written on it. Words that would propel her grandmother backwards into pain and grief she undoubtedly was struggling to overcome after losing her beloved daughter. I wondered what the repercussions would be for me because I showed Erica how to write them. I wanted to write the words for Erica. I really did. I understood what the little girl was asking me for and why, but in the end, I couldn't bring myself to do it.

The love I received from the children of Northside Child Development Center and the love I was able to give them in return helped me heal from the loss of my baby. Looking forward to seeing my preschool students gave me a reason to get up each day. Those little children were like stars that lit up my world. Seeing life through their eyes as they learned new things each day renewed life for me, as well.

CHAPTER 29

Half White

One day, as I was standing in front of the round mirror that hung on the wall of my bedroom combing my hair, I observed my face, which looked no different than it had every other day of my life. I took note of my freckles, which continued to pepper my complexion, my thin lips, my pug nose, and my light-bright skin, and was suddenly horrified by a possibility that had never crossed my mind. I could hear my mother in the kitchen cooking dinner and decided to ask her to clarify what had suddenly become apparent to me in a way it never had before.

"Mom, was my real mother white?" I asked, dreading her answer.

"Yes, she was" was my mother's nonchalant response.

"She was white?"

"Uh-huh."

I could not believe my ears. How had I lived seventeen years on earth without knowing such an important factor about myself and my racial identity? I felt sick inside. White people had been the conscious and unconscious, spoken and unspoken, enemy of my people—Black people—my entire life. How could I be half white? It wasn't possible.

Why hadn't anyone thought it was important enough for me to know?

What did it mean?

What, if anything, did it change about me?

I could remember when I was a child being asked from time to time by children at school or in the neighborhood, "Are you mixed?"

I had always replied, "No," because my mom and dad were Black. I knew being mixed meant being half white and half Black. Most of the time in my neighborhood, it meant having a white mother. There may have been a few mixed kids I knew with a white father, but in most cases, he was out of the picture, so it was unverifiable.

Perhaps the discovery that I had a white mother somewhere should have changed my self-identity, but it did not. I grew up during a time that wholeheartedly adhered to the one-drop rule: If you had one drop of Black blood, you were Black.

Not knowing my white mother or her relatives nor having any details about my European ancestry and heritage made it difficult for me to identify with whiteness in any way. What I knew about white people—how they had enslaved, discriminated against, and oppressed Black people, how they had stolen land from the Native Americans, how they often made me feel whenever I encountered them—made me ashamed of being part white. So after a day or two of bewilderment and racial confusion, I resumed having a 100 percent Black identity. It was all I knew. Percentages be damned.

There have been times in my life when it has been clear to me that my perception of my racial identity does not match up with an outsider's perception. I have at times been rejected, ostracized, and challenged, which seemed to be based on my light-skinned and mixed-race appearance alone. I have encountered Black people who by their actions I could tell do not view or accept me as being fully Black.

Maybe in their eyes, my skin is not dark enough.

Maybe in their eyes, my body is not graceful enough, nor my butt round enough.

Maybe in their eyes, my rhythm and dance moves are not African enough.

I have had all those same thoughts; however, when my identity was being formed, I was socialized as an African American by my family, friends, and community, so that is who I am.

CHAPTER 30

The Drake Relays

◈ ◈ ◈

Marita told me that Alana, Blue's main hooker, was in jail. Because of her numerous prostitution busts, she had received a ninety-day sentence in the workhouse. Marita and I were at the Old Timers Club, where grown men gambled. Marita liked it because she could often pull a trick out of there. I liked it because I could usually get a ride home from the Northside after the buses had stopped running.

I ran into Marita right after she made a quick thirty dollars from one of the gamblers. Marita was a free spirit who liked to have a good time, and she was usually quite generous with the money she made. She and I had formed a bond of sorts since the fight I had with Cherie on her behalf at the Cozy Bar. Prior to that, Marita had been somewhat jealous of my friendship with Tina. I had known Tina since grade school, but she and Marita had become friends more recently. Marita couldn't see what Tina saw in me as a friend because I was so-called "square," meaning not living my life in the fast lane.

Marita had gradually warmed up to me, and now we were cool with each other. One thing we had in common was that we were both reckless. Marita used to mess with Blue and possibly still did on occasion. I forgave Marita for this transgression because there were very few men Marita had not messed with. She took men in stride, didn't take them too seriously, and rarely got hung up on one. Marita mainly lived life from day to day and seemed to take the song "Love the One You're With" to heart. So when I suggested that we go over to Blue's house to see what was going on with him, Marita nonchalantly agreed.

"Do you think he has any blow?" she asked, her primary concern.

"I don't know. He might."

"How much money do you have?" asked Marita.

"About ten or fifteen dollars, why?"

"Want to go in on a half a gram if he is at home?"

"Yeah, okay."

I often used the pretense of buying cocaine as an excuse to show up at Blue's door, so this was nothing new. I hadn't visited him lately because he had moved out of his mother's house and into his own apartment. Alana lived with him, but now that Alana was in jail, she ceased to be a factor to consider when I entertained the thought of going to visit him.

"Let's go."

"Okay, just a minute," replied Marita. "I see this one sap over there. Let me see if I can get a few more dollars out of him. I know he's good for a drink at least."

Marita returned in a few minutes with two drinks. She passed one to me.

"Here you go," she said.

"What is it?"

"Rum and coke, I think. That's all they had left."

The Old Timers Club was both a gambling and a bootlegging joint.

"Okay, you all got to go," rumbled Jake, the owner of the club. "You young girls don't bring nothing but trouble and attention to the joint. Finish your drinks and get on out of here."

"Bye, baby," purred Marita as we exited the Old Timers Club. Jake's face softened a little bit, but he didn't smile.

"Damn, he's hard," I commented once we were on the street and headed in the direction of Blue's place.

"He knows he's going to jail the next time his joint is busted, so he's jumpy," explained Marita. "He even stopped selling liquor out of there for a while."

"Blue's home," I interrupted. "I can see his car."

"Girl, we're still two blocks away. How can you see his car?"

"Look, you can see the TV antenna. He's parked right under the streetlight."

Marita squinted. "Sure can. Go on with your bad self. You know you can spot your man anywhere!"

"You mean Alana's man."

"Yeah, as long as she keeps paying him, that's her man," snorted Marita contemptuously.

Once we got onto his block, I could see lights on in his unit. That was a good sign. I didn't want to wake him up or disturb him if he had other female company. Marita pushed the door of the four-plex open; Blue's apartment was one of two on the first floor. His door was on the left side. I knocked. I could vaguely hear music and men's voices through the door.

"That chump ass Devin must be over there," Marita declared in a stage whisper. "I hear another voice."

"You know he is," I agreed. "Blue doesn't travel very far without his flunky."

"Girl, be quiet before they hear us," Marita cautioned as she knocked a little louder. Suddenly the door flung open, and I was face to face with Blue.

"Hey, Devin, look who we have here." Blue threw his head back and laughed.

I nervously joined in. I never knew what to expect from him, whether he would accept or reject me. He seemed a bit more friendly since I had gotten my own apartment. He had even asked me for a set of keys. I gave him the keys to my apartment willingly with the hope that I would come home from work one day and find him there or that he would surprise me in the middle of the night by stopping by. So far, neither scenario had transpired.

"Well, come on in," he said. Marita and I went into the apartment.

It was the first time I had been inside, so I looked around. There was very little furniture. It definitely looked like a bachelor's pad. One large gold, crushed-velvet chaise longue sat in the middle of the floor occupied for the moment by Devin. There was a huge sound system against the wall that included four large speakers and a turntable. Positioned in the corner was a black leather bar with two swivel bar stools in front of it. There was a chrome and glass table in the dining room surrounded by four matching chrome and velvet chairs. Next to the dining room table sat an ironing board with a pair of blue jeans draped across it. On the floor next to the ironing board was a laundry basket full of what appeared to be clean clothes.

Devin, who was laying back in the chaise longue and looking like he was posing for a magazine cover, thrust a joint in our general direction.

"Want a hit?" he drawled in a low voice while holding in reefer smoke.

Before I could answer, Marita grabbed the joint from Devin and flopped down on the chaise longue next to him. Devin's long brown permed hair fanned out around his shoulders like a girl's. The fingernails of his delicate-looking golden brown hands were painted with clear nail polish. I seriously doubted if he had ever done as much as bounce a basketball with his hands, let alone put in an honest day's work. Devin was the epitome of a gentleman of leisure whose goal was to rest, dress, and collect his dividends from working girls.

When Devin glanced in my direction, I rolled my eyes. Something about him rubbed me the wrong way. He definitely fit the stereotype of a pimp who did not like women. He was too soft for me, but some hardcore women went for his feminine traits and long, flowing hair. When I really stopped to think about it, the main thing that got on my nerves about Devin was his lack of originality. Every time I was within earshot of him, he was quoting some line out of an Iceberg Slim novel.

"Come here," Blue gestured. "I want to talk to you."

I followed him to his room. I was not surprised to see his bed still had three or four mattresses piled up on top of each other as they had been when he lived at his parents' house. I stepped on a chair placed next to the bed and climbed up. After popping a tape into the tape player, Blue climbed into the bed and relaxed against a backrest at the head of the bed. I sat near the foot, swinging my legs over the edge. A red bulb glowed from a lamp in the corner of the room.

"Come up here so I can talk to you," Blue said, beckoning to me.

I complied. I laid my head in the crook of his arm, and Blue ran his fingers through my hair. Marvin Gaye's hit record, *Let's Get it On*, crooned from the speakers, adding to the mood of the moment. I didn't know what stroke of good fortune had landed me in that place at that time, but I appreciated where I was and hoped nothing would spoil the mood.

As it turned out, nothing did. Blue and I laid back, talked, laughed, and had a good time listening to music and enjoying one another's company. Blue dumped a package of coke on the mirror and cut it up, and we each tooted a few lines. Eventually, we went back into the living room and joined Devin and Marita.

"Hello, strangers," Marita greeted us.

It was obvious she was pleased to see us return. It was equally as obvious she was not having as good a time with Devin as I was having with Blue. What was good about Marita was that she was no party pooper. She firmly believed in the song's message, "Love the one you're with," because she usually went with the flow whether she was with the one she loved or not.

"You know what we should do? We should go to the Drake Relays down in Des Moines," she suggested. "Except I don't have any money."

"Don't let that stop you, baby, get off your money maker and go make some money," challenged Devin.

Marita peered out the window. "You must be crazy. It looks like it's going to rain."

"Walk between the raindrops, bitch," was Devin's reply and a direct quote from an Iceberg Slim book.

Everyone ignored him.

"Yeah, we should go to the Drake Relays," I agreed, not wanting the moment with Blue to ever end.

I knew I had a couple hundred dollars in my savings account that I could pull out with my bank card. It was money I was saving for some new furniture, but I would gladly part with it for a weekend trip with Blue.

"A brother needs his hair done before he can even think about going out of town," noted Blue, peering in the mirror at himself, forever vain.

"That ain't no problem. Take me to the cash machine," I offered.

Blue raised his eyebrows at me as if he was wondering if he had finally broken me down. "Let's go then," he agreed.

The four of us headed towards Blue's navy-blue Cadillac Brougham and piled in.

"No beauty shops are open at this time of morning," commented Marita.

"I know one over in Saint Paul that's open all night long," Blue replied.

Devin was driving. Blue hardly ever drove himself but always kept someone around to do his driving for him. Soon he pulled up to a cash machine. I jumped out of the car. I couldn't believe what I was doing. It had taken me forever to save that money, and I was going to blow it all just like that. The most I could withdraw in one day was two hundred dollars, so that is what I did. Blue reached over and removed the crisp twenty-dollar bills from my hand when I got back in the car.

"Leave this to me," he said, flashing a smile.

I smiled back, but inwardly I was sick. I didn't understand how some women could give up all their money every day. It didn't come naturally to me, but I was learning. I felt it was worth a try if I could spend some quality time with Blue. This was the nicest he had been to me since before we lost our baby. I wanted the night to last forever.

Devin got on I-94 and headed to Saint Paul. Before long, he pulled in front of a small storefront beauty shop. I had no idea where I was. Although I had lived in the Twin Cities all my life, Saint Paul was totally foreign to me. We all got out and went inside.

"Hey, Blue," the proprietor greeted him. She was a middle-aged woman with a street wise but unhardened face. "Ain't seen you for a good little while. What can I do for you?"

She took a drag from the cigarette that was dangling from her lips as she awaited Blue's response.

"We all want a wash and set."

"Well, you sure came at a good time. Business just slowed down for a minute. You know everybody been in here all night long getting their hair done for the Drake Relays. Are you all going?"

"We were thinking about it," Blue replied evasively.

I looked at Blue from the corner of my eye. "We better be going," I mumbled under my breath.

"What was that?" Blue gave me a warning glance.

"Oh, nothing, just that we were thinking about going."

Satisfied that I hadn't violated one of his always-respect-your-man pimp rules, he strode confidently to the washbowl and sat in the chair, awaiting his shampoo. Another woman came from a back room and gestured to me to come to the other bowl. I sat down and leaned back until my neck rested in the shampoo bowl. The attendant turned on the water, tested it, and began to dampen my hair. Soon she began to massage some shampoo into my wet hair and work it into a thick lather. Her fingers felt good on my scalp. She scrubbed lightly with her fingernails in a circular motion. I closed my eyes and went with the good feeling.

After the shampoo, the stylist rolled my hair on large rollers and led me to a dryer across from where Blue was already drying. Marita suddenly bolted from her dryer towards the front door. When she returned, she told me she had been sick to her stomach.

"Must have been that dog," I suggested, referring to the heroin Marita had snorted at the Old Timers Club. Marita absently nodded her head in agreement.

When we were all dried and styled, Blue paid with what had very recently been my money. I looked forward to our trip to the Drake Relays. Once we got back into the car, Blue headed back towards Minneapolis on I-94. However, once he merged onto 35-W south, he got off on the first exit instead of continuing south towards Iowa.

"Where are we going?" I wanted to know.

"I'm going to drop you ladies off. We really don't have enough money to go to Des Moines anyway. And it's raining too damn hard," he added, turning the windshield wipers on high for added emphasis.

I was stunned. I couldn't believe he was playing me like that. I knew Blue was doggish, but this beat all. He unceremoniously dropped Marita and me off at my apartment building and pulled off. I decided to let it slide without comment when I got out of the car. When wronged, my vindictive Scorpio nature rarely let anyone or anything slide, so I knew I was going to get revenge in some way. I just didn't know how or when.

I went to the Nacirema Club to hear Mocha and her sisters sing a week later. The name of the band was Myst and Network. They were always good to listen to. As usual, before I went to the Nacirema, I stopped by the Spruce Lounge to have a drink. The Spruce was a small private club owned and operated by the Masons. The bar was inside what used to be a house right next to the Masonic Temple in the 3800 block of 4th Avenue South.

As I sat at the bar nursing my drink, I noticed a young lady sitting at the end of the bar laughing and talking with a few friends. I had noticed her a few times before because we looked alike, and I was not used to encountering people who looked like me. We had the same eyebrows, light complexion, dark hair, and similar body build. It was a coincidence, I was sure, but she never failed to attract my attention.

I quickly finished my drink, placed a tip on the bar, and headed out the door towards the Nacirema Club, a block south of the Spruce. As always, Mocha with Myst and Network put on an outstanding performance, which I thoroughly enjoyed. I was proud that Mocha was my friend, so I never let an opportunity pass to applaud loudly and let everyone know I was one of her number one fans.

After the bar closed, I decided to pay Blue a visit. The buses had stopped running, so I caught a ride from an old man who was leaving the Nacirema at the same time I did. I recognized him as a member of St. Peter's AME Church, where I had attended Sunday school as a child, who sang in the choir. This fact, however, did not stop him from offering me money for sex.

"How much would you charge me to lick it?"

I was repulsed. I often saw the man with his wife at the grocery store and around the neighborhood. I quickly calculated the situation: I was asking him to drive me all the way over North, but he lived about a block from the Nacirema. If I showed him how much he disgusted me, he might decide not to give me a ride. I decided to play the innocent role, which always worked for me.

"Lick what?" I asked, looking at him with wonder.

"You know what I'm talking about."

"How's Mrs. Pearson doing?"

Mr. Pearson began to stutter like I knew he would. "She–she's fine. How are your parents?"

Mr. Pearson shifted himself around in the car seat and straightened up a bit. Right before my eyes, he transformed himself from a lecherous near-child molester into the pillar of society that he pretended to be most of the time.

"My parents are fine, thank you," I replied.

"You ought to be careful being out this time of night," Mr. Pearson advised. "Especially on that Northside. You know how bad it is over there."

"Yes, sir," I agreed.

I was always amazed by the fact that the very people who were the most harmful to my health and well-being were always giving me advice on how to stay out of harm's way. We rode along in companionable silence. Mr. Pearson seemed to be proud of the fact that he was seeing me safely to my destination despite the fact that a few minutes earlier, he had propositioned me, a teenager, and the daughter of his neighbors. I was proud that I had put him in his proper place but had still managed to get a ride to where I was going.

I could see the lights on in Blue's apartment. I thanked Mr. Pearson for the ride and asked him for a few dollars if I needed to catch a cab home. He handed me the bills, and I got out of his car. I had figured correctly that his feelings of guilt would be worth a few dollars.

Devin opened the door to let me in. Blue was relaxing in the chaise longue and seemed to be in a good mood. He actually seemed happy to see me; for this, I was glad. After sending Devin to the all-night convenience store for some cigarette papers, Blue invited me back to his room. I climbed up onto his towering bed, which seemed more like a throne fit for a king.

I thought about all the times I had wanted to be with him, but circumstances had prevented me from doing so. I wrapped my arms around him and held him close as we kissed passionately. Blue had always been a good kisser, and that night was no exception. Being with Blue intimately again felt like coming home after being gone for a long, long time; however, before the morning sun lit up the sky, Blue surprised me out of my blissful state by shaking me and saying, "You need to get ready to go."

"Go?" I asked, confused.

I had planned to spend the entire night with him. I didn't want anything to interfere with my illusion of love. Deep in the zone of relaxation and peace I feel right before drifting off to sleep, the last thing I wanted to do was get up and go back outside.

"And don't come back over here until you have some money."

It took a nanosecond before what he was saying registered. Something deep inside clicked, causing the force of my anger and resentment to propel me up and out of bed. I dressed quickly. Blue got up and pulled on his pants, so he could walk me to the door.

"Don't come back over here until you have some money," I mocked him as I unlocked the door. "Fuck you, black motherfucker. Kiss my ass."

True to form, Blue ran up behind me and punched me on the side of my face. I broke out running down the stairs and was heading north on Oliver Avenue just as Devin turned the corner in Blue's car and pulled to a stop.

"You can leave the car there if you want to, but I guarantee you it won't have any windows in the morning!" I was beside myself with rage. "You punk ass bitches; faggot motherfuckers!"

Blue ran towards me and knocked me to the ground. He grabbed a thick wooden two-by-four from off the ground and began beating me in the back and head with it while kicking me in the side.

If he kicks my teeth out, I'm killing him.

I rolled away from the attack. After a few more well-placed kicks to my rib cage, Blue turned and started towards the car. Propelled by fury and adrenaline, I jumped up from the ground and ran behind him.

"You bitch-ass-nigga," I screamed hysterically. "I swear to God, I'm gonna kill your black ass, punk!"

All the hurt and anger I had contained over the past two years since my baby was stillborn and Blue had rejected me resurfaced. I was blind with rage and out of control. I cursed and paced back and forth in front of him, calling him every derogatory name I could think of.

"Give me the keys," Blue finally told Devin, eyeing me warily.

The look on Blue's face seemed to say, *I have given this bitch the very worst ass kicking I could muster. I have done everything I possibly could to beat the dog shit out of her and break her down to the lowest common denominator. But this crazy motherfuckin' bitch is still up in my face talking mad shit.* In a nutshell, Blue looked wary and uncertain about the turn of events.

"Yeah, motherfucker, get the keys because I swear before God, if you leave that car out here tonight, birds are going to be building a nest in it before morning, sorry ass bitches!" I continued to pace, rant and rave.

Blue and Devin got into the car from opposite sides and drove off. I searched the immediate vicinity for a rock. I didn't have to look far. A nice fat, gray brick that must have been sent straight from the heavens above peaked out from underneath the bushes. I grabbed it and hurled it right through Blue's front plate-glass picture window. The sound of tinkling glass gave me a sense of satisfaction, and I craved for more. Searching frantically around the darkened front yard, I spotted another rock. I ran around the side of the four-plex and stopped at what I believed to be his bedroom window. I trotted back a few paces and then slammed the rock through the windowpane.

"Yeah, motherfucker, kiss my ass," I yelled as I headed for the alley.

I knew that Blue would be coming back soon, and the police were possibly even on their way, so I wanted to get as far away from the area as possible. I decided to walk to Tina's grandmother's house, where Tina was living for the time being. Her apartment building was on the other side of Olson Highway. I needed to use the phone to call a cab.

When I finally made it over there, I rang the buzzer with trepidation. I did not want to wake her grandmother up if she had returned from her trip to Chicago.

"Who is it?" I heard Tina's garbled voice through the intercom.

"It's Colnese. Buzz me up. I'm stranded over North." Nothing happened, so I rang the intercom again.

"I got company," Tina yelled.

"Well, call me a cab then," I yelled into the speaker.

Tina was the only one of my friends who changed so dramatically when a man was around. How would it hurt her to let me in to use the damn phone? I surely was not over there trying to look at her man. He was cute but not my type. Plus, on general principles, Tina and I didn't sample each other's fruit, so I didn't know why Tina was tripping.

I kept periodically ringing the buzzer but got no response, so I finally left and began walking down Olson Highway with my thumb out. I didn't have to hitchhike long before someone pulled over and offered me a ride. A young teenage girl walking down the highway in the middle of the night was a temptation few men could refuse.

The following day, I was feeling a lot of pain. I looked in the mirror and saw blood crusted over my left ear, and I had black and blue marks all over my arms and back. A hangover had me terribly thirsty, but I didn't even feel like getting up out of bed to quench my thirst. I eventually got up, though, because I knew I had to go face the music. I had broken Blue's windows out, but to effectively send the message of contempt

I intended for him to receive, I couldn't hide out. I had to get right back on the scene and in his face.

Slowly and painfully, I got dressed and then caught the bus to the Northside. I got off the Plymouth bus at Penn Avenue and headed up the street. One of the first people I ran into was Pontiac, Blue's father, who hung out at the Old Timer's Club. One of his jobs was to watch out for the police when he wasn't gambling himself. I glanced up at the narrow window that served as a lookout post as I walked by, and sure enough, my eyes met Pontiac's. His face disappeared from the window, and soon his entire body emerged from the club.

"Girl, you know that wasn't right breaking my son's windows out like that. You know he ain't no earthly good, so you just need to make up your mind to stay on away from him."

I whirled around and yanked the shirt off my shoulder. "Look what your son did to me!" I said furiously but in a modulated tone. He was, after all, Blue's father and not some lame off the street. Pontiac's always-hard expression stayed the same, but he shook his head after surveying the damage his son had inflicted on me.

"I told you that boy ain't no earthly good. You a good girl and don't have no business even foolin' with him. He don't mean you no good. I would tell you to stay out of his way, but he's locked up. He checked in this morning at the workhouse. He has fifteen days to do."

That was news to me, and I supposed it was good news. I understood that the situation had escalated to the boiling point. To save face, I knew Blue would have to do something bad to me when he saw me, something even worse than what he had already done. I also knew I wasn't going to let that happen. Somebody would get seriously hurt. Blue's cold-hearted nature would seek to hurt me. On top of that would be his need to make an example out of me so that Alana, and whatever other whores he had out there, would continue to respect him and see no signs of weakness or softness in him.

On the flip side, I had reached the point where I wanted to see him dead. The only thing up to that point that had kept me from killing him was my love for his mother. I thought back to when I had stood over his bed while he was sleeping with a pair of scissors clutched tightly in my left hand. He had hurt me and, therefore, I believed he deserved to die, but the thought of his beautiful mother had stopped me. Mrs. Lockett didn't deserve to have her son taken out in such a brutal, calculated, and cold-hearted manner. Blue's mother had always been kind to me, and for the most part, so had the rest of his family.

Wherever he is at this moment and whatever he's doing, he needs to drop to his knees and thank God for his mother. If it wasn't for her, his ass would have been dead a long time ago.

To Pontiac I replied, "When he gets out, I'll stay out of his way. Thanks for letting me know."

"Yeah, all right. Are you going around to the house? My wife's at home. Go on over there and talk to her."

"Okay, I will," I agreed and headed towards the Lockett's house. I was glad I no longer had to look over my shoulder, at least for the time being.

CHAPTER 31

On the Rebound

♦ ♦ ♦

One late summer afternoon, Tina and I were enjoying happy hour at the Blue Note Lounge when, without warning, DeAndre's sister Jada ran up behind Tina and slashed her face with a razor blade. I was aware that Tina had been spending some time with Jada's boyfriend Kyle, a popular disc jockey, so I assumed she did it out of jealousy. It all went down so fast I was caught off guard. Tina began rummaging through her purse in mad pursuit of a knife.

"Get her off me," she yelled out.

Tina's friend Chantal, who was tall, big-boned, and muscular, jumped between them and pushed Jada backwards. A group of Jada's friends beckoned to her from a nearby car.

"Girl, you better come on before the police get here."

Jada did not have to be told twice. She jumped into the car with them, and they sped off, going south on Lyndale Avenue North. Tina and Chantal hurriedly jumped into Chantal's car and drove off in another direction.

Shook up by the entire episode, I walked slowly up Lyndale Avenue towards Plymouth Avenue. I was headed to the Cozy Bar. Everything had happened so quickly, and I needed time to process what had gone down. Coincidentally, when I arrived, I noticed Jada's brother, DeAndre, at the bar with another guy that I soon learned was their older brother, Eugene.

They were standing at the bar having a drink. DeAndre approached me not long after I sat down on one of the nearby barstools. I was in the process of staring at myself in the mirrored wall behind the liquor bottles, something I often did while seated at the bar. It was a good way to gauge the condition of my appearance while also keeping a watch on what was going on behind me.

"What you drinkin'?" DeAndre asked.

"Champale," I replied.

I was mildly surprised that DeAndre was even talking to me. Like Catfish, he was an Undertaker, sworn enemies of Blue and his brother, Apollo, due to the incident in which Apollo's car had been set on fire allegedly by Renard, DeAndre's best friend, and the Undertaker's ringleader. I knew about the Undertakers through Tina, who at one time had been involved with Renard.

The summer before, I had gone over to Renard's house with Tina. On that day, there had been a few white boys who looked like hippies, smoking angel dust out of a pipe. They each took a hit and then passed the pipe to Tina and me. I took a puff, instantly becoming paranoid and couldn't shake the thought that Renard and the Undertakers were rumored to be known for gang rape. I sat on the couch as close to Tina as was humanly possible. I knew that if anything went down, there was strength in numbers. It seemed like Renard could sense my paranoia because when he offered Tina and me a drink of water, he brought the entire pitcher out of the kitchen and poured it into our drinking glasses right in front of us, which I deeply appreciated. Luckily nothing went down.

At that moment, however, I didn't care about DeAndre's affiliation with the Undertakers or that they were at odds with Blue and his brother, Apollo. After the window-breaking incident and the events leading up to it, I considered myself officially done with Blue and was on the rebound. As far as I was concerned, I had tied up two long years of my teenage life in a no-win situation. I was a living, breathing cliché—a woman who loved a man, who did not love her in return. To go even deeper, I loved a man who seemed to hate me, as well as every other woman in the universe.

Blue was an aspiring pimp. I heard the phrase, "Pimpin' ain't easy," used in a joking manner, but on a serious note, pimping seemed to come very easy to men like Blue, who hated women. Pimping was a money game. The golden rule was that a pimp should never have sex with a woman for free. In that way, pimping was a form of prostitution. Who couldn't control his sexual impulses if he did not like women in the first place? The cold-heartedness and brutality that went hand in hand with pimping were par for the course. Who couldn't be cold-hearted and brutal towards women if he did not like or respect women to begin with?

I had finally seen the light. The idea of Blue and I ultimately winding up together as a loving couple seemed completely hopeless. It had become crystal clear to me that the likelihood of ever getting him back was slim to none. We had reached an impasse. I wound up leaving the Cozy Bar with DeAndre that night. Together we walked down Lyndale Avenue and headed to his home in the projects. That night kicked off a summertime fling between us that kept my mind occupied and off Blue.

CHAPTER 32

After Hours Joint

One night after the clubs closed, I went over North to Mr. Ribs, an after-hours joint on Broadway Avenue hosted by Odell. At Mr. Ribs, there was always good music, as well as food and drinks that could be purchased until dawn. As I walked through the front door, I ran into Gee Rich, my so-called friend. Gee Rich made it hard for me to think of him as a true friend because he could be such a shyster. Half the time, we were cool, and the rest of the time, he was doing me in. Gee Rich kept me guessing, so I never knew quite what to expect from him. One time, he gave me some pills he said were downers, but they turned out to be Thorazine, a psychotropic medication.

In fairness, Gee Rich had warned me not to take more than one, so I promptly took three. I didn't trust him because of his past scandalous moves, like the time he sold me what he said was cocaine, but turned out to be a nonnarcotic powder that smelled more like peppermint candy. When the Thorazine kicked in, I passed out in the doorway of Othello's Bar on Hennepin Avenue in downtown Minneapolis. After being helped to my feet by the bouncer, I somehow made my way down the street about half a block before collapsing in a doorway. It was just my luck that as I sat there in a zombie state, Sporty, the brother of a known rapist, happened to walk by.

"Colnese, are you good? Do you need a ride or something?"

"Am I good? No," I stammered. "I mean, yeah. Yeah, I'm good."

I wasn't sure if Sporty was a rapist like his brother or not, but I wasn't taking any chances. Thankfully, Sporty nodded and continued on his way. The threat of potential rape penetrated my drug-induced impairment, and I somehow managed to get to my feet. I did the Thorazine shuffle all the way down the street to my bus stop. After nodding off on the bus, I came to just in time to get off at the correct stop. I concentrated on putting one foot in front of the other and slowly made my way down the four long blocks home where I slept off and on for the next three days.

I never knew what to expect from Gee Rich, yet for some reason, I continued to interact with him whenever I saw him. He spotted me when I came through the front door of Mr. Ribs and sauntered over to where I was. After a bit of small talk, Gee Rich asked me if I wanted to go in on a half gram of cocaine. Having loved the euphoria cocaine produces since my very first experience with it when I was sixteen years old, I was game, so I willingly handed over twenty dollars. After Gee Rich made the purchase, we went into the bathroom for a toot of blow. I wasn't surprised to see his sidekick Geno trailing us to our destination. Because Gee Rich and Geno were tight friends, you seldom saw one without the other.

I first met Geno back in late 1973, when Mocha was staying with Gee Rich over at Chirene's place. At that time, like so many of the young men I knew, Geno was an up-and-coming young pimp. Geno and his hooker, Butter, traveled to Detroit to make some money. When they returned to Minneapolis, Butter took up temporary residence at Chirene's apartment. Geno often breezed in and out while picking up Butter for "work."

Slenderly built, he moved quickly and gracefully. Geno had a pecan complexion with caramel-colored eyes. His auburn-colored hair was processed into a mass of waves combed to the back. He left one perfectly curled shock of hair hanging towards his eyes, similar to Elvis Presley. Geno had been groomed by his parents to be a ladies' man. Even as a teenager, his manners were impeccable but calculated.

After Geno joined Gee Rich and me in the bathroom of Mr. Ribs, Gee Rich opened the package of cocaine, dipped his gold-plated coke spoon into the sparkly white powder, and gave me a toot up each nostril. After we had each had a toot of blow, he folded up the package and put it into the breast pocket of his tan jumpsuit.

We stood around chit-chatting for a minute or two until the cocaine began to wear off. I then asked Gee Rich for another hit, to which he replied, "No."

I shook my head as if to clear it. Surely, I had not been denied a toot of the blow my money had helped to purchase.

"No?" I asked incredulously.

No had never been an answer I took graciously.

"I went in half with you," I reminded Gee Rich heatedly. "What do you mean, no? I know I'm good for at least another hit."

My voice escalated with indignation as I reached into Gee Rich's breast pocket for the small package. Gee Rich clamped one hand over my hand on his pocket while snatching my coin purse with his other hand and tossing it across the bathroom to Geno. I darted towards Geno while leaping and grabbing at the air in the direction Gee Rich had thrown it. Geno gracefully intercepted the coin purse and threw it back to Gee Rich, and I became the pickle in the middle.

"Give me my damn purse!" I yelled, lunging for Geno. His fawn-colored eyes widened, and I thought I saw just the slightest hint of alarm just before he stepped to one side and tossed the purse over my head back to Gee Rich. Right then, Odell came storming through the bathroom door.

"What the hell is going on in here?" he demanded. Big, black owlish-looking glasses framed his narrow face.

"They're trying to rob me," I protested angrily. Inwardly, I felt relieved help had finally arrived.

"You're gonna have to get on up out of here," Odell said threateningly to me.

"They got my purse! What do you mean I have to get out of here?"

"Let's go," Odell said, grabbing my upper arm roughly and shoving me unceremoniously towards the hallway exit. Suddenly, I found myself outside on the sidewalk in the dark. Seconds later, Gee Rich and Geno exited the same door.

"Give me my purse, Gee Rich!" Hot, angry tears trickled down my cheeks. "You're supposed to be my friend," I reminded him.

Gee Rich calmly passed my coin purse to me. "I don't want your purse. I was just trying to teach you a lesson—not to go in a pimp's pocket."

Oh, my God. Gee Rich is a pimp, too? When did that happen?

Having gotten me straight on the proper etiquette of how to treat a pimp, Gee Rich turned to Geno, "Let's roll, man. Come on, Colnese, you can ride with us."

Indignantly blinking back tears, I obediently followed Gee Rich and Geno to the car and—not wanting to break another rule of the pimp game—got into the backseat. Instinctively, I knew pimps rode in the front and women rode in the back. Another variation of the phrase, "Pimps up, 'ho's down."

Geno headed downtown, so he and Gee Rich could "check their traps." We found Gee Rich's woman working on a corner on 9th Street, not too far off Hennepin Avenue. Gee Rich got out of the car and talked to her for a minute. I watched from the backseat as she handed him her earnings thus far that night. After exchanging a few more words with her, Gee Rich got back in the car, and we drove off.

Geno was three-deep, meaning he had three prostitutes working for him. Two were white, and one was Black. We spotted the blonde, but she was busy leaning into a car talking to a potential trick, so we kept on going. It was in the wee hours of the morning, and I was getting tired. As we headed north on 7th Street back towards the Northside, I asked Gee Rich and Geno to drop me off in the projects where DeAndre lived with his family. After dropping me off, I waved goodbye, and they pulled off. As I knocked on the door, a white car pulled up full of women. At that moment, a voice on the other side of the door asked, "Who is it?"

I responded, "Is DeAndre home?"

One of the women in the car yelled angrily, "No, DeAndre's not home. No, he's not home!"

As the car screeched off, I recognized that the angry voice had come from none other than DeAndre's sister, Jada. I thought back to the day she sliced my friend Tina's face with a straight razor at the Blue Note over her boyfriend. Apparently, she associated me with Tina, or maybe she just disliked me based on my status as a Southsider. Whatever the case, the hate was real. Soon the door opened, and DeAndre invited me in.

CHAPTER 33

Expecting Again

◆ ◆ ◆

The next time I saw Blue, I was six months pregnant by DeAndre and huge. Even so, I had decided to go out to Othello's to party with some friends. It was hot and smoky in the club, and because I was pregnant and not drinking, I wasn't having any fun, so I decided to call it a night. I left the club to go home long before the last call for alcohol.

As I was walking down 8th Street towards the Nicollet Mall to catch the bus home, I saw Blue walking towards me with a couple other guys, who I did not recognize. As we passed one another, Blue noticed my big stomach, and he turned completely around in his tracks to stare at me. As I walked past, I looked back at him but kept right on walking. Thankfully, the shock of my pregnancy made him temporarily forget the beef we had in the summer about his broken windows. As for DeAndre, I had told him in early July 1976 that I was pregnant by him. His reply had been, "We're not ready for kids. As good as you look, you could make cash money."

To me, it seemed that tired line was coming out of every young man's mouth in Minneapolis. The reality of the situation was that I was not going to get an abortion to become a prostitute. I was eighteen years old. At that point in my life, I really didn't have a game plan, but I knew prostitution wasn't it, so I ignored DeAndre's pimp dream and continued on with my pregnancy. When rumors began to spread around town that I was pregnant by DeAndre, he became furious and called me on the phone.

"You fat motherfucker, you're not pregnant by me," DeAndre hollered into the phone and then hung up in my face.

His words caught me off guard with their abrasiveness. What would cause him to go from zero (mildly suggesting our unpreparedness for parenthood) to a hundred (calling me a fat motherfucker and denying our baby was his)? Those words were the last words DeAndre uttered to me for the duration of my pregnancy. I didn't hear from him again until after I delivered.

Surprisingly, I wasn't devastated by us parting ways. Simply put, DeAndre didn't have my heart. While I was shocked and offended that he denied any responsibility for my pregnancy, I was not invested in him emotionally. Yes, we'd had a few good times over the summer, but ours was a rebound relationship. I needed something to take my mind off Blue and the heartbreak he had caused me, and DeAndre had magically appeared.

Life was strange. I was expecting a baby by a man who didn't want to claim it, while the baby that Blue and I both wanted had been so tragically lost and was forever gone. Regardless of what DeAndre wanted or didn't want, I decided to move forward with my pregnancy and my life regardless of any negative feelings he had towards me.

Not long after discovering I was pregnant, Tina became pregnant, too. I was happy that we were expecting babies at the same time. We both went to the Minneapolis Public Health Clinic in downtown Minneapolis for prenatal care. It was a free clinic, which was right up my alley since I was unemployed with no income. I had applied for Aid to Families with Dependent Children, which would kick in after I was five months pregnant.

Once a month, I went to the clinic to receive my prenatal vitamins and WIC coupons. I got undressed, put on a paper gown, and sat on a chair in the hallway next to other pregnant women and waited my turn to have my blood pressure checked, my blood drawn, my weight recorded, and a pelvic examination performed.

My nurse, Patty, was friendly, understanding and seemed genuinely interested in my well-being. In addition to being my prenatal nurse, Patty functioned in my life as a sort of counselor and confidant. I told her everything I was going through with my pregnancy and everything I was going through in my life in general. I thoroughly enjoyed having Patty's listening ear as a sounding board.

One day I arrived at the clinic full of enthusiasm and expectation. I had a picture of DeAndre I wanted to show her, but upon checking in, I was told that Patty was sick and another nurse would be seeing me that day. Tina was in the waiting room when I returned from my visit with the random substitute nurse, who was nothing like Patty. Tina took one look at the expression on my face and knew something was up. My face was flushed, and I was almost in tears.

"What's wrong with you?" Tina asked.

"My nurse isn't here," I explained.

Tina nodded sympathetically. We were both emotional to begin with, and pregnancy had only intensified our feelings. "Then who saw you?"

"Some green-eyed tramp."

Tina doubled up with laughter and couldn't stop. Seeing her laughing so hard made me laugh, too, and soon I felt much better.

When the year-long lease was up at my apartment on Blaisdell, I decided to move back to my old neighborhood to be closer to my parents after I had the baby. I found a nice, modern one-bedroom apartment on 32nd and Portland, which I moved into in December 1976. As my pregnancy progressed, I found myself spending more and more time at my parents' house. Being alone in the apartment was boring, and pregnancy made me more homebound. One day as I was at their house lounging around in my nightgown and talking on the phone to Tina, the doorbell rang.

"Hold on, girl, somebody's at the door," I told her.

I got up from the floor where I had been lying down on my back talking, raised the window shade that covered three small windowpanes at the top of the front door, and peeked outside. I was speechless to see DeAndre standing there on the front steps looking downwards and dressed in a forest green Minneapolis Housing Authority uniform. He hadn't seen me, so I quickly dropped the shade and hurried back to the phone.

"You're not going to believe this," I said in a low voice. "DeAndre's at the door."

"Well, are you gonna let him in?" Tina asked.

I dropped the receiver once again and went back to the door. This time when I raised the shade, I watched as DeAndre returned to the City of Minneapolis vehicle he was driving. I guess I could have opened the door and called him back, but everything had happened so quickly, and then it was too late. DeAndre jumped into the driver's seat, started the engine, and merged into traffic. Just as quickly as he had appeared, DeAndre was long gone.

CHAPTER 34

Single Motherhood

My due date was February 28, but when I went past that date, the clinic's OB-GYN doctor decided to do a stress test to determine whether or not the baby was in distress. He gave me a huge bleach bottle and told me to save all my urine in it for a few days and then bring it back into the clinic to be tested.

When my urine was tested, it turned out that my baby was indeed in distress, so a decision was made to induce labor. As my luck would have it, on March 4, 1977, the day my labor was scheduled to be induced, there was a huge snowstorm. I walked over to my friend Pam's house carrying my huge jug of pee and asked her brother, Pop, if he would take me to the hospital if I gave him three dollars' worth of gas money. He agreed, so we loaded into his car and headed slowly down the snowy streets to Hennepin County Medical Center (HCMC). I couldn't think of a nicer person than Pop to take me to the hospital to have my baby. Two years younger than Pam and me, Pop was one of the kindest and level-headed young men I knew.

After Pop dropped me off, I went up to the labor and delivery floor where I was asked to change out of my clothes and into a hospital gown, so they could begin to induce my labor. When my mom got off work, she came down to the hospital to be my breathing coach.

Six intense hours later, Destiny was born weighing nine pounds, three and a half ounces, and twenty-one inches in length. In my eyes, she was the most beautiful newborn baby girl ever born. Because of her large size, she looked to be at least a month old at birth. Her cheeks were plump, and she had a head full of black hair. Her hair was curly on top, but very straight on the back of her head near her neck. Destiny's skin was initially a light shade of peanut brown, but I could look at the pigmentation along the edges of her ears and tell her skin would darken up to a toasty brown.

When my labor was initially progressing at a slow pace, the intern at HCMC increased the level of Pitocin (a drug used to induce contractions) so high, I almost hemorrhaged to death after Destiny was born. The labor and delivery team massaged my uterus to stop the blood flow. Because I had never delivered a full-term baby, I had no idea that the situation was so critical. I found out later that they were concerned they might lose me. Thank God their efforts worked, or I wouldn't be here to tell my story.

I was on cloud nine in the recovery room. The euphoria I experienced was above and beyond any other high I had ever had. I thanked God for giving me a healthy baby while simultaneously forgiving all my enemies. I was thankful to finally have a living, breathing baby girl, someone blood-related to me. I had no way of getting in touch with DeAndre to tell him the news because he was in the work-release program at the Hennepin County Workhouse. After a four-day hospital stay, standard in 1977, my brother Ira picked us up at HCMC to take Destiny and me to my parents' house. I planned to spend a couple of weeks recovering from childbirth and receiving help with my newborn from my mom and dad.

As we drove through downtown Minneapolis, I caught a glimpse of Blue walking down Hennepin Avenue and turning into Moby Dick's Bar. Even with the joy of being a first-time mom, the sight of Blue still caused my heart to jump inside my chest, and I knew he still had a hold on me. Despite everything that had transpired, I was definitely not over him, not by a long shot.

Not many days after Destiny was born, Tina saw DeAndre in the parking lot of the SuperValu grocery store on Glenwood Avenue near the projects. After telling him I had given birth to a baby girl, DeAndre went on another rampage. He was right in the midst of vehemently denying Destiny was his baby when Tina cut him off.

"I don't want to hear that mess," she told him bluntly. "That baby looks just like you."

Because DeAndre was still on work release at the Hennepin County workhouse, he wasn't able to come see Destiny until the following Saturday. I hadn't spoken to DeAndre since he had hung up on me after calling me a "fat motherfucker" and denying I was pregnant by him. However, while he was locked up, I had written him a letter the day after Christmas, but he had not responded to it.

December 26, 1976

DeAndre,

I haven't seen you or talked to you in months, so I don't know whether you have the same attitude you had the last time we talked. At that time, you started out by saying that you didn't want any kids, so I should get an abortion and ended up saying that it wasn't your baby.

Do you still feel that way? If you do, there's nothing I can do to change your feelings. But you should check yourself out. You were out there trying to pimp, which takes a man, but you're not man enough to claim your own baby. I don't believe that shit, that you really don't think it's yours. I think you want the easy way out.

I don't know what's the sense in saying the baby's not yours if it is. I don't want no more out of you than you care to give. I'm not the type of person that would try to pin a baby on you that is somebody else's. That would make me the fool. On the other hand, who's the fool when you're denying something that everybody knows is yours? Think of it this way, what would I gain by lying? You don't have no more than the average man. Why would I pick you to lie to?

I'm glad I found out where you're coming from. You're only good as long as times are good and as long as things are going your way. What do I need with a man whose hand is always out but can't stand up when times are bad? My baby is due sometime in February. I'll let you know when I have it. If you want to see it, that's cool, and if you don't, that's cool too.

Sincerely,
Colnese Hendon

P.S. If you're so against having kids, next time don't be so quick to jump in bed. You're a grown man; you know what makes babies.

When DeAndre rang the doorbell to see Destiny for the first time, she was two weeks old. It was a bit awkward seeing him after he had missed the majority of my pregnancy. Nevertheless, the visit went smoothly. The Sloe Gin and 7-Up we were drinking helped relax the tension between us. Instantly, DeAndre warmed up to fatherhood and to his newborn baby girl. He expressed his happiness that I had given her a first name similar to his. When the visit was over and he was leaving the house, he told Destiny, "Your dad will be back to see you soon."

◆ ◈ ◈

I soon found out that motherhood is not for the faint of heart. Destiny and I shared a bedroom in my new apartment. Getting anything done, including getting enough sleep, was a huge challenge since Destiny cried whenever I wasn't holding her. She wanted to be held in a very specific way—upright and looking over my left shoulder. If held in any other position or put down somewhere other than in her wind-up swing, she would cry. Years later, I would discover that Destiny was lactose intolerant. It was the Similac with iron that most likely caused her so much distress, but as a nineteen-year-old mother, I didn't have a clue.

Destiny was a big baby, and she developed very quickly, so by the time she was a couple months old, she could hold her own bottle, and by five months old, she was crawling. Destiny probably would have been an early walker as well, but like DeAndre, she was pigeon-toed. Her pediatrician at the Minneapolis Public Health Department's Well Baby

Clinic referred me to a podiatrist, who prescribed corrective shoes with a bar between them that forced her feet to turn outward rather than inward. It took a while for her to figure it out, but soon Destiny was crawling all over the apartment in her new corrective shoes with the bar in between. She even figured out how to pull herself up to a standing position and balance against the coffee table.

The reason I wanted a girl was so I could dress her up in cute clothes, get her ears pierced, and show her off like a real live baby doll. When Destiny was five weeks old, I dressed her up in a pair of lime green stretch pants with a matching striped, green, yellow, and blue top. I bundled her in a pink sweater with a matching pink cap, then swaddled her in a blue bunting. I carried her down 4th Avenue to a neighborhood beauty shop on the corner of 37th Street and 4th Avenue to get her ears pierced. The sign on the wall said that infants needed to be three months old to have the procedure done.

When the proprietor of the beauty shop asked me my baby's age, I replied, "Three months old," and held my breath as the lie floated around in the air.

"Your baby's big for her age," was the woman's only response.

I smiled and let out a sigh of relief. Destiny was asleep when her first ear was pierced. She flinched a little when the ear-piercing gun fired the silver post into her earlobe. I gave Destiny her bottle to lull her back to sleep and keep her calm while her second ear was pierced.

After the ear piercing was completed, the lady gave me instructions on how to keep Destiny's ear lobes clean while they healed, and then I carried her back home.

I know every mother thinks her baby is beautiful, but mine really was. As my dad used to say, "Every crow thinks hers is the blackest." Destiny's brown skin complemented the brightly colored baby clothes I kept her decked out in. She had a head full of black curly hair, bright and shiny round eyes, and plump, healthy legs. Destiny was everything I wanted in a baby girl. Because of her brown skin, Tina nicknamed her Brownie. When Destiny was four months old, I started feeding her rice cereal and fruit, mainly apple sauce and bananas. Eating solid foods obviously agreed with her because she stopped crying so much. Praise the Lord!

At nineteen years old, I was a welfare mother. I received two-hundred sixty-two dollars per month from Aid to Families with Dependent Children (AFDC). Hennepin County, my benefactor, wanted me to name the father of my baby, or they would cut me off welfare, so I complied. Soon DeAndre was paying Hennepin County seventy-five dollars per month for child support. The fact that the welfare department was collecting child support from him pissed him off and caused DeAndre to despise my status as a welfare mother.

"You need to get off your ass and get a job," he said in a nasty tone of voice.

CHAPTER 35

Career Goals

◈ ◈ ◈

The welfare department often sent out communications with my monthly AFDC check. One month they offered welfare recipients interested in a career an opportunity to schedule an appointment to take an aptitude test. I took them up on their offer and was surprised to discover from the test results that pursuing a career in banking would be a good option for me. My dad worked as a personal banker at Northwestern National Bank, so I knew a little bit about banking.

I had taken a few classes at Minneapolis Community College during my pregnancy, and I planned to return in the fall. I wondered what type of courses I should take with the goal of a career in banking. I looked in the want ads of the newspaper to see which banks were hiring and what type of jobs were available. Fifth Northwestern Bank had openings for full-time and part-time tellers. They listed their phone number in the want ad, so I called the number. Marty Corbin, their personnel director, answered my questions.

"Many people enter the field of banking through an entry-level position and work their way up the ladder," he explained. "I'll tell you what. The next time I have an opening, I'll give you a call."

"Okay, sounds good," I agreed.

Marty took my contact information, and then we said our goodbyes. I didn't really expect to hear from him again. I thought he was just making small talk, but a few months later, Marty was as good as his word. He called to tell me he had an opening in the bookkeeping department as a check filing clerk. He also told me if I was interested in the position, to come in and fill out an application, and he would interview me.

On the interview day, I dressed up in my three-piece navy-blue pantsuit. I prepared for the interview by talking to my friend Glenda, who worked in the bookkeeping department of a different Northwestern

Bank. She filled me in on her job duties, which gave me a better understanding of what work to expect in the bookkeeping department. Our conversation also helped me feel more confident during the interview. Apparently, I interviewed well because after all was said and done, I was offered a full-time job with benefits as a check filer at Fifth Northwestern Bank. It was located right off the intersection of Lake Street and Hennepin Avenue in Minneapolis's Uptown area.

One of my mom's close friends, Aunt Dorsella, recommended Barbara Nell, one of her friends from the Kingdom Hall, to babysit Destiny. Barbara Nell charged thirty dollars a week. She lived on 37th Street and 4th Avenue, right on the number nine bus line and only a couple of blocks from my apartment building. I could walk to Barbara Nell's house, drop Destiny off in the morning, and then cross the street to catch the bus to work. I was relieved when I found out Barbara Nell was related to Mocha. I knew her extended family and trusted that Destiny would be well taken care of.

I was twenty years old when I started working at the bank. A white girl, whose name was Jenny, trained me in as a check filer. She pulled up her chair next to me at my workstation, known as the 56 File, and proceeded to teach me how to file checks and answer phone inquiries.

The first thing she said after sitting down was, "My name is Jenny Bates. Have you ever heard of Jenny Bates or Jessi Bates?"

"No," I responded.

"You've never heard of Jenny Bates or Jessi Bates?" she asked incredulously.

"No, I haven't," I replied, wondering where the line of questioning was going.

Jenny tossed her thick and wavy light brown hair over her shoulder. "I went to Bryant Junior High School, and I hated it. Did you go there?"

Bryant Junior High School was the predominantly Black junior high school in the South Minneapolis neighborhood where I grew up, but I had not gone there. As Jenny continued to train me on the 56 File, I told her I had gone to Breck and described my experiences while attending the predominantly white prestigious private school.

CHAPTER 36

Breck School

One day during the summer between sixth and seventh grade, my mom told me we were going to Breck School, so I could take an admissions test. I absolutely did not want to go to Breck, a private school, because that would mean I would miss out on going to Bryant Junior High School and be separated from my friends.

As fate would have it, I passed the entrance exam. Before I knew it, I was shopping for the school uniform instead of doing regular school shopping for more stylish junior high school clothes. The uniform consisted of a navy-blue blazer with the school emblem on the breast pocket, a white collarless blouse, a blue and green plaid skirt, navy-blue knee-highs, and navy-blue penny loafers. I had never before worn a uniform, and the idea of being dressed like everyone else for every single day of the school year did not appeal to me.

On the first day of school, I walked to the corner of 38th Street and Portland Avenue to wait for my school bus. I felt conspicuous standing there in a school uniform as my neighborhood friends headed to Bryant Junior High School in their sharp new school clothes. Riding to school in a bus filled with privileged white children from the suburbs was also a very different experience since I was used to walking to school with not-so-privileged Black children from the city.

But nothing could have prepared me for the culture shock I was in for when I got to Breck. Chapel was the first activity of the day, which amounted to a church service complete with hymns and a sermon. Before I went into the Chapel, I saw a Black girl named Tamara, who used to live on my block, standing with a group of her friends. I approached her smiling and happy to see her after such a long time, but she snubbed me completely. She turned to me, greeted me with an unenthusiastic hello, and then turned back towards her friends, who stood by with

181

their pointed noses lifted towards the high ceiling of the Chapel with an air of frosty snobbery.

I was taken aback by Tamara's rebuff and her distance. Initially, I suspected she was paying me back for our childhood days on the block before her move to Burnsville. I had begun to play with Tina more than I played with her after Tina moved onto our block into a house directly across the alley from Tamara. The three of us could have played together, except Tamara did not like Tina at all.

My theory about the root of Tamara's snobbish behavior came crashing down after I had been attending Breck for a while. I discovered there was a completely different social hierarchy at that school than what I had been accustomed to in my neighborhood school. At Bancroft, there had also been groups of students who hung around together because they were friends. Unlike Bancroft, at Breck the cliques were much more exclusive. There was the in-crowd made up of the "cool kids," and then there was everyone else. Since most of the cool kids had known one another since kindergarten, I was relegated to membership of the out-crowd, which in seventh grade consisted of two Jewish girls, Rachel and Katy, and a few others who did not fit the category of WASP (White Anglo-Saxon Protestants) and/or had not attended Breck School since kindergarten.

I hated attending Breck School with a passion. I missed my neighborhood; I missed my childhood friends; I missed inner-city Black people. The few African Americans sprinkled throughout Breck's upper and lower schools lived in the suburbs, where their working knowledge and understanding of Black culture seemingly had been completely stripped from their vocabulary and behavior.

Admittedly, it was hard to hold on to African American culture, or any other culture, for that matter, other than that of WASP, in an environment like Breck School in my seventh-grade year, 1969 to 1970. There was tremendous pressure on everyone to be just like the next person. The word diversity had not yet been introduced into American society. Each student seemed to be trying so hard to be a snobbish clone of the next one that you were teased or ostracized if you fell outside of that norm.

For example, wearing natural hairstyles was being embraced by Black people all over the country instead of continuing to wear pressed or chemically relaxed hairstyles. "Black is beautiful" was the new concept of the times and one that the majority of African Americans were buying into. I wanted to wear my hair natural, so finally, my mom and dad gave in and let me cut my hair, so I could wear an Afro. As a result of my newly expressed Black pride, a few of Breck's white boys teased me about my hair, saying, "Hey Colnese, did you stick your finger in a light socket?" I refused to cave in and straighten my hair, however. I simply did what any self-respecting inner-city girl would do–I threatened to kick their asses.

"Oh, Colnese is a tough girl!" was their amused response, but they did not let up on taunting me about my hair.

The way I pronounced certain words was also mocked. At the lunch table, when I asked Mr. Kingsbury, my homeroom teacher, to pass me the bread, the boys would repeat, "Pass me the bray-ed." It was nerve-wracking, to say the least. Although it was a struggle at times, I was determined to hold on to my Blackness at all costs. Because I refused to assimilate, I was called a weirdo.

I remember going on a field trip with my seventh-grade classmates to the Minneapolis Institute of Art to see a play. I ran into some of my neighborhood friends from Bryant Junior High School. As we were boarding our buses to return to our respective schools, my neighborhood friends and I waved goodbye to one another. I was standing on the sidewalk near the Bryant Junior High School bus as a group of my neighborhood friends waved and called out to me from the windows of the school bus. Kate, one of the Breck girls, asked me in a haughty tone of voice with a sneer on her face, "Who *are* those people? What are *they* doing here?"

"They're my friends," I said longingly. I wished so desperately that I could click my heels together three times and be on the school bus with them heading back to Bryant Junior High School instead of returning to Breck.

Eighth grade at Breck was much better for me because a Black girl named Shonda began attending the school. She was from the 46th

Street neighborhood of Minneapolis, which was a few blocks south of my neighborhood and less rowdy. Shonda was both smart and down-to-earth. She also wore her hair in a natural hairstyle. I began to hang around with Shonda both in and out of school, so I got to know her friends, who hung out at Field School's playground after school. It was such a relief to have a friend at school that I could truly relate to, which caused me to relax and enjoy Breck School more.

Despite my relief due to Shonda's appearance at Breck, I still could not see myself going there all the way through high school. Constantly being around privileged white kids with a few members of the Black upper echelon sprinkled in felt stifling to me. I wanted to return to public school to lead what I considered to be a more normal life with a variety of people with different life experiences.

Finally, my parents relented and said I could go to Central High School's magnet program the following year. The magnet program attracted students from all over Minneapolis because it was an accelerated program, making it possible for me to skip ninth grade and graduate in three years. Because I had started kindergarten when I was four years old due to my November birthday, it meant I would begin tenth grade when I was only thirteen years old and potentially graduate at age sixteen if everything went well. I couldn't wait to get to Central High to reconnect with all my long-lost neighborhood friends.

◆ ◆ ◆

After sharing my story of attending Breck School during junior high with Jenny, she shared what she and her sister, Jessi Bates, had endured at the hands of the Black girls at Bryant Junior High School. According to Jenny, who was quite convincing, she and Jessi were forced to hold their own at Bryant by fighting nearly every day. I believed her. I knew most of the girls she referenced, and they were known bullies. Most of the white girls probably backed down from them, but not Jenny and Jessi Bates. They fought back and made quite a name for themselves.

When Jenny saw me on my first day at Fifth Northwestern Bank, she automatically thought of the Black girls at Bryant and wondered whether I would be like them. After telling her my story, which was equally as horrific as hers, we became very good friends. We had much in common, including our one-year-old daughters. Her baby's name was Arielle, but she went by Ari.

Jenny and I often picked our daughters up from daycare after work, and together we would head to the park or to one of our apartments for happy hour. Our toddlers would play together while we sipped from bottles of Pink Champale. Other times, we would ask the girls' fathers, DeAndre and Tim, to pick up the girls from their babysitters, so we could join the other bookkeeping staff after work for a real happy hour. The Uptown Bar and Grill was about a block from the bank. It had good drink specials and even better burgers.

Working at Fifth Northwestern Bank was fun, mainly because so many young women worked there. Most of us, who worked in the book-keeping department, were in our twenties. There was also a group of older ladies who got together every day to chit-chat during their coffee break. It was a super cool place to cut my adult working teeth. I started out as a check filer, and in less than a year, I was promoted to overdrafts clerk. A short time later, I was trained to be a teller.

CHAPTER 37

Trouble in Paradise

◆ ◆ ◆

When Destiny was around two or three years old, I caught on to a pattern that was emerging in my rocky relationship with DeAndre. I began to see how his mood swings and resulting behavior affected our on-again, off-again relationship. I noticed how he was more open to being actively involved in a relationship with me and our daughter, as long as he had no outside women interests. I also noticed how as soon as some other woman caught his eye, he went missing in action, leaving me and my hope for our future as a family ground into the dust.

If DeAndre had simply disappeared, maybe I could have handled it better than I did. But DeAndre's parting words were always caustic, rejecting, and harsh. They were also sudden and came bursting forth unexpectedly from a storm cloud that suddenly appeared in an otherwise clear blue sky, catching me off guard during those rare occasions when things seemed to be going right between us.

"Why don't you go find you a man and leave me alone?" he would snarl.

DeAndre's frequent about-face turns regarding our relationship opened the door to my desire to rekindle a romantic relationship with Blue. Because I knew Blue's first love was the almighty dollar bill, I knew money would always be the road to his heart. My strategy was simple: I liked cocaine. Blue sold cocaine. I would buy cocaine from Blue.

Money exchange would be my ticket into Blue's world. This arrangement worked just fine for a while. It helped that Blue liked cocaine, too, which meant that when I bought it from him, he was usually game to snort some blow with me. Soon we became involved again.

I thought we had a mutual understanding. I understood that he had a girlfriend and a baby and that he was involved with his baby's mother. When Destiny was three years old, Blue's girlfriend, Janelle, had given birth to a baby boy, who they named Royal Blue. I was happy about the baby because he was my deceased daughter's brother, as well as Blue's son. I saw Royal Blue whenever I visited the Lockett household. Because I continued to maintain my friendship with Blue's mother and sisters, I visited every so often.

Janelle was a few years younger than me, I thought, but I wasn't sure. She was pretty, petite, and dark-skinned. I had gone to Central High School with one of her brothers, Jerry, who had transferred from North High. He was extremely attractive with chiseled features and dark eyebrows. Janelle was just as attractive as Jerry, just a female version. I was surprised that Blue had settled down with a woman that was not a prostitute since he adhered so closely to the rules of the pimp game. I could tell he really cared about her. As far as I knew, Blue was also still involved with Alana.

Because I accepted his relationship with his son's mother, I thought Blue understood that my daughter's father, DeAndre, was also still in the picture. I had a great deal to learn about men and their double standards. Our so-called understanding all came crashing down one weekend after Blue had compromised his strict standards and spent the night with me. I owed him some money from our cocaine escapade the night before, so after my mother dropped Destiny off in the morning, we headed for the cash machine so I could pay him his due.

The next day was Sunday. When DeAndre came over to visit Destiny, we decided to go out to the Nacirema, a private club in South Minneapolis near the corner of 39th Street and 4th Avenue.

Because there wasn't much happening in the club scene on Sunday nights, everybody who wanted to party on Sunday went to the Nacirema, which had a live band, good drinks, and a sizeable dance floor. For some reason, that night, DeAndre and I dressed alike. He had on a maroon velvet suit, and I also had on a maroon velvet pantsuit. When I spotted Blue across the club, I acknowledged him by nodding my head, and he did the same. Other than that, the night was pretty uneventful. DeAndre and I had a few drinks, and then we headed home. Everything was all good. Or so I thought.

The following week, as I sat filing checks at Fifth Northwestern Bank and answering phone inquiries from customers about their checking account balances and what checks had cleared their accounts thus far, a call came in on the last phone line. I knew it was a personal call because incoming banking business calls rarely rolled over to that line, so that was the phone number I gave my family and friends to reach me during the workday.

"Is Colnese there?" I recognized Blue's voice.

As per usual, adrenaline shot through me. His voice and presence never ceased to elicit an emotional response.

"This is Colnese," I responded with a smile I hoped Blue could hear in my voice.

"Yeah, bitch, you gave me a disease, and you owe me some money," Blue said harshly.

I sat up straighter in my chair. "A disease? What are you talking about?"

"You know what I'm talking about. I got gonorrhea, and you owe me at least a couple hundred dollars. I'll be by there tomorrow to pick up my money, and you better have it."

"I didn't give you no disease, so you don't have nothing coming."

I knew my body well enough to know that if I had a venereal disease, I would have symptoms, which I did not. This I knew for certain, so I put the entire situation out of my mind for the time being. I knew, and Blue knew, that I wasn't the only woman he was dealing with intimately. I concluded that I was being used as a scapegoat. There was also the distinct possibility that Blue was lashing out in retaliation against me because of his male ego. He had seen me with DeAndre, so it was highly likely he was applying the age-old double standard which, for the life of me, I did not understand—men can have more than one woman, but women can have only one man. I ignored Blue's threat believing that he would eventually calm down and that his common sense would be restored.

The following Sunday, I went out to party at the Nacirema like I often did on Sunday nights. That night, the live band featured Sue Ann Carwell, a Saint Paul entertainer who could really sing. The night was nice but uneventful. The club was full but not overly packed. I briefly saw Gee Rich, but he left the club shortly after I saw him.

After Sue Ann had sung her final song, I filed out the front door behind the other clubgoers to head home and immediately got ambushed. Blue stepped out from the shadows behind the door and punched me in the face with all his might. He then disappeared into the night. My face right underneath my eye along my cheekbone split open upon impact, and my blood poured out onto the pavement in front of the Nacirema.

Mr. Ruffin, an older man from the neighborhood who did odd jobs for my parents on occasion, was walking out of the Nacirema right behind me. He saw what happened and offered to drive me to the hospital. I was stunned but nodded and followed him to his car, parked immediately across the street. The entire way to Hennepin County Medical Center's emergency room Mr. Ruffin lectured me about "no good men." I had heard enough stories about Mr. Ruffin when he was a younger man to firmly believe he was included in that category, but I refrained from commenting on it. Having no way of knowing for certain if the rumors were true, all I could do was sit there, listen, and occasionally nod to his advice about the importance of avoiding no good men as he transported me to the hospital.

Mr. Ruffin dropped me off at the emergency room and continued on his way. I checked in at the triage desk in the ER, had my vital signs checked, and was then assigned to a curtained-off cubicle where I stretched out on a hospital bed. After a considerable amount of time waiting to be seen, medical personnel finally showed up to cleanse my wound and tape it together using Steri-Strips. Next, I was given an opportunity to make a police report about the incident and was sent on my way. I caught a cab home, having no one else I could call at that time of night.

The assault by Blue ultimately cost me my relationship with DeAndre. He didn't want to get involved in any way because he said I didn't have any business messing with Blue in the first place. I learned a hard, cold lesson about the double standard between men and women in real time. In a very short length of time, I went from having two men to having none, and that's the way it stayed for a long, long time. DeAndre and I had always had a rocky relationship, but the incident with Blue made it even rockier. Every now and then, we would get back together for a short spell and then break up shortly thereafter. That pattern continued for a few more years.

When the fifth-degree assault case against Blue came before the judge, the city attorney offered Blue and me the opportunity to go to mediation to resolve the matter out of court. I was game to go through mediation, but Blue was not. The alternative was for me to press charges against him for domestic violence.

"If you press charges against me, I'm gonna whup your ass," Blue threatened me.

"Well, then that's one ass kicking I'm gonna have to take," was my sarcastic response.

"It's not gonna be one ass kicking," Blue clarified. "I'll whup your ass every time I see you."

In my misguided state of mind, I saw mediation as a way to work out my differences with Blue and get back on good terms with him, but he wasn't going for it. Seeing no possible way to come out ahead in the situation, I dropped the charges and cut my losses.

The force of the blow Blue inflicted gave me a black eye in addition to the gash under it. Destiny, who was two years old at the time, questioned me about it while we were on the bus on our way from the babysitter's house after work one day.

"What happened to your eye?" she wondered aloud as she sat facing me on my lap.

"Blue hit me," I replied.

"Blue hit you?" she questioned. She looked worried about the new development in my life.

"Yeah, Blue hit me," I responded and then turned to look out the bus window.

I did not believe in sugarcoating the facts of my life, no matter how raw they might be, even to my own child. Hopefully, showing Destiny what life was all about—the good, the bad, and the ugly—would help her avoid the pitfalls I had stumbled upon thus far in my life, which were many.

CHAPTER 38

Searching

◆ ◆

The final showdown with Blue coupled with my up-and-down, in-and-out relationship with DeAndre caused the question about my birth mother and biological family, which always lurked just beneath the surface, to resurface and float back into my consciousness. It was not the first time. Another incident had taken place shortly after I had moved into my own apartment when I was eighteen years old. At that time, I attempted to obtain information about my adoption from my brother's godfather, Raymond Cannon, the attorney who had presided over my adoption.

Raymond Cannon lived in San Diego, so I called him long distance and asked him if he had any records related to my adoption. After a few minutes of catching up with one another about our respective families, he told me he would look into it and get back to me. Several days later, he called and gave me my birth mother's name, Nancy Hanson.

I immediately looked in the White Pages phone book and was overwhelmed by the number of Hansons listed. I knew there was no possible way I could find my birth mother without assistance. When I contacted the Hennepin County Department of Vital Statistics, the person who answered the phone told me the steps I would need to take to initiate a search. These included writing a letter to the Department of Vital Statistics, which would contact the adoption agency. In my case, it was the Children's Home Society. The process sounded too daunting to undertake. Just like when I was a child, I wanted immediate answers. Not being able to get them frustrated me, so at that time, I let the idea of conducting a search for my birth mother go.

After the big breakup though, I decided that the time to search was now or never, so I moved forward and kicked off the search by writing the requisite letter to the Department of Vital Statistics. Unfortunately, Mayiko Ito, the caseworker who contacted me shortly thereafter from the Children's Home Society, encountered the same hopeless situation I had. Finding a Nancy Hanson in Minnesota, who was unmarried at the time of my birth, but who was possibly married by that time, was highly unlikely.

"I'm sorry, but I just don't see any viable way of locating your birth mother without additional identifying information," she said.

I was disappointed, but I took the news in stride. I was twenty-two years old, and I had not known who my birth mother was or where she was for my entire life. I would simply have to continue down the same path I had been on up until that point. I had to accept the bitter fact of being completely lost with no way of finding out who I was, and therefore, having a difficult time determining where I was going in life. My entire focus was on my identity or lack thereof. Until that issue was resolved, my life and its possibilities remained on hold.

CHAPTER 39

Transitions

◈ ◈ ◈

All good things must come to an end. After two years of working at Fifth Northwestern Bank, I lost my job because I called in sick one time too many. I was still partying, and sometimes I partied too hard and didn't feel like getting up in the morning and going to work. Lois, my boss, refused to call in sick because of partying. She explained her philosophy to me one day after the team had gone out drinking the night before. Our desks were right across from one another, so we often chatted during the day. Lois was admittedly hungover, but she had dragged herself to work anyway.

When I questioned her about why she hadn't just stayed home, she said simply, "When you play, you gotta pay."

It made sense, but still, I called in one day after being out at an after-hours party so late the birds were singing when I finally left the party to go home. My plan was to sleep an hour or so and then get up and go to work, but when the time came, I just wasn't up to it.

I was crushed when I lost my job, but I wasted no time looking for another one. The next day I called First Bank Plymouth, a bank on Plymouth Avenue right in the heart of the 'hood. Millie, the branch manager, told me they had an opening for a teller and gave me an appointment to come in and fill out an application. I was hired on the spot. Ecstatic to have a second chance, I vowed to myself to never frivolously call in sick again. It is said experience is the best teacher, and in the case of losing my job, it has proven to be true. After being fired, I fully understood what Lois meant by her wise words. It is perfectly fine to have fun, but your responsibility to your job comes first, since that is how you earn your bread and butter.

Working at First Bank Plymouth was very similar to working at Fifth Northwestern Bank in many respects: The type of work that was done, the various banking products, and the processes used to transact banking business. At the same time, it was very different. Where most of the staff and customers at Fifth Northwestern Bank had been white, the majority of the staff and customers at First Bank Plymouth were Black, which caused the bank to have a completely different vibe. It was much more laid back. For example, instead of elevator music, we jammed to KMOJ Radio, the local soul station, while we worked.

Fifth Northwestern Bank was located within walking distance of Lake Calhoun and Lake of the Isles, where wealthy people lived in huge mansions. Conversely, First Bank Plymouth was located in a poor to middle-class Black neighborhood where many people lived in public or subsidized housing. Others lived across Penn Avenue in the Willard Homewood neighborhood in beautiful homes that had been formerly owned and occupied by well-to-do Jews. That was prior to their fleeing the neighborhood and relocating to St. Louis Park, a first-ring suburb, after the race riots of the 1960s. Now many prominent African American families occupied those spacious and lovely homes.

My mom worked a couple blocks from the bank at Pilot City Health Center. Estes Funeral Chapel, home of a Black-owned mortuary, was a block from the bank. The bank's clientele was made up primarily of a mixture of poor, working-class, and middle-class Black people, and a few white customers and a mixture of Black and white business owners. Most of my co-workers on the teller line were also in their twenties, and we had a blast at work pretty much every day.

Not long after I started, an opening for a customer service position was posted. I applied for it and received a promotion. My new job duties included opening new accounts, helping customers reconcile their accounts, and cross-selling the bank's other products, for example, certificates of deposits, money-market accounts, and savings and checking accounts. I also continued to back up the tellers when they needed help.

One day, as the afternoon progressed, I looked up at the clock on the bank's wall. As far as I was concerned, three o'clock p.m. could not arrive fast enough. I was way past ready to get up from my desk and lock the doors of the bank, so the tellers could begin to balance their drawers before I could call the workday a done deal. I was just about finished helping Mr. Small, an old man sitting in front of me and stalling his way through the process of opening a bank account.

I had opened an account for him at least three times before, so I already knew it was a blank mission. He would put ten dollars in the bank to avoid a check cashing fee, and then by the end of the month, he would come into the bank full of ignorant oil and close his account. It was always a dramatic occasion. He would rear back on his legs, stick out his scrawny chest, and when all eyes were on him, he would declare in an angry and demanding tone, "Give me *all* my money out of this here bank!"

I knew from past experience that Mr. Small couldn't read and write very well, so I retrieved the bank application and pen from him and began to walk him through the questions to speed the process along, but he was being rebellious.

"Sir, what is your phone number?"

"Phone?" he asked, looking perplexed by the question. "I don't have a phone."

"Okay," I said.

I wrote "N/A" in the box on the application where his phone number was supposed to go. I then moved on to the next question.

"What is your social security number?"

But Mr. Small was not in the mood to be hurried along.

"How much a phone cost a month?"

"I don't know, maybe about fifteen or twenty dollars a month," I answered. "Your social security number is . . . ?"

"How much would the phone cost for a whole year?" he asked while wrinkling his brow and studying me intently.

"Uh," I stalled while I used my calculator, math not being my strong point. "About two hundred and forty dollars a year."

Mr. Small looked at me as if I had lost my ever-loving mind. "Two hundred and forty dollars a year? Hell, I could buy two hundred and forty dollars' worth of beer!"

What a character.

I rested my forehead in my palm and shook my head. Right when I thought I had seen and heard it all, here comes Mr. Small with his off-base logic. The two of us obviously thought about how to spend money in a completely different way. In my way of thinking, a telephone was like a lifeline to the outside world; therefore, I would much rather spend my money talking on the phone for a year than guzzling down two hundred and forty dollars' worth of beer. But as they say, "Different strokes for different folks."

I glanced out the bank's huge plate glass window across the street to the parking lot of Staten Liquor Store, where Mr. Small's running buddies spent the better part of their lives sipping on wine from the bottle, usually under the cover of a brown paper bag, or guzzling cans of beer and philosophizing about the world in which we live. Just as I couldn't imagine my life without a phone, Mr. Small couldn't imagine his life without beer.

Oh, well, to each his own.

I smiled pleasantly at the old man across from me.

"You're sure right," I agreed.

After we had reached a consensus on the value of beer compared to the cost of having a phone, we were finally ready to quickly finish the application. I made Mr. Small's ten-dollar deposit, gave him his receipt, and sent him on his way. I was resigned to the fact that before the end of the month, he would close out his account and retrieve the ten dollars it took to keep it open.

There were truly some real live characters who visited First Bank Plymouth. They helped to make my day. Without the excitement of the bank customers' varied personalities, my days would not have been quite so interesting. After being entertained by the customers all day, on Tuesday evenings after work, the bank staff went roller skating at the Northgate Roller Rink down the street.

Working at First Bank Plymouth also made it possible to work close to my mom around the corner at Pilot City Health Center. She was a nurse practitioner assigned to work with pregnant women. There were very few women in North Minneapolis of childbearing age who did not know her. I had a feeling having my mom as their nurse kept me out of some fights in the neighborhood. There continued to be rivalry between the Northside and Southside, but once they knew I was Bernese

Hendon's daughter, the love and respect they had for my mom helped neutralize the situation and cause would-be adversaries to leave me alone. My mom was very popular with her patients because of her caring and compassionate nature. She was a mother to her core and could not seem to help mothering anyone within range.

Not long after I began working at First Bank Plymouth, I decided to transfer Destiny to Northside Child Development Center, which was right down the street from the bank. I knew it was a good preschool because I had worked there when I was eighteen years old. Many of the staff I had worked with were still there. But I was a bit worried about how my daughter, Destiny, would adjust to Northside Child Development Center. She had been cared for by Barbara Nell since she was a year old. Barbara Nell had made Destiny an honorary member of the Caldwell family. There were days when I arrived late to pick her up only to find Destiny sitting at the dinner table with Barbara Nell, her husband, and their four children eating pork chops or fried chicken with macaroni and cheese, green beans, and all the fixings.

Destiny and I would miss the loving care Barbara Nell and her family had always provided, but now it was time for Destiny to move into a preschool setting where she would be in closer proximity to my new job. I hoped she would thrive at Northside Child Development Center the same way I had.

CHAPTER 40

Mulatto Blues

◆ ◈ ◈

My relationship with DeAndre was in shambles, and I did not want to run into him celebrating the holiday with someone else at one of the popular hangouts where Black people regularly gathered over holiday weekends like Glenwood Lake, Powderhorn Park, and the North Beach of Lake Calhoun, now known as Lake Bde Maka Ska. Therefore, I decided to go to Chicago for the Fourth of July weekend. I wanted and needed a break from Minneapolis, so I decided to visit my dad's sister, Auntie Marge.

We spent the holiday having a cookout over at her son Norval's house with his family, which included his wife, Odessa, and their three sons, as well as Odessa's sister and her daughters. Destiny played with their youngest son, Doug. On Sunday morning, we were sitting together in my Auntie Marge's living room watching the news and reading the Sunday paper when she posed a question. "You know what I've always wondered?"

"No, what's that?" Because we were watching the news, I assumed she wondered something about what was on the screen.

"I've always wondered why as dark as my brother is, your mother would go out and adopt such white-looking kids."

For a few seconds, I was speechless. In my extended adoptive family, I had never heard my adoption mentioned. In fact, after my mother read *The Adopted Family* to Ira and me when we were very small, adoption was never again mentioned in our immediate family. It was a deeply buried secret. If my adoption was talked about, it was never in front of me, so I was doubly shocked. I was shocked the subject had been brought out of the closet into the light. I was even more shocked that after twenty-four years of being a part of the family, my skin tone was still such a source of discomfort for my Auntie Marge.

After a few seconds of silence, I attempted to help resolve the mystery for my aunt by hazarding a guess, which was probably not far from the truth. "I don't know. Maybe there weren't any darker-skinned kids to choose from."

The Black families I knew kept the children of family members within their family, including those born out of wedlock and those in need of care due to other extenuating circumstances, such as incarceration, drug addiction, alcoholism, and other factors. Grandmothers and aunts often raised the children of unmarried family members and those too young to take care of their babies.

Thinking back to the taunts about dark skin on the playground of Warrington Elementary School, the hurtful rhymes we sang as we jumped rope, and Nettie's comment in first grade about my "ole black daddy," I understood from firsthand experience the ugliness and negative impact colorism and being "color-struck" had on the Black community. I also knew my brother Ira wasn't the only light-skinned child who was ever bullied by darker-skinned people because of skin tone alone. Many in the Black community believed light skin equaled weakness, or they were resentful of those possessing it because of the persecution they may have experienced because of their darker skin.

I even understood my aunt's initial concern about the importance of my mom and dad adopting children whose skin tone and looks more closely resembled those of my dad's. But, in spite of her concern, I knew beyond a shadow of a doubt that my dad loved me and accepted me as his daughter despite my light skin, and up until that moment, I thought she did, too. My aunt's words hurt me deeply. They reminded me that despite all the years I had been a member of the family, I continued to remain an outsider. Apparently, my light skin and lack of blood ties continued to set me apart.

CHAPTER 41

First Bank Plymouth

◈ ◈ ◈

My day just wasn't going right at First Bank Plymouth. On top of finding out the bank was closing and the majority of us were going to lose our jobs, I had taken a bite out of a fish sandwich that belonged to a nasty-looking old white man with a dirty beard. My friend Pat's teller window and mine were side-by-side. It was the first of the month, as well as Friday, so the bank was packed with people wanting to cash their welfare checks, SSI checks, and paychecks, as well as to conduct other banking business. There had been no time for a break, and I was hungry.

Pat was at the back counter encoding a cashier's check with the requested dollar amount when I spotted a half-eaten fish sandwich on her side of the teller space we shared. I held it up in her general direction and raised my eyebrows quizzically. She nodded, so I took a big bite out of it. A few customers later, I asked if I could have another bite.

"Oh, I threw that sandwich in the trash," she answered.

"Girl, as hungry as I am, you threw your sandwich in the trash?" I asked incredulously.

"That wasn't my sandwich. That was that old white man's sandwich," she replied nonchalantly.

"Not that old white man with the beard that looked like bugs were crawling around in it?

"Uh-huh," she answered casually as she handed her customer his cash-filled envelope.

"Do you mean to tell me you let me eat after that man?" I asked in a shocked tone of voice.

"I thought you knew it was his. Didn't you see him hand it to me to throw away? I just hadn't gotten around to it. Is that why you were showing it to me? You wanted a bite?" Pat asked mildly. "I thought you were fixing to throw it away."

"Girl, hell no. I thought it was yours, and I was asking you for a bite of it. I think I'm going to throw up," I declared, leaning over the trash can melodramatically.

Pat looked at me sympathetically for a couple of seconds and then turned to face the customer making her way to the teller window. Pat's low-key demeanor was why we got along so well. Pat was always cool, calm, and collected while I tended to fly off the handle. Our opposite personalities offset one another. Except, that is, until later that day when a customer slapped Pat in the face because she wouldn't cash his check. That's when Pat lost it.

The offending party was on his way out the bank door when Pat picked up her heavy glass Coke bottle and aimed it at him. Mr. Warder, the bank president, saw what was happening and ran across the bank lobby to place himself between Pat and the customer. The primary problem was that it was far too late in the game to cease the action.

"Young lady!" Mr. Warder uttered while frantically shaking his head no at Pat and waving his finger from side to side. He had started walking towards her when, in her uncontrollable fury, Pat let go of the bottle. In my mind's eye, I can still envision the pop bottle flying through the air in a perfect arc before hitting Mr. Warder's belly with a resounding thud.

Mr. Warder let out a gasp, and his open mouth formed the letter "O." Meanwhile, Pat was yelling all types of curse words at the customer's retreating back. When I saw the bottle hit Mr. Warder in the stomach, I froze. The stool I had picked up to assist my friend was still cocked back over my left shoulder, ready to swing.

After a second or two of silence, Mr. Warder regained his ability to speak. "Colnese, do you want your job?" he asked, giving me a stern look. "I want to see the both of you in my office."

Pat and I looked at each other wordlessly and then obediently followed Mr. Warder across the bank lobby towards his large corner office. Since childhood, I had known Mr. Warder because he and my dad were both members of Zion Baptist Church. As I followed him into his office, I hung my head in shame. I knew Mr. Warder's stomach had to be hurting badly, so I felt contrite and humble. Meanwhile, Pat was still pissed off.

Both of us took a seat in one of the two chairs facing his mahogany, executive-sized desk. My heart was pounding hard because I sincerely believed Mr. Warder was going to fire us. Instead, he looked at us gravely before asking, "Should we pray?"

Pat and I glanced at each other out of the corner of our eyes before bowing our heads and praying silently along with Mr. Warder's heartfelt prayer. I began to relax. Whenever Mr. Warder suggested prayer, it usually resulted in him being in a more forgiving mood afterwards. Indeed, divine providence was on our side because that is exactly what transpired. After praying with us, Mr. Warder lectured us about professionalism and how to handle a situation like that if it ever were to occur again in the future.

"Do you have anything to say for yourself?" he asked Pat.

"Only that I'm sorry, but he didn't have any business putting his hands on me."

"You're absolutely right. He didn't have any business putting his hands on you, but that is why we have a security guard on the premises. You are too nice of a young lady to be carrying on like that," Mr. Warder said firmly.

Pat nodded her head somberly.

"And what about you, Colnese? What were you planning on doing with that chair?"

"Well," I began hesitantly, not wanting to get Mr. Warder riled up again. "I guess I was scared when I saw him slap Pat, and I wanted to protect myself in case he decided to double back and slap me, too."

"Now, Colnese, you and I both know that you were far from being scared. You wanted to retaliate against him with that chair for slapping Pat, now, didn't you?"

I hung my head and nodded with what I hoped came across as a remorseful and contrite attitude.

"In the future, you leave that to the security guard, hear?" he demanded.

"Yes, Mr. Warder." I agreed in a meek voice.

Satisfied that we had learned our lesson, Mr. Warder dismissed us with a final warning. "Don't let anything like that ever happen again."

After we both nodded our heads in agreement, Pat and I got up to leave Mr. Warder's office. We were pleased to find that the bank had closed, and it was time to balance. We closed our teller windows, ran our cash-in and cash-out totals, and began to count our cash drawers.

"Do you want to go down to the Elks Club to play Ms. Pac-Man?" I asked.

"Yeah, I don't care," agreed Pat.

"Okay, I need to get me some quarters then."

I grabbed a couple rolls of quarters and dumped them into my purse. Pat also grabbed a roll of quarters and stuffed it in the pocket of her sweater. On payday, we would return the coins to their proper place in our coin cabinets. Then we each locked the rest of our coin trays in the lower cabinets beneath our teller windows, slid the covers to our cash drawers into place, and locked them. We then lifted them up and out of our drawers to carry them down to the vault downstairs in the basement.

Mrs. Summers, the stylishly dressed comptroller, who was old enough to be our mother, was sitting at her desk in front of the vault.

"Good evening, ladies. Are we in balance?"

"Yes, ma'am," replied Pat.

"Yes, we are," I agreed.

"Good," intoned Mrs. Summers. We went through the same ritual every evening, so we all understood and played our roles perfectly.

CHAPTER 42

The First of the Month

◆ ◆ ◆

Once again, it was the first of the month, which was always a busy time at First Bank Plymouth. The North Minneapolis neighborhood was alive and full of activity on the first. People had money in their pockets, places to go, and people to see. I had spent most of my day opening bank accounts and okaying checks to be cashed. As I glanced up from my desk towards the teller line, I was pleasantly surprised to see my good friend, Leora, standing in line waiting to cash her check.

"Leora!" I called out and waved to catch her attention. I got up and walked over to where she stood in the teller line.

"Hey, girl? How you doin'?" asked Leora, her signature dimple deepening attractively in her right cheek. My enthusiasm and excitement to see my friend and the mother of my godchildren bubbled over.

"I'm good. How're you doin'? It's good to see you—you're lookin' good, as usual."

"Honey, please, I'm just trying to get this check cashed, girl, get this money right quick, but this line is too muhfuckin' long. Could you help me out?" Leora asked. "I left Leon at home watching the kids, so I got to get back to the house soon. I ain't got all day to be up in here. Johnny is coming by later to drop me off a package, if you know what I mean, so I got to be there to get it."

"Okay, girl, hold up. Go sit at my desk—I'll be right back. Give me your ID. You know how they be trippin'."

Leora dug into a large, oversized bag and handed me her ID, then went and sat down on one of the two chairs facing my desk. I went behind the teller line, handed my friend Pat Leora's check to cash, and soon I was on my way back to the desk with a bank envelope and a cashier's check.

"Here you go, Miss Lady. Here's a cashier's check for your rent and the rest of your money. I can't have you blowing your rent money on cocaine."

"Girl, and you know it! Good lookin' out, Colnese. You know what they say, one hit is too many, and a thousand hits ain't enough," Leora said laughing. "But seriously, though, you should come by the house later on when you get off work. We're gonna be partyin' girl, groovin', and you know your godchildren would love to see you."

"I wish I could, but you know I have to go to group tonight, Education for Cooperative Living. I'm court ordered to go."

"Damn, what the fuck did you do, bust out DeAndre's windows again?"

"Hell-to-the-yes. I most certainly did break out his windows with the quickness."

"How many times does this make?" Leora asked with her lips pursed, causing the dimple in her cheek to be even more pronounced. "You're a mess, girl. You are too much. James Brown got the words wrong, talkin' 'bout 'Papa Don't Take No Mess.' He should have been singin' 'Colnese Don't Take No Mess.'"

"It was my third time, but this time I went to jail, girl. I offered to pay restitution, but the judge sent me to this class to 'learn how to manage my anger'—that's what the judge said. I know how to manage my anger. All DeAndre needs to do is stop playing with my emotions, and then we'll be straight. Poof, anger all gone."

"Every time y'all break up, Colnese, you end up breaking that man's windows out. Maybe you need to call it quits. He's just bringing you down."

"You're right. I made up my mind when I was in that jail cell that this time I am done. He cheats too much, and when he gets caught cheating, he talks shit. This time he went too far, though, which is why he got his windows broken out.

"I called over there, and he told me, 'I got company. Go find you somebody else and leave me alone.' And girl, we had just got back from taking a trip down to Oklahoma together, so Destiny could meet his people down there. I thought things were looking up in our relationship. Then without any warning, he pulls some mess like that a week after we got back to Minnesota, so you know I had to spank that ass.

"I went to his house, right? And the coward wouldn't come outside, so what choice did I have but to break out his windows? Something about the sound of glass breaking gives me such a release of tension that if I could bottle up that feeling and sell it, I'd be rich, know what I'm sayin'? And with his whorish ways, at least once a year, I get to the point that if I don't release some tension, I'm going to kill him, I swear to God I am."

"All I can say is, you need to leave him alone once and for all," advised Leora. "As my mama would say, there's too many fishes in the sea."

"Yeah, I guess you're right. Gloria, the lady who leads my group, is a therapist. She says most likely the reason I go off like that is because of my inability to tolerate rejection. She thinks it stems back to my feelings about being adopted."

"No tellin'. Adopted or not, nobody wants to be mistreated, and De-Andre takes the cake. He acts like his shit don't stank. Well, anyway, I got to go, but thanks again for helping me out. Come on by after group and have a drink and a toot of blow if you want to."

"Yeah, I'll see—I might come by. If so, I'll see you later."

After Leora left, the head teller came over to my desk.

"Colnese, would you mind covering the teller line for about a half hour while the other tellers take their breaks?"

"No problem." I got up from my desk and went over to the teller line to relieve one of the tellers. After I unlocked my drawer and got situated, the next customer stepped over to my teller window.

"Good morning, Ernestine," I said. "How are you doin'? How can I help you?"

"I can't complain. I need my check cashed, and I need to get three money orders—one for 32 dollars and 15 cents, one for 26 dollars and 52 cents, and one for 257 dollars and 92 cents. Lord, my gas bill is so high this month. Well, actually, it's been high since wintertime. I'm paying it down little by little. Once it's paid off, I'm going to get on the budget plan. That way, I only have to pay 60 dollars a month."

"Yeah, that sounds good," I responded. "Here, just write your account number on the back of the check. As you know, there is a service charge of one dollar for each money order. Have you ever considered opening a checking account? We have a dime-a-time account—no minimum balance and just one thin dime per check, which beats paying a dollar per money order."

"Yeah, I thought about it, but not this month. I guess I'm old school. I like to cash my check and have my money readily available. Too many people I know with checking accounts have gotten their money gobbled up in overdraft charges. But I will definitely think more about it and get back to you next time I'm in the bank.

"On another note, I saw your baby daddy, DeAndre, standing in front of the bank just now right before I walked in here talkin' about he's getting married. Who is he getting married to, you?"

"Hell no. That's the first I've heard of it, but I wouldn't be surprised. I'm done with him and all his drama. Let the next woman deal with his philandering ways. Let me get you your money orders so you can be on your way."

I turned away from my customer and went to the counter behind the teller line to encode the money orders. Upon my return to my teller window, I used the adding machine to determine how much cash Ernestine had coming back to her after deducting the money orders and fees. Finally, I went into my teller drawer to count out her change.

"Ma'am, here are your money orders, and you have 217 dollars and 41 cents coming back to you." I counted it out to her aloud. "Have a nice day."

"All right then, you too. Thanks so much."

"May I help whoever's next?"

Donny walked up to my window.

"What's up, Colnese? When you gonna get with me? You know you like me."

"Quit playing, Donny. Yes, I like you, but not in that way. What can I do for you, Donny?"

"I need you to cash this check for me. I don't have my ID, but you know me, Colnese."

"Donny, do you have an account with First Bank Plymouth?"

"I used to, but I closed it last month. I needed that ten dollars, but I'm gonna open it up again, probably next month."

"Well, in that case, there is a three-dollar check cashing fee for non-customers."

"Come on now, baby, don't do me like that. I can't afford no three dollars. How about you let me put that three dollars to the side, and I promise you, I'll buy you a drink next time you come down to the Elks Club. You still drink Christian Brothers and Coke?"

"And you know it. All right, Donny, you're getting on my nerves. I'll waive the fee this time, but don't ask me again. I'm not fin' to lose my job over a check cashing fee."

"Thanks, baby. Did I ever tell you how beautiful I think you are? You really need to give me a chance, especially since DeAndre is getting married. He's posted up out there in front of the bank right now, running his mouth about it. When I heard it, I thought to myself, opportunity knocks, so what do you say, Colnese?"

"I say, 'Here is your money, Donny. Now go on.'"

"All right, Colnese," he replied, chuckling while extending his hand to retrieve his funds from me. "Enjoy your day. Thanks, hear?"

I nodded and beckoned to help the next person in line. I was tripping, but I was trying hard not to show it. So DeAndre was standing outside my job, telling everybody who passed by on their way into the bank that he was getting married to another woman. That was the type of behavior that, in the very recent past, had caused me to go off on him. But since I had spent the night in jail for criminal damage to property after taking my hammer to his garden-level apartment window, I was determined that I was not going to continue down that road with him. DeAndre obviously loved the negative attention he received after provoking me. As far as I was concerned, the game was officially over.

I went on with my day at the bank as if my child's father was not standing literally twenty steps away from where I was helping customers attempting to publicly humiliate me in front of my coworkers and friends. From past experience, I now recognized it for what it was—an obvious attempt to stir up my emotions and provoke my wrath once again. But with God's help, I was getting stronger.

◈ ◈ ◈

One evening as I was on the 4th Avenue bus headed to my parents' house after work, I noticed an older man looking at me. He was medium brown-skinned, had a prominent nose, was slender built, and appeared to be in his mid-forties. First, he glanced back at me nonchalantly, and then he turned all the way around in his seat to take a harder look. As I glanced in his direction, I was surprised that he continued to stare at me intently with a penetrating glare.

The man's continued stare caught me off guard. I was accustomed to people averting their eyes when caught in the act of staring. Uncomfortable by his unwavering gaze, I was finally forced to look away. During the awkward moments of the stare-down between the man and me, I became convinced that he must be a little off, so I was relieved when he rang the bell signaling the bus to stop, so he could get off. My relief dissipated somewhat when I saw him heading down the aisle my way. I was seated immediately behind the rear exit.

Here we go.

I was expecting some type of drama from him as he exited, so I was surprised when he just nodded his head and simply said, "Later."

Oh, well, maybe he's not so strange after all.

I pulled the cord to alert the driver of my intent to exit the bus and thought no more about it.

CHAPTER 43

Discovery

◆ ◆ ◆

In addition to backing up the teller line at First Bank Plymouth, I also backed up the receptionist occasionally by answering the phone.

"Good morning, First Bank Plymouth. May I help you?"

"May I speak to Colnese Hendon, please?"

"This is Colnese Hendon speaking."

"Colnese, this is Mayiko Ito from the Children's Home Society."

"Mayiko, what a surprise; how are you? We haven't spoken for, what, three or four years? How did you track me down? The last time we talked, I was working at Fifth Northwestern Bank."

"You're right, Colnese. It has been quite some time. The last time we talked, I told you I was unable to locate your birth mother because her last name, Hanson, is such a common name here in Minnesota because there are so many Scandinavians," Mayiko recalled. "I am about to retire very soon. There were a few files, in addition to yours, that I decided to make one more attempt to resolve prior to my retirement."

"Okay," I prompted when Mayiko paused.

"When I looked back over your file, I noticed that your birth mother had three brothers at the time of your birth—Erick, Rune, and Leo. Because the names Rune and Leo are not so common, I attempted to locate them. Colnese, I am happy to tell you I was successful. I was able to contact your Uncle Leo, and through him, I found your birth mother, Nancy. I spoke to her today, and she wants to meet you."

I was so shocked and overcome with emotion, I was unable to respond. Tears spilled out of my eyes and rolled down my cheeks.

"Hello, Colnese, are you there?"

Voice thick with tears, I answered, "Yes, I'm here."

"Are you still interested in meeting your birth mother? She is very anxious to meet you."

"Yes, I am. I want to meet her."

I simply could not believe what was happening to me. This could not be real. The news had come out of the blue, and I was having a hard time holding it together. I'd heard of the term "out-of-body experience," which clearly fit the description. In my wildest dreams, although I had hoped for this day, I had never imagined what it would actually feel like if I ever found my birth mother, and now that it was happening, I was overwhelmed by my sense of relief and the intensity of my emotions.

"Is it all right with you if I give her your phone number at the bank so she can call you and make arrangements to meet?"

"Yes, it is. Thank you so much, Mayiko," I said. "You have no idea what this means to me."

"I think I do. I am so pleased that I've been able to help you with your search. I'm going to call Nancy back and give her your contact information. Take care, Colnese, goodbye."

"Thank you so much, Mayiko," I responded. "Bye."

I hung up the phone, covered my face with my hands, and with my shoulders heaving, shed tears of tremendous joy and relief.

Nancy and I spoke on the phone for the first time not long after that and made plans to meet later that day at her house, on the Northside of Minneapolis, not far from the bank where I worked. After work, I picked up Destiny from Northside Child Development Center and caught the bus to my parents' house to tell them the news that I was going to meet my birth mother. I cared about how my parents felt about the news, but meeting Nancy was something I needed to do.

"Maybe you should leave Destiny over here," my mom suggested. "After all, we are the only grandparents she has ever known."

I agreed that I should leave Destiny with them while I met my birth mother for the first time. Destiny was only six years old and would find it confusing and hard to understand that I had another mother. It was mind-blowing to me, as well, and I was twenty-six years old. We talked a bit more about how Mayiko found Nancy and my subsequent conversation with Nancy. Then I got ready to catch the bus to the address Nancy had provided. I walked two blocks to 4th Avenue, where I caught the number nine, Glenwood-4th Avenue bus to the Northside.

After getting off the bus at Glenwood and Knox Avenues and walking north a block and a half, I found myself standing in front of my birth mother's house. It was hard to believe that all the time I had wondered who and where she was, she was living right on the Northside. Her house was only a short distance from Zion Baptist Church where I had attended services with my dad most Sundays while growing up; Phyllis Wheatley Community Center, where I had worked at Camp Parsons during my teen years, was right down the street; First Bank Plymouth where I worked was only blocks away. She lived in close proximity to Pilot City Health Center where my mom still worked. Nancy's house was not far from where DeAndre's family lived in the projects or from Blue's family's home on Sheridan Avenue. It was mind-blowing that Nancy lived so close to the most important and meaningful places I frequented. Right smack dab in the middle of my everyday life, Nancy was nearby.

The moment I had been waiting for most of my life had finally arrived. I looked around my birth mother's yard and at her house. *The house looks decent enough, and the yard is well kept,* I thought. I stood there for a few seconds trying to get up the nerve to approach the house. Finally, I squared my shoulders, mounted the stairs, and rang the doorbell. I could hear a dog barking within the house, and then a walnut, brown-skinned man with a medium-sized, slender frame opened the door. He was smiling broadly and held his hand out to shake mine.

"Hi, how are you? I'm Lou, Nancy's husband. Come right on in. We are so excited to meet you."

A few feet behind Lou standing in his shadow was Nancy, a slender white woman with long, wavy, mixed grey hair cascading down her back and bangs framing her face. A pretty, mixed-race teenage girl with light skin, slanted eyes, and long dark brown hair with highlights, stood next to Nancy, holding an adorable baby boy with black curly hair. She was also smiling widely. Nancy and I embraced, but surprisingly there were no tears. Nancy stepped back to take a good look at me.

"I've often wondered if you survived," she remarked.

I was startled by the irony of her comment. My birth mother, the primary person responsible for protecting my life, had instead given me up for adoption and then wondered over the years if I had survived. I tried to think of an appropriate response.

"Yes, I did survive," was the only response I could come up with as scenes from my childhood and turbulent teen years flashed through my mind.

I returned from my trip down memory lane initiated by Nancy's question about whether I had survived and refocused on the real-life scene playing out in front of me. I was meeting my birth mother after twenty-six years of life in which she had played no role other than the mysterious phantom mother as the backdrop to my life. Her husband Lou jumped into the conversation and alleviated the awkwardness of the moment.

"Well, Colnese, have a seat. Make yourself at home."

"I've seen you before," the pretty teenage girl said, beaming at me.

"Colnese, this is my daughter," Nancy introduced us. "Your sister, Davetta."

"People call me China," my sister said.

"I've always wanted a sister," I exclaimed. "I'm so happy to meet you."

"Did you grow up with any siblings?" Nancy wanted to know.

"Yes, I have a brother," I replied. "He's a few years older than me. I think I've seen you somewhere before too, China. You look familiar."

I shifted my attention to her baby. "What's his name? How old is he? He's so cute!" I rattled. "Do you think he'll let me hold him? I can't believe I'm an auntie."

China passed the baby—my nephew—into my outstretched arms.

"His name is Brian Keith. He just turned seven months. Do you have any children? It seems like I've seen you with a little girl."

"Yes, I do. I have a little girl named Destiny. She's six."

"Where is she? Why didn't you bring her?" asked Nancy.

"Oh, I dropped her off at my parents' house. My mom and dad thought it was best if I met you first."

"Oh, I understand, but I'm anxious to meet her, so we'll have to get together again real soon."

"Yes, definitely," I agreed. "My parents are in support of me meeting you but said that Destiny has always known only them as grandparents.

I'm sure they'll eventually come around, but it might take some time. They understand how important the reunion is to me, and even though they accept me meeting you, having Destiny meet you at the same time would be quite a bit for them to swallow all at once."

"I can imagine that it would be," Nancy agreed. "I guess things will work out eventually."

"This is blowing my mind," exclaimed China. "Every time I see you, I can't help but stare at you. Now that I know you're my sister, it makes sense. It almost seems like I must have subconsciously sensed some type of connection with you."

"Where have you seen me?" I asked.

"Mainly up on Plymouth Avenue."

"Yeah, I work at First Bank Plymouth. I've been working there for about four years."

"Oh, really? I bank there!" exclaimed Nancy. "It's such a small world."

"You bank there? I wonder why I've never seen you."

"I usually go through the drive-through every other week on payday Friday."

"No wonder then. The only time I work the drive-through is on Saturday mornings once or twice a month."

"Every time I see you, I can't help but stare at you," continued China. "And now to find out you're my sister is unreal."

"Why do you stare at me, China?"

"There's just something about the way you carry yourself. For one thing, you walk with your head held high, and I'm looking at you thinking, 'Who does she think she is?'"

"Oh, yeah? I didn't know I came off like that," I chuckled. "That's too funny."

I looked around the room. It was full of boxes stacked on top of one another. There was a dog cage in the living room where the dog was confined, but not much else. A path between the boxes led into the dining room where there were more boxes.

Nancy must have followed my eyes because she said, "Please excuse the house. We've been having some work done. Let's go have a seat in the den."

"Can I get you something to drink?" Lou asked. "Name your poison."

"Do you have any brandy?"

"How about some Christian Brothers?"

"You hit the nail on the head!"

"How do you like it, straight up?"

"No, let me get that mixed with Coke."

"Coming right up."

Lou mixed the drinks and then handed one to Nancy and me. He opened up a Miller beer for himself.

"Where's mine?" asked China, somewhat teasingly.

"One Coca Cola coming right up. You're not eighteen yet. Next month it will be a different story, but until then. . ." Lou trailed off.

"Do you have any questions," asked Nancy as we sipped our drinks. "I mean, what would you like to know?"

"There's so much, I don't know where to start."

"Well, I guess I should begin with my health history. Polycystic kidneys run in the family."

"Yeah, I have polycystic kidneys," China added. "And my grandma died of a heart attack."

"One of my brothers has polycystic kidneys," Nancy continued. "How are your kidneys? Maybe you should have them checked out."

"No, my kidneys are fine," I answered a bit defensively, not yet ready to accept my biological connection to their health problems.

"Well, I've had polycystic kidneys all my life. I've already had two surgeries. It's hereditary, you know," China chimed in.

"I've never heard of it, but I'm pretty sure I'm healthy. My mom's a nurse. Not too much gets past her health-wise. She works at Pilot City Health Center."

"Pilot City Health Center? That's the clinic that killed my mom!" Nancy announced with an angry tone of voice.

"Killed your mother how?" I asked, a bit startled by her outburst.

"She was having pain in her chest and arm, so I took her up to Pilot City," Nancy explained. "But they just let her sit there in the waiting area. By the time I got tired of waiting for a doctor to look at her and left Pilot City to take her over to North Memorial Hospital, it was too late. I had no idea she was having a heart attack. That's how she wound up dying."

"Oh, I'm sorry to hear that. How long ago did it happen?"

"I was fifteen years old, so almost three years ago," China replied.

"Yes, she's been gone just about three years. She had just turned 80 when she passed away. I was a change-of-life baby. She was around 40 when I was born," Nancy explained.

"What about your father?"

"Oh, he died the year before you were born."

"Tell me about that. My birth, I mean. What happened? I mean, why did you give me up for adoption?"

"Lou, why don't you and China go out and get a pizza or something. That will give me a chance to talk to Colnese privately."

"Oh, man, I want to talk to my sister," China complained.

"Don't worry. I'll be right here when you get back. I want to get to know you better, too," I responded with a smile.

"What do you like on your pizza, Colnese?" asked Lou.

"Pepperoni, sausage, mushrooms, green peppers, onions . . . Whatever you get is all right with me. I'm easy when it comes to pizza."

"All right then, come on, China. We'll be right back."

After the front door shut, Nancy turned to me and said, "You have no idea how hard it was for me to give you up. I didn't have much choice. I was only sixteen when I found out I was pregnant, and my brothers weren't having it. After my dad died, they stepped in and united to play the role of a father figure to me. And if the truth be told, they hated Black people. You'll have to ask Lou what happened the day I brought him by my brother Leo's house to introduce them before we got married.

"To make a long story short, Leo's son hurriedly escorted Lou to the corner bar for a beer. Lou enjoyed the beer but was wondering why he was at the bar rather than meeting my brother as intended. As they made their way back to the house, Leo's son informed Lou that the detour was based on the fact that his father, apparently preparing for the visit, was sitting at the kitchen table cleaning his gun when Lou knocked on the front door."

"Wow."

"And I'll never forget the day Leo finally picked China up. She's eight years younger than you, so several years had passed since your birth. China was on the floor crawling around, and she crawled over to him. Leo wouldn't even look at her for a while, but when China began to pull herself up on his knee, I guess he had no choice but to notice her. Leo picked her up and started to cry. 'Poor little baby. No one wants you. The white race doesn't want you, and neither does the Black race.' After that, he became fiercely protective of China."

"Wow," I repeated. "I'm so glad that wasn't me."

I was outraged by the thought of having a racist white uncle. Sitting there talking to my white mother about her prejudiced white brother felt surreal.

"What do you mean you're so glad it wasn't you?" asked Nancy.

"I mean, I can't even imagine a grown man being so racially prejudiced that he would take it out on a baby."

"So were you adopted by a Black family?"

"Yes, I was."

"I kind of figured you would be adopted by a Black family. Did you grow up around here?"

"No, I grew up in South Minneapolis, but I work over here on the Northside and have quite a few friends who live over here."

I took another sip of my drink before continuing. "So who is my father?"

"His name is Larry. Larry Henderson."

"Larry Henderson? Where did he live? Was he a Northsider?"

"No, as a matter of fact, he lived in South Minneapolis. His mother's name was Cassie Walters."

"No way! There's no possible way Cassie Walters is my grandmother."

"You know her? I can't believe it."

"If it's the same Cassie Walters I know, she used to work at Phyllis Wheatley. She was my supervisor when I worked at Camp Katherine Parsons day camp as a junior counselor during the summer when I was a teenager."

"What happened? Why don't you like her?"

"She slapped me in the face and fired me from my job."

"She slapped you! Why?"

I thought back to that summer day in 1974 when Clive said my baby had died of gonorrhea, and I had gone upside his head with a stick.

"It's a long story. I'll have to tell you about it sometime," I told Nancy.

"Well, now that you bring it up, there's something that's been in the back of my mind ever since you walked through the front door. It's partially why I asked Lou and China to go out and get a pizza. I have something to tell you that I didn't want my husband and daughter to hear."

"What's that?"

"Well, you know I told you Larry Henderson is your father?"

"Uh-huh," I nodded my head.

"All these years, that's what I thought until I saw you. Now that I have laid eyes on you, I don't think Larry is your father."

"What? Well, who do you think my father is?"

"Lloyd Gross."

"Damn, and here I was just getting used to Larry," I remarked sarcastically. "Are you serious? Wasn't I born back in the fifties when women wore aprons and stuff? What are you saying? You don't actually know who my father is?"

"Lloyd and I had sex only one time, and then I got into a relationship with Larry. That's who I always thought was your father. Lloyd was kind of thuggish. Back then, there used to be boxing matches down at the Phyllis Wheatley Community Center. Me and my girlfriends used to go down there to watch. That's where I met Lloyd. He was cute. I always liked men with tight butts, and Lloyd's butt was really tight."

Nancy looked off into the distance as her mind traveled down memory lane.

"So, he had a tight butt, and then what?" I asked in an attempt to bring her back to present-day reality.

"I used to date this guy they called Cat Daddy, who was real smooth. To make a long story short, one night after the boxing match at the Wheatley, Lloyd and I were chatting a bit as we walked out the door, and he asked me if I was a virgin. I told him, 'Yes, of course, I'm a virgin.' Then he said, 'No way you're going out with Cat Daddy, and you're still a virgin.' So, to prove to Lloyd I was a virgin, I had sex with him."

I shook my head as I pondered the startling facts surrounding my conception and how surprised I was by Nancy's revelations.

"How irresponsible," was my jaded response.

"And I never really saw him again after that until after you were born," Nancy continued. "In the meantime, I had started dating Larry, so when I found out I was pregnant, I assumed he was the father. That is, until today when I met you. When I first saw you, I pretty much knew right off the bat that Lloyd is your father. You look just like him."

"What do you mean he was a thug?"

"Well, I just remember he hung around with a tough group of guys, and then he was sent away to Red Wing Training School."

"For what?"

"I'm not sure. I think he committed a robbery or something."

"Wow, Lloyd is my father, not Larry. I'm relieved, I guess, that Mrs. Walters is not my grandmother," I admitted. "I'm sure she would be relieved too if she knew, but I'm still surprised that all that was going on back in the fifties. I guess I have an unrealistic view of the fifties, having grown up watching *Leave It to Beaver*, *Andy of Mayberry*, and *Father Knows Best*. I thought girls were good back then."

"And some were," Nancy commented. "But others were pretty fast."

"I guess my next question is, why did you give up your white privilege to date Black guys?"

"It just happened like that. I didn't think about it in those terms. One day a friend and I were dialing random numbers and making prank calls, and we wound up talking to this Black guy on the phone. He invited us to come down to Phyllis Wheatley the next day after school, so we did.

"Back in those days, if the white guys at my school found out you had dated a Black guy—or colored guy as Black people were called back then—you got a bad reputation, and they wouldn't go out with you anymore. They used to say, 'If you go Black, then you can't go back.'"

I sat there for a few moments sipping my drink, trying to take it all in, everything I had just learned about my birth and the facts leading up to it.

Soon Lou and China returned with the pizza. After we finished eating, Nancy brought out a photo album. She turned the pages until she got to a baby picture.

"This is a picture of you shortly after you were born," Nancy told me.

"This was me? Oh, my God, I can't believe it! It says here, Teresa Marie. Was that my name? You named me Teresa Marie?"

"Yes, my mom was Martha Marie; I'm Nancy Marie, Davetta's or China's middle name is also Marie, and when you were born, you were named Teresa Marie."

"I was so cute!" I enthused. "Who is the baby on the opposite page? Is that China?"

"Yes, that's me," China confirmed. "I was cute, too!"

"Yes, you were." I agreed. "How did you get this, Nancy? I mean, were you supposed to have this picture?"

"No, I wasn't. During my pregnancy, I was staying at St. Luke's Home for Unwed Mothers in Duluth. I wasn't supposed to go back to the hospital ward after I was discharged. I overheard one of the other mothers mentioning that the newborn photos had been delivered, so I took a chance and went back to get your baby picture. I've treasured it all these years."

We talked awhile longer and then said our goodbyes. Nancy gave me a ride home, and I promised to visit again soon and bring Destiny the next time.

That night it took me a while to fall asleep. Thoughts and images of the visit with Nancy kept on replaying in my mind. I was excited to have a sister, but I had mixed feelings about my birth mother. Meeting her was emotionally overwhelming for me. It felt strange to me that even though she was white, I could see myself in her appearance and in her demeanor. She reminded me somewhat of the actress Mae West. She was a white woman with some spunk and a bit of an attitude, which is how I viewed myself. I was happy to have some of my questions about my origins answered, but there were many more questions that were still unresolved. Hopefully, they would be revealed in time.

CHAPTER 44

Imagining the Day of My Birth

❖ ❖ ❖

Based on what Nancy told me, this is how I imagine the day I was born:

The labor pains were over, but for Nancy, the pain of saying goodbye to her newborn baby girl had only just begun. It was nighttime, and except for a dim nightlight, the lights in the hospital ward were out. Nancy could hear the other women shifting around in their beds trying to get comfortable. She looked wistfully down the darkened hallway in the direction of the nursery. Hot tears seeped from the corners of her eyes and ran down the sides of her face into tangled tresses of her auburn hair.

She knew that the brief glimpse she'd had of the baby before they whisked her away may very well be her last. Her throat tightened and she turned over and pressed her face into her pillow. She could not breathe for the tears that constricted her throat. The pressure of despair welling up inside made Nancy feel like screaming, but she knew that crying out would not help her and would only serve to further betray her family roots. The blood of her Scandinavian ancestors coursing through her veins demanded that she remain stoic in the face of adversity.

She tried to be strong, but the memory of her baby's pursed lips, her wavy black hair, and her little arms thrashing about before she was swaddled made Nancy's seventeen-year-old body tremble with grief. Oh, how she longed for her mother's firm embrace to help her through this night, but her mother was far, far away from St. Luke's Hospital in Duluth, Minnesota. Nancy pressed her fingers into the corners of her eyes. Her mother was at home in Minneapolis, and Nancy had not seen her for the entire five months she had been away in Duluth.

For the first four months of her pregnancy, her mother had insisted that she not walk across the floor of their upper-level duplex during the day for fear that the downstairs neighbors would wonder why Nancy was not in school. Her father had died the year before. Nancy's Norwegian immigrant mother, who could barely speak English, had to take over the job of supporting them financially, so she worked long hours as a ho-tel maid downtown. Nancy did not want to make her mother's burden, which was already heavy with the stigma of having an unmarried, preg-nant teenage daughter, any more burdensome than it already was, so she obediently sat quietly until the school day was over.

Now that Nancy had given birth, she could go back home, probably as early as the following week, and resume her life as it had been before pregnancy interrupted it. After tossing and turning a while longer, Nancy finally fell into a fitful sleep.

A few days later, one of the sisters from St. Luke's Home for Unwed Mothers came to assist her with signing the adoption papers and with being discharged from the hospital. Sister Mary Theresa walked solemnly in front of Nancy towards the chauffeur-driven car waiting for them at the hospital's entrance.

"Sister Mary Theresa, please wait. I forgot something," Nancy said suddenly.

"What is it? We mustn't dawdle. We are expected to be back at the Home at a certain time."

Sister Mary Theresa looked back at her with an expression of disap-proval on her already stern face, but after seeing Nancy's look of urgency, she relented.

"Run along, dear, but please hurry. Would you like me to go with you?"

"No, Sister, I shouldn't be very long."

Breathlessly Nancy hurried up the long flight of stairs to the maternity floor. She remembered hearing one of the women on the ward mention that the photographer would return the babies' photographs to the hos-pital that morning. Nancy approached the volunteer Candy Striper at the front desk of the maternity ward and was relieved to see that the girl looked to be about the same age as her. She slowed down and caught her breath as she walked towards the desk with what she hoped was dignity and restraint.

"Excuse me, but I have come to collect my baby's photographs, please," she intoned with exaggerated maturity in her vocal inflection.

"What is your first and last name?" the Candy Striper inquired, also posturing maturity and professionalism.

"Nancy Hanson."

The Candy Striper rifled through a stack of large envelopes. "I can't seem to find it," she said as her eyes scanned the desk. Panicked, Nancy's eyes darted back and forth across the desk, as well. "What about that envelope over there?" she suggested. Relief was evident in her tone.

"Oh, I didn't see that one. I wonder why it isn't with the rest of the photographs?"

Nancy remained silent.

"Here it is—Baby Girl Hanson," she confirmed as she handed the large envelope to Nancy. Mission thus accomplished, Nancy turned and headed for the stairwell.

"Excuse me!" the Candy Striper called out to her.

Nancy froze and slowly turned to face her, believing that the little charade was over.

"You forgot your baby's birth certificate," the Candy Striper said, holding the document towards Nancy with an outstretched arm.

Nancy returned to the desk and took the birth certificate from her. She then rushed down the staircase towards the front door and fled the building. The car sat idling at the curb. She quickly got in and shut the door.

"Is everything all right?" asked Sister Mary Theresa.

"Yes, Sister. I forgot something important, but everything's all right now."

Later, after she had returned to her room at St. Luke's Home for Unwed Mothers, she opened the envelope and read the handwritten birth certificate:

St. Luke's Hospital

Duluth, Minnesota

Certificate of Birth

This certifies that Teresa Marie Hanson was born to Nancy Hanson in this hospital at 5:57 o'clock p.m. on Thursday, the twenty-first day of November 1957. In Witness Whereof the said Hospital has caused this certificate to be signed by its duly authorized officer, and its official seal to be hereunto affixed.

Signed, Clyde K. Fox, Superintendent.

Nancy turned it over. Sex of child: Female. Weight at birth 7 pounds 3 ounces. Length 20 inches. She gasped when she saw her baby's tiny footprints pressed lightly on the back of the birth certificate. She vaguely remembered the hospital attendant pressing one of her thumbs and then another onto an ink pad shortly after the birth and then rolling them one by one from right to left on the card. Now she saw the reason why. Nancy's very own thumbprints framed the tiny footprints.

Next, she examined the photograph. To Nancy, her baby was breathtakingly beautiful. Teresa's wavy hair was brushed upwards, so that little waves and curls were clustered on top of her head. Her closed eyes appeared to be slanted. Her pursed lips were moist. Something about her little chin suggested strength and stubborn determination even at birth.

From the expression on her face, there was something evident about her character beyond that, Nancy realized. Was it only wishful thinking? To Nancy, she appeared to be a very stoic baby indeed. A sudden realization washed over her:

"She is going to make it," she thought. "My baby is going to survive." Nancy's spirit brightened somewhat at the thought, even as a tear made its way down her cheek. "Without me," she added aloud as she sadly brushed the tear away.

Nancy packed the birth certificate and photograph into her suitcase with care. The next day she would go back home with the precious keepsakes in tow. Despite her baby's absence, the images contained on the birth certificate and photograph were proof positive that her life and the life of her baby had, in fact, intersected, if only for a brief period of time. Throughout her pregnancy and during the time it took to press their thumbprints and footprints on a sheet of card stock, Nancy and Teresa had shared a special place in one another's lives. The indelible ink on the birth certificate recording their names, thumbprints, and footprints bore witness to that fact.

Nancy closed the suitcase and pressed the metal latches until they clicked into place. With a determined set to her chin, she was ready to return to Minneapolis and face the future. As for the little dark-haired baby she was leaving behind, Nancy wondered what her future would be and who would be there to help her pave the way. With no way of knowing, she shrugged her shoulders and swallowed her tears.

CHAPTER 45

Meeting Lloyd

Not long after meeting my birth mother, Nancy, I decided to also search for my birth father, Lloyd Gross. Since Nancy had supplied his name, it didn't take much effort. In fact, it happened almost effortlessly. I looked in the White Pages and found an L. Gross. I dialed the number listed, and the phone was answered by a teenage girl, who turned out to be my half-sister, Andrea.

It felt a bit awkward making the call since I wasn't one hundred percent certain Lloyd was my father based on the story Nancy had told me, so when Andrea answered the phone, I lost no time with small talk. I jumped right into my story of being adopted and having recently met my birth mother, who had told me Lloyd was my birth father.

"Dad doesn't live here. The 'L' in the phone book listing stands for my mother, Loni, not Lloyd," she told me. "I'll give you his number, though. We just went through a similar situation last year. Another relative had a baby she gave up for adoption, Aunt Janet. Anyway, last year Janet found her mother, and we all met her, so your phone call doesn't surprise me like it probably would have before Janet showed up."

In two short days, I had gone from having no known birth relatives to meeting my birth mother Nancy, my sister China, and my nephew Brian a couple days before. Now, I discovered yet another sister and learned about an aunt who, according to Andrea, was only a year older than me. That she had also been given up for adoption was mind-blowing.

After sharing that juicy tidbit of information, Andrea gave me Lloyd's phone number, which I dialed immediately after our phone conversation ended. When Lloyd picked up the phone, I told him my name and then went into the purpose of my call.

"Do you know Nancy Hanson?" I asked.

"Yeah, sure, I know Nancy," Lloyd confirmed.

"Well, I'm adopted, and I met her a couple of days ago. She's my birth mother, and she told me you're my father. But you might not be because first, she told me Larry was my father."

"Yeah, yeah, yeah, I know all about Larry," Lloyd admitted. "But whether you're my daughter or not, I'd like to meet you anyway. I'm just happy you're finding out who you are."

I was stunned but elated by his response. Coincidentally, I was seated at the kitchen table in the same room where I had been approximately twenty years earlier when I first made the call to Hennepin County attempting to locate my birth mother but had failed miserably.

Hearing Lloyd's welcoming words helped to quench my life-long thirst for acceptance and belonging. In my heart, I hoped he was my father. I liked his accepting attitude. We arranged to meet the following day. I gave Lloyd my friend Pam's address because I didn't want to meet him by myself. He said he'd pick me up at her house around noon. Next, I called Pam to give her the scoop. She rushed right over to my mom's house, where I was camped out at the time to hear all about it. I had known Pam since grade school. We became tight friends in fifth grade.

Because we were so completely opposite as children, we were an unlikely pair: Where I was big-boned and plump, she was all skin and bones. Where I was light-skinned and freckle-faced, she was dark-skinned with a flawless complexion. Where I was rather shy, she was bold and talkative. When I told Pam I had found out who my real father was and then told her his name, she knew right away who he was.

"You know whose brother Lloyd is, don't you?"

Pam knew everything about everybody, so I was not surprised.

"No, whose brother?"

"Lloyd is Ronnie Gross's older brother."

I remembered going to Ronnie's after-hour parties after the nightclubs closed when I was a teenager. I didn't know him well, but I knew of him from the after-hours parties and from living in my neighborhood.

"What? Are you trying to tell me Ronnie could possibly be my uncle?"

"Yep, and he's Kathy's uncle, too." Kathy was Pam's close friend from Saint Paul. "I always said you and Kathy looked alike with all those freckles."

I was stunned. I had never met Kathy, but I had heard her name mentioned countless times by Pam over the years.

"I'm supposed to meet Lloyd on Saturday," I told Pam. "Would you go with me?"

"Girl, yes!" she agreed.

I already knew that would be her response. Pam loved drama and enjoyed nothing more than being front and center as it was going down.

The next day, I went over to Pam's mom's house, who lived in the next block, to wait for Lloyd to pick us up. When her Aunt Belle (pronounced Aint Belle because they were from Memphis, Tennessee) heard what we were up to, she looked at me, sucked her teeth, and rolled her eyes in disgust.

"That's why I cain't stand no adopted kids. They always searching for they parents. I don't know why y'all don't just leave well 'nough alone."

I had spent nearly every day of my life over Pam's house since we were in fifth grade, so I didn't take offense to what Aint Belle said. She spoke whatever was on her mind to all the kids in Pam's family, and I was no exception.

When Lloyd arrived, he came to the door and introduced himself to Pam's mother, Celestine, and Aint Belle. He politely shook their hands and made small talk, and then we followed him to his car.

"Yep, that's your daddy," Pam co-signed. "Look how he raises one of his eyebrows like you."

I glanced over at Lloyd, and sure enough, one eyebrow was arched higher than the other one. I wasn't sure if that was officially enough proof to establish paternity, but it was a step in the right direction. Yet I was surprised that his skin was walnut brown and not the deep mahogany brown I had expected. My stillborn baby and my six-year-old daughter Destiny both had dark brown skin. My skin was high-yellow, so I had always assumed my biological father was dark-skinned.

Lloyd's skin had a reddish undertone. His nose was like that of the Native American on the nickel, so I guessed he had some Native American in his bloodline, which he later confirmed. As I took in Lloyd's appearance and mannerisms, Pam was busy chatting with Lloyd about his niece Kathy and several other family members she knew. I listened with interest. Once again, the scene was surreal.

"I've seen you before," Lloyd said to me. "One time, I saw you on the 4th Avenue bus, and I couldn't take my eyes off you because you look so much like my oldest daughter, Kathy. I was on my way to my brother, Ronnie's, house."

"Your daughter's name is Kathy, too?"

"Yes, my niece and my daughter are both named Kathy. It was a popular name at the time," Lloyd explained.

"That's why you look so familiar to me!" I exclaimed. "I remember that day. I wondered why you were looking at me so hard. I know who Ronnie is. I used to go to his after-hours parties all the time."

"I was usually at his after-hours, too. I was either in the kitchen frying chicken or helping him bartend. It's a wonder we never ran into each other."

"We probably did. We just didn't know we were related."

Soon we got to Lloyd's building. He lived in a studio apartment in an older building in downtown Minneapolis. His place was neat, clean, and compact, and the bed let down out of the wall, which I thought was pretty cool. I wanted a drink but decided against mentioning it since Lloyd had told Pam and me that he was a recovering alcoholic. Since his baby girl Letoyia was born, he had been sober for the past few years.

"You have a baby girl? How old is she?" I asked.

"Letoyia's three going on four. Her birthday is next month."

"Ooh, I want to meet her."

"I'll give you her mother's phone number, and you can call her and make arrangements."

"Okay, that's cool."

Besides Letoyia, Lloyd also had five more daughters—Evelyn, Kathy, LoRay, Andrea, and Kelly—and a son named Courtney. My cup was overflowing with siblings. I had always wanted a sister, and through Lloyd and Nancy, God had blessed me with seven sisters and one more brother.

The longer Lloyd and I talked, the more people we discovered we knew in common. I also asked him about the rumor Nancy had told me that he had served time at Red Wing when he was a juvenile. Lloyd confirmed that he had done time at the state training school in Red Wing but that after his brush with the law when he was a teenager, he had gone on to have a successful and fulfilling career on the railroad. He had worked for several years in the dining car of the train on the Great Northern Railway.

Working on the railroad as Pullman porters and in other positions on the train were coveted jobs for Black men during that era. It equaled steady employment and status in the community. I was shocked and excited to find out that Lloyd knew O. Donald Smith. I knew him as Don or Donny Boy, as my dad and our family called him while I was growing up. Don was my dad's best friend, who had brought Ira and me our puppy, Frisky, on the train from Chicago when we were small.

"Me and the other porters called Lloyd, Grossie," Don had explained to me after I told him I had met my biological father and who he was. "I knew his dad and the whole Gross family from Saint Paul. Boy, did Grossie ever have a bad temper! He could go from zero to sixty in a minute. Me and the other porters had to hold him back from fighting a lot of times. You're just like him!"

Don had a good laugh about how much I was like Lloyd and the rest of the Grosses. Thanks to Donny Boy telling me that little tidbit of information, I figured out one more piece of the puzzle that was me. It was hard to absorb it all. It was overwhelming. All those years I was blinded to my true identity, my biological father had been just down the street and my extended family right around the corner. All those years, I had wondered who and where my biological relatives were, they were right within arm's reach.

Lloyd told me that not long after I was born, he and his first wife, Virginia, were visiting friends, socializing, and listening to music. Nancy, her husband, David, also known as Punkin, and some other friends were in the group.

"Nancy had a picture of you when you were first born that she passed around. I can remember looking at the picture and commenting to Virginia about how much Nancy's baby looked like our daughter, Kathy."

It turned out I knew Lloyd's daughter, Kathy. I had seen her over the years around the neighborhood and at the Spruce Club, a neighborhood bar. I was awestruck.

"I used to stare at her because we looked so much alike," I told Lloyd, shaking my head. "What's tripping me out is that I just thought it was a coincidence, but the reason we look so much alike is because we are actually sisters. There I was sitting at the bar a few seats away from my sister, but I just didn't know it."

Pam and I visited with Lloyd a while longer, rehashing the past and examining the present turn of events, and then Lloyd took us back home. We asked him to drop us off at my mom and dad's house. As I got out of the car, we promised to stay in touch.

My parents were not at home, so Pam and I went down in the basement, fixed some drinks, and got comfortable, so we could process and debrief the visit and the multiple connections we had discovered. Between her phone calls and Lloyd's phone calls to his extended family members, the news had traveled rapidly through the grapevine.

About an hour later, we heard the doorbell ring. I went upstairs to see who was at the door. I pulled back the shade and saw a group of people on my front steps that I had never seen before, but in an instant, I could tell they were my blood relatives. I could hear their muffled voices through the door,

"Yep, she has our eyes," said one young woman to another.

"Look at her freckles," was the other one's reply.

Pam had come up the stairs behind me. "That's Kathy and Jossie, Lloyd's nieces, and their kids."

I opened the door with a smile and invited them in. There was a flurry of animated conversation between us. I was glad Pam was there with me since she already knew everybody. It helped to break the ice between me and my kinfolks. Jossie said she would be hosting Thanksgiving dinner at her house, and she invited me to join them, which I accepted.

After everyone went home, I called Tina's younger sister, Stacy, in excitement to tell her everything that had transpired. In the middle of telling her about all the people I was related to that she also knew, I broke down crying. I was completely overwhelmed by the knowledge that many of my relatives were people I knew in passing, had interacted with over the years, and shared friends in common with. All that time, they had been so close, but yet so far.

◈ ◈ ◈

Over the next few weeks, I met several more of my relatives on Lloyd's side. I had not yet met any of Nancy's relatives except for her brother Leo, a North Minneapolis policeman. I met him on the day First Bank Plymouth was robbed a few months after I had met Nancy and Davetta. I had been on my break taking a nap in the ladies' room, which had a couch in it, when Pat came in and woke me up.

I had been out the previous evening nearly all night long partying. I'd caught a cab home early in the morning, laid down for about an hour, bathed and changed clothes, and then caught a cab to work. Destiny had spent the night over my parents' house, which she often did when I went out at night.

"Colnese, wake up! The bank just got robbed," Pat exclaimed as she grabbed my arm and shook it to wake me up.

I was groggy and hungover, but I got up and followed her upstairs. I went back to my desk and sat down. The bank was swarming with police and FBI agents. Soon a tall, white policeman came over to me and asked, "Are you Colnese Hendon?"

"Yes," I responded, nodding my head and trying to look alert.

"Can I speak to you in private?" he asked.

I said yes and obediently followed him into the hallway.

"Hi, I'm your Uncle Leo," he said as he stuck his hand out for me to shake.

I was stunned. Until that moment, when I heard the word uncle in relation to me, it always meant somebody Black. All my uncles, godparents, and family friends I called uncle were Black men. Suddenly, a white man was standing in front of me, referring to himself as my uncle. Unbelievable! I quickly recovered from my shock and shook his hand.

"You look just like your mother," he added. "We'll have to do lunch sometime."

"Sure, that sounds good." I agreed.

But I never saw him again. Not long after the bank closed a couple months later, Uncle Leo died. When I asked Nancy why she hadn't introduced me to any of her family members, she said, "I'm not very close to my family." I suspected it was because of racial issues, but she never came out and said so.

Meanwhile, I was meeting more and more of Lloyd's seemingly endless number of family members. One Saturday, he picked me up and drove me across the Mississippi River to Saint Paul, where I met his aunts, Cookie and Josephine, his father's sisters.

His father, Lloyd Sr., had been killed in a car accident when Lloyd was only six years old. He showed me a picture of his father, and I could see myself in his face. He had arched eyebrows just like mine and was a very handsome man. Lloyd Jr. had also been a handsome man in his youth.

While in Saint Paul, we also visited his sister Rozetta (Rosie) McGee, who was only a year older than Lloyd. She was the mother of seven children, including Jossie and Kathy. Her other children included Randy, Nacey, Hattie, David, and Paul Kevin. Aunt Rosie was also the grandmother of many children. Their family was closely knit.

What was most astonishing was the fact that most of my biological family members had been so near to me my entire life. As it turned out, Lloyd's mother, Hattie—my grandmother—had lived right across the street from Warrington Elementary School. Her house faced the playground I played on during recess each day for the first four years of my grade school experience. I can imagine my grandmother looking out the window or door of her house and seeing me playing right across the street in the schoolyard, but just not knowing I was her granddaughter.

Candy, the youngest sister of Nancy's first husband, Punkin, had been in my third-grade classroom. We had danced together on the last day of school. The night I fell in love with Blue, we had partied at my Uncle Ronnie's after-hours party. Unknown to me, Lloyd had been in the kitchen frying chicken that night. Ronnie's daughter, Bavette, lived with her family on the corner of 39th of Portland within view of my family's house. At the time, she had been a cute little six-year-old girl, who I can remember playing outside with her two little sisters.

Lloyd told me that he used to hang out with a few of DeLady's older brothers when he was younger. DeLady was from a large family. She had seven sisters and eight brothers with the same father and mother. We had been together at a track meet the day my baby was stillborn. We had been out partying together the night we got into the big brawl with Leora, her sisters, and cousin behind the Filling Station.

Cousin Kathy McGee and Pam were friends at the same time that Pam and I were also friends. Kathy was on one side of the Mississippi River, and I was on the other side. Nancy banked at First Bank Plymouth, where I worked for several years. China walked past the bank on a regular basis with her friends. These are just some of the ways my life had brushed up against the lives of my birth family members over the years. We had been just like ships passing in the night.

Being separated from my family of origin at birth, adopted at five months old, and then reconnecting with my birth family twenty-six years later taught me it takes more than blood ties to define a family. Just like Dorothy in *The Wizard of Oz*, I searched for something that was there all the time. I now define family as the people I love and those who love me. These include my adoptive family, blood relatives, multiple generations of godchildren, and close long-term family friends too numerous to count. My heart is wide open to the infinite possibilities of family that exist when you are willing to give and receive love.

CHAPTER 46

Bonding

◆ ◆ ◆

It was a warm summer day in early September 1998. I was sitting at my desk in front of the computer screen, focused on completing a grant proposal, when the phone rang.

"Good afternoon, Sabathani Community Center," I greeted the caller.

"Colnese, if you want to see Nancy before she dies, you need to go visit her today. She's at North Memorial's Hospice in Brooklyn Center." It was Lynn, my sister China's husband.

It had been nearly fifteen years since I met Nancy when I was twenty-six, and she was forty-three years old. After our initial reunion, we had not developed a close relationship. I could not get over being given up for adoption, nor could I transcend the racial and cultural gap between my African American upbringing and Nancy's Norwegian heritage. Apparently, neither could Nancy's extended family. The only other relative I had met on her side of the family was her brother Leo, a North Minneapolis police officer. Meeting him was happenstance. It had taken place only because the bank where I worked at the time had been robbed, and he was one of the officers dispatched to the location.

Despite my distance from Nancy, I was able to develop a relationship with my sister, China, and her immediate family, which included my niece, JaQuala, three nephews, Brian, Christopher, Trehahn, and their father, Lynn. After asking Lynn for directions to the hospice, I left work and drove straight over there. In early June, Nancy had been diagnosed with lung cancer, which had metastasized to her brain. Although she had undergone chemotherapy, the cancer was too far gone. Now she was dying.

When I arrived, Nancy was sitting up in bed eating chunks of fresh fruit from a small bowl. The brightly colored cantaloupe, watermelon, and honeydew looked inviting. Her failing organs had infused her normally pale white skin with varying shades of olive green. A colorful silk scarf covered her head.

When I had asked the men in her life to tell me about my mother, they had described Nancy's hair to me before describing anything else about her. Her first husband, Punkin, reminisced about how Nancy's long, thick, wavy hair had glowed beautifully in the sunlight with hints of auburn. He described how her long hair cascaded down her back and nearly reached her butt as she walked down the street in the summertime. I remembered how on the day I met her, my baby nephew, Brian, cuddled in her arms and rubbed her hair between his small fingers as he fell asleep. Now Nancy's trademark hair was all gone.

I sat down in a chair near her bed and attempted to talk with her.

"Are you afraid?" I asked.

Nancy shook her head and firmly said, "No."

I believed her. Although I didn't know her very well, our shared bloodline helped me understand her. I saw in her expression my own firm resolution when I held a strong opinion or belief. As I sat there, I noticed Nancy staring at me unwaveringly. It was as though she was attempting to commit to memory all my facial features, each strand of hair on my head, and the placement of every freckle on my face.

I looked away for a moment, and when I turned back to her, I saw that her eyes continued to be locked on mine. I was reminded of the day my daughter Destiny was born. I recalled the intensity of her eyes as she stared into mine when I held her shortly after her birth. The attending nurse had explained it was one of the ways infants bonded with their mothers.

I realized with a start that Nancy had never bonded with me as a baby. During the 1950s, when I was born, mothers placing their babies for adoption were not allowed to hold them nor spend any time with them. Now that she was dying, Nancy was spending some of her last moments on earth to finally bond with me. As I left the hospice room, I patted her on her foot and said goodbye. It was the last time we saw each other, but it was also the first time.

CHAPTER 47

This Is My Story; This Is My Song

◈ ◈ ◈

The first words from my birth mother when I met her were, "I've often wondered if you survived." When I look back over my life, no one is more amazed than me that I did, in fact, survive. Because I felt so lost, so full of anger, I often threw myself right into the path of destruction.

But God.

I imagine He looked down from his throne and decided I was worth saving. He saved me the first time by placing me with my adoptive parents, Coleridge and Bernese Hendon. I could not have asked for better parents. After they raised me, they also helped me raise my own children since it would be many years before I finally grew up and settled down enough to do the job right.

When I finally met my biological family, my journey to healing had only just begun. Learning to love myself took place over a long period of time. It was not until I returned to church and reestablished a relationship with the Lord that my self-destructive path finally came to a halt.

Listening to the lyrics of hymns and gospel songs each Sunday, absorbing the messages of weekly sermons, as well as reading and hearing Bible scriptures reinforced my understanding that God has a purpose for my life. In fact, He has a purpose for all our lives. Knowing that helped me believe that my life has value and that the Lord did not make a mistake when I was conceived. Even though my conception happened in the most random way I can think of, as the result of a bet between Lloyd and Nancy that she was not a virgin, here I am.

Meeting my biological family helped me see and embrace my inner and outer beauty. When I look at the faces of my biological relatives and can see their intelligence and beauty, it is like looking into a mirror that enables me to see and believe I am smart and beautiful, too.

From my adoptive family, I learned strong values and ethics. I grew up in a stable household and experienced what it feels like to be truly loved. My adoptive parents endeavored to give me every possible advantage life has to offer spiritually, culturally, and academically. When I was finally able to knit the two halves of myself together—nature and nurture—which amounted to my biological family and my adoptive family, I was finally able to become a whole person.

And last but certainly not least, there is my Lord and Savior, Jesus Christ. When the time was right, the Lord called me out of darkness into His marvelous light.

> But you are a chosen people, a royal priesthood, a holy
> nation, a people belonging to God, that you may declare
> the praises of him who called you out of darkness into his
> wonderful light.
>
> —1 Peter 2:9

My Answer to Being Called Mulatto

◈ ◈ ◈

I am a rainbow.
I am a rainbow of African, European, and Native
    American.
In America, they call me Black.

"What kind of baby is this?" asked my mother's family when
    I was born. "Never saw one like this before."

"I'm a rainbow," I cooed.

But they didn't want a rainbow.

"You can't keep this baby," they told my mother. "This baby's
    not white."

And with that, they turned to go and left me in the world
    all alone.

As the days turned into weeks, and the weeks turned into
    months, God held me in the palm of His hand.

"Don't worry. I'll find you a family, Little Rainbow," He said.
    And He did.

One day a Black family came to claim me. "We want her,"
    they said. And then they took me home with them and
    made me their own.

"Let's name her after us," said Coleridge to Bernese. "Let's take Col from Coleridge and Nese from Bernese and name her Colnese." And so, they did.

And their family became my family.
And their values became my values.
And their culture became my culture.
And their Black pride became my Black pride.

What color am I?
In America, they call me Black.
And they're right.
I am a beautiful Black rainbow.

Acknowledgments

Thank you to the following individuals and arts organizations that nurtured my creative journey:

Bread Loaf Writer's Conference, Middlebury, VT

Hurston/Wright Foundation, Washington, DC

Kim Johnson, manuscript review

Billy Jones, manuscript review, marketing, and webpage design

Roots. Wounds. Words., Nicole Shawan Junior, Founder/CEO/
Teaching Artist, Brooklyn, NY

Strive Publishing, Mary Taris, Publisher/CEO, Robbinsdale, MN

The Givens Foundation for African American Literature, Minneapolis, MN

The Loft Literary Center, Minneapolis, MN

- Writers of Color and Indigenous Writers Class, David Mura, Teaching Artist
- Year-Long Memoir Writing Project, Nicole Helget, Teaching Artist

The Write of Your Life 2019 Cohort Group, Sophfronia Scott, Teaching Artist, Veneto, Italy

Ari Tison, author, manuscript review and book endorsement

VONA: Voices of Our Nations Arts Foundation

A heartfelt thanks to all the interesting and colorful characters I encountered along the way, who made my life so rich, poignant, and worth capturing on the pages of this book.

Thank you to my children, grandchildren, and family members:

By Adoption.

By Blood.

By Choice.

Much love to all!

About the Author

Colnese M. Hendon enjoys writing memoir, short stories, and poetry. She is a fellow of the Givens Foundation for African American Literature (2009), the Hurston/Wright Foundation (2014, 2015, and 2018), VONA Voices (2017), the Bread Loaf Writer's Conference (2019), and the Write of Your Life writer's workshop in Venice, Italy (2019). Her poetry and short stories have been published in Ishmael Reed's online *Konch Magazine* and the Minnesota Literacy Council's *Black Literacy Matters Anthology*.

Colnese's educational background includes a BA degree in professional communications/public relations and an MA in public and non-profit administration from Metropolitan State University. In addition to her work as development director at Isuroon, she volunteers as a guardian ad litem in Hennepin County's Fourth Judicial District, where she advocates in court for children in the child welfare system.